RISKS, COSTS, AND LIVES SAVED
Getting Better Results from Regulation

RISKS, COSTS, AND LIVES SAVED
Getting Better Results from Regulation

Edited by Robert W. Hahn

Oxford University Press
New York and Oxford

The AEI Press
Washington, D.C.

1996

Oxford University Press

Oxford • New York • Athens • Auckland • Bangkok • Bombay • Calcutta • Cape Town • Dar es Salaam • Delhi • Florence • Hong Kong • Istanbul • Karachi • Kuala Lumpur • Madras • Madrid • Melbourne • Mexico City • Nairobi • Paris • Singapore • Taipei • Tokyo • Toronto and associated companies in Berlin • Ibadan

Oxford is a registered trademark of Oxford University Press.

Library of Congress Cataloging-in-Publication Data

Risks, costs, and lives saved: getting better results from regulation / edited by Robert W. Hahn.
    p. cm.
Includes biographical references and index.
ISBN 0-19-521174-X (alk. paper)
    1. Risk assessment—Government policy—United States.
2. Health risk assessment—Government policy—United States.
3. Environmental risk assessment—Government policy—United
States. 4. Risk management—Government policy—United States.
5. Safety regulations—United States. I. Hahn, Robert William.
HM256.R59   1996
363.17—dc20   96-33644
                                                                       CIP

THE AEI PRESS
Publisher for the American Enterprise Institute
1150 17th Street, N.W., Washington, D.C. 20036

Printed in the United States of America

CONTENTS

PREFACE

There is a growing sense among U.S. citizens that government regulation has become excessive. People no longer believe that more government will necessarily cure society's ills. And they are right. This book will show that the government regulation of risks could benefit from a serious reexamination of how risks are assessed and managed.

The government's record on regulating risks has been decidedly mixed. In some cases, such as removing lead from gasoline and requiring the use of seat belts, the economic benefits of the regulations appear to have substantially outweighed the costs imposed on consumers. On the other hand, recent major laws and regulations, such as the 1990 Clean Air Act Amendments, would not pass an economic cost-benefit test, even after including health benefits.

A growing body of evidence, which subsequent chapters will review, shows that many recent expenditures on risk reduction have done very little to actually reduce risk. Indeed, in some cases, those investments are likely to have increased risks to human health. Even when the government requires the private sector to spend money on reducing health risks, there is ample evidence that many more lives could be saved through a judicious reallocation of resources.

Despite the growing skepticism about government regulation, public opinion polls show strong support of policies that promote environmental protection, human health, and worker safety.

The amount of money spent on managing health, safety, and environmental risks is quite large. The Environmental Protection Agency estimates that the expenditures for environmental protection will exceed $160 billion in 1996. Other regulation of health and safety risks could add another $50 billion annually.

Two obvious questions arise in the management of health, safety, and environmental risks. Have we chosen the right goals? Are we achieving those goals at the lowest possible total cost? Until recently, the policy debate did not focus on those questions. The presumption in most legislation was that goals should be set without attention to cost. Moreover, the means for achieving specific goals were rarely scrutinized with an eye toward choosing the least costly method. Instead, policy makers generally made decisions on the basis of political pragmatism. If the costs of a regulation were not readily visible to the consumer, and it did not result in plant closures, then the agency could promulgate the regulation, even if it conferred very few benefits.

The discussion of goals and means for risk management is now changing. Indeed, we are in the midst of two profound revolutions in the management of health, safety, and environmental regulation. The first involves a serious discussion of the means by which goals are achieved. The 1990 Clean Air Act Amendments, for example, used a "market-based" approach to achieve an ambitious ten-million-ton reduction in sulfur dioxide emissions by the year 2000. That approach, in which regulators set the total target but allow individuals and businesses maximum flexibility in achieving those goals, replaced a more traditional "command-and-control" approach, in which regulators prescribed specific technologies for achieving environmental goals. The market-based approach has the potential to reduce the cost of regulation by more than $10 billion.

The second revolution in social regulation concerns the debate over appropriate policy goals. The ever-growing reach of regulation has in large part precipitated that debate. As constituencies affected by regulation become more vocal, Washington has begun to respond, most notably with a wave of proposed legislation aimed at "streamlining" regulation. Bills that promote cost-benefit analysis, limit unfunded mandates, and restrict the government's ability to take property without compensation have all received serious consideration in the current policy debate.

New constituencies are being created that will serve as a counterbalance to existing "public interest" groups, such as environmental and consumer organizations. The new political alignment will help shape the next revolution. But so too will ideas.

The principal objective of this book is to help define the intellectual terms of the debate underlying the emerging revolution in risk management—and particularly the government's role in the regulation of health, safety, and the environment. Because risk assessment and risk management involve several disciplines, this book draws on scholars from several disciplines. The book aims to provide the reader with a deeper understanding of some of the key scientific, economic, and policy issues underlying risk assessment and risk management.

Robert W. Hahn

ACKNOWLEDGMENTS

This book would not have been possible without the support of several people in addition to the authors. I would like to express my gratitude to Leigh Tripoli, Ed Dale, Elizabeth Drembus, and Jonathan Siskin for their help in editing the manuscript. To the extent the book exhibits a stylistic coherence, it is due to the hard work of those people. In addition, I would like to thank Chris DeMuth for encouraging me to pursue new academic frontiers in reforming regulation.

Robert W. Hahn

CONTRIBUTORS

BRUCE N. AMES is professor of biochemistry and molecular biology and director of the National Institute of Environmental Health Sciences Center at the University of California, Berkeley. He is a member of the National Academy of Sciences (NAS). He was formerly on the board of directors of the National Cancer Institute (National Cancer Advisory Board) and the NAS Commission on Life Sciences. Dr. Ames has been the international leader in the field of mutagenesis and genetic toxicology for more than twenty years. His work has had a major influence on basic and applied research on mutation, cancer, and aging.

LOIS SWIRSKY GOLD is director of the Carcinogenic Potency Project at Lawrence Berkeley Laboratory and the University of California, Berkeley. She has published more than fifty articles on the results of animal cancer tests, interspecies extrapolation in carcinogenesis, and issues related to the use of bioassay data to assess cancer risks to humans. Those analyses are based on the Carcinogenic Potency Database, which she has directed for sixteen years. The database includes analyses of 5,000 chronic, long-term carcinogenesis bioassays on 1,200 chemicals. Dr. Gold has served on the panel of expert reviewers for the bioassay program of the National Toxicology Program and on the board of the Harvard Center for Risk Analysis and was a member of the Harvard Risk Management Reform Group.

BERNARD D. GOLDSTEIN is director of the Environmental and Occupational Health Sciences Institute, a joint program of Rutgers University and the University of Medicine and Dentistry of New Jersey (UMDNJ), and chairman of the Department of Environmental and Community Medicine at the UMDNJ-Robert Wood Johnson

Medical School. Dr. Goldstein is a physician specializing in environmental and occupational medicine and served as a faculty member in the Departments of Environmental Medicine and Medicine at New York University Medical Center. Dr. Goldstein was assistant administrator for research and development of the Environmental Protection Agency, and he was a member and chairman of the NIH Toxicology Study Section and of the EPA's Air Scientific Advisory Committee.

JOHN D. GRAHAM is professor of policy and decision sciences at the Harvard School of Public Health, where he teaches methods of risk analysis and benefit-cost analysis. Dr. Graham is the founding director of the Harvard Center for Risk Analysis and president of the International Society for Risk Analysis. Since joining the Harvard faculty in 1985, Dr. Graham has focused his research on toxic chemicals, automobile fuel economy, HIV infection, drinking and driving, and risk analysis. He is the author of four books, including *In Search of Safety: Chemicals and Cancer Risk*, and dozens of scientific articles. He serves on the international editorial boards of *Risk Analysis* and *Accident Analysis and Prevention*.

ROBERT W. HAHN is a resident scholar at the American Enterprise Institute and an adjunct professor of economics at Carnegie Mellon University. From 1991 to 1994 he was an adjunct faculty member at the Kennedy School of Government, Harvard University. Before that he worked for two years as a senior staff member of the President's Council of Economic Advisers. Mr. Hahn frequently contributes to general-interest periodicals and leading scholarly journals including the *New York Times, Wall Street Journal, American Economic Review,* and *Yale Law Journal.* In addition, he is a cofounder of the Community Preparatory School—an inner-city middle school that provides opportunities for disadvantaged youth to achieve their full potential.

WILLIAM R. HENDEE is professor of radiology, biophysics, radiation oncology, and bioethics and dean of the Graduate School of Biomedical Sciences at the Medical College of Wisconsin. Dr. Hendee is past president of the American Association of Physicists in Medicine and the Society of Nuclear Medicine. The author or coauthor of more than 350 scientific articles and twenty books, Dr. Hendee has also edited several books and has produced a large number of monographs. His research interests are in diagnostic imaging, with an emphasis on visual perception and cognition and on technology assessment in medicine.

LESTER B. LAVE is the Higgins Professor of Economics and University Professor at Carnegie Mellon University. In addition to his appointments in the Graduate School of Industrial Administration and Heinz School of Public Policy and Management, he is professor of engineering and public policy in the College of Engineering. He is also the director of Carnegie Mellon's university-wide program on Green Design (Product and Process Design for the Environment). Before joining Carnegie Mellon, he was a senior fellow at the Brookings Institution and has served as a consultant to federal and state agencies. His early risk analysis assessed the benefits and costs of the 1968 automobile safety standards, and he has published on a wide range of issues related to risk, including *Air Pollution and Human Health* and *The Scientific Basis of Health and Safety Regulation*.

RICHARD S. LINDZEN is the Alfred P. Sloan Professor of Meteorology at the Massachusetts Institute of Technology. Previously, he was a member of the faculty at the University of Chicago and at Harvard University, where he directed the Center for Earth and Planetary Physics. The author of *Dynamics in Atmospheric Physics* and the coauthor of *Atmospheric Tides*, Dr. Lindzen is a fellow of the National Academy of Sciences, the American Association for the Advancement of Science, the American Geophysical Union, the American Meteorological Society, and the American Academy of Arts and Sciences.

TAMMY O. TENGS is an assistant research professor in the Center for Health Policy Research and Education at Duke University. She completed her doctorate in health policy and management at the Harvard School of Public Health in 1994. Dr. Tengs directed the four-year Lifesaving Priorities Project at the Harvard Center for Risk Analysis, where she supervised a team of twenty that amassed cost-effectiveness data for more than 500 life-saving interventions. Her research interests include the rational allocation of social resources devoted to promoting health and the economic efficiency of investments in science.

W. KIP VISCUSI is the George G. Allen Professor of Economics at Duke University and an adjunct scholar at the American Enterprise Institute. Dr. Viscusi's research focuses primarily on individual and social responses to risk and uncertainty. He has published numerous books and articles dealing with different aspects of risk, including *Fatal Tradeoffs: Public and Private Responsibilities for Risk*. He has consulted for the U.S. Office of Management and Budget, the Environmental Protection Agency, the Occupational Safety and Health Administration, the Federal Aviation Administration, and the U.S. Department of Justice on issues pertaining to the valuation of life and health. Dr. Viscusi is founding editor of the *Journal of Risk and Uncertainty* and serves on the editorial boards of several other journals, including the *American Economic Review*.

RISKS, COSTS, AND LIVES SAVED
Getting Better Results from Regulation

Chapter 1

INTRODUCTION

Robert W. Hahn

Since the creation of the Environmental Protection Agency in 1970, the United States has embarked on a major regulatory effort to protect the environment, health, and safety. That effort has produced some unquestionably desirable results—such as cleaner rivers and cleaner air—but also much controversy.

We have learned a great deal about regulation since 1970. Perhaps most important, we have learned that regulations have significant costs, not just benefits, and that analysis of risk is an indispensable component of sensible regulation. It has become clear that more sensitivity to costs not only would yield greater net social benefits but would actually improve regulatory outcomes such as a cleaner and safer environment.

Making that statement does not, however, imply that the matter is settled. Profound disagreements remain—more among the public and politicians than among economists and scientists—about the implications of being more aware of costs and of assessing comparative risk in making regulations. Emotions often run high, as recent congressional debates over the major regulatory reform legislation have made amply clear. Most noneconomists, for example, have an instinctive aversion to putting a limit on what they would be willing to spend to reduce different kinds of risks, although doing so is fundamental to certain kinds of regulatory analysis.

This book, consisting of ten chapters, will bring the interested reader up to date on the latest thinking and evidence on regulatory issues. Two of the chapters contain completely new databases of a type never before compiled, which provide previously unavailable means of evaluating regulatory interventions. The chapters range in tone from the coldly mathematical to the almost impassioned, but they all reach conclusions that are important to sound thinking about regulation.

The book does not present a monolithic viewpoint. Indeed, Lester Lave's strong critique of benefit-cost analysis goes farther than some of the other authors would accept. Nevertheless, all the chapters perform the essential function of exposing the latest thinking, evidence, and analysis on regulatory issues. Without exception—though by different routes—the authors reach the conclusion that sensitivity to costs and relative risks will lead to better outcomes for society. But the chapters generally also implicitly and explictly conclude that regulations can be and often are beneficial in improving the environment, health, and safety.

The following three chapters are by scientists and illustrate in various ways the scientific approach to regulation. The fifth chapter raises a large warning flag about the misuse of science in reaching political decisions—legislative or regulatory. The final five chapters are by economists and public policy analysts and bring to bear the insights of those disciplines on various regulatory questions.

Chapter two by Bruce N. Ames and Lois S. Gold examines cancer. It distinguishes between the truly important causative factors in cancer—smoking above all—and the marginal effects of such factors as air pollution or pesticides, where carcinogenicity is often deduced mistakenly from huge doses of the suspect substance in animals.

William R. Hendee's chapter examines the particular case of one presumed hazard—exposure to ionizing radiation—as a case study of the process of assessing risk. He notes that scientists themselves disagree on some aspects of the issue but that, despite this, a "no-threshold" model for measuring radiation risk has emerged as the standard. Hendee concludes that this may not be the best model; yet it has huge consequences in such areas as the cost of radiation cleanup.

The fourth chapter, by Bernard D. Goldstein, places risk assessment—an essentially scientific approach to regulation—in perspective. While emphasizing the great value in regulatory decision making of risk assessment and analysis that are properly carried out and used, Goldstein cautions against many pitfalls that can lead to misuse and poor results.

In the fifth chapter Richard S. Lindzen cites the current case of global warming and the nearly century-old case of eugenics and immigration as two compelling examples of the misuse of science, which can occur when science, advocacy nominally based on science, and politics interact.

In chapter six, the first economics-based chapter, Lester B. Lave casts a highly skeptical eye on the use of cost-benefit analysis in scrutinizing regulations. While he acknowledges that the technique can be valuable, he worries that far more is expected of it than can be delivered in practice.

Chapter seven, by W. Kip Viscusi, assesses the efforts to date to bring more cost consciousness into the regulatory process. There is both good and bad news concerning the balancing of costs and risk, but clearly much regulatory activity continues to be misdirected. Viscusi finds considerable promise in legislation on regulatory process reform that Congress is considering.

The following chapter, by Tammy O. Tengs and John D. Graham, compiles new data on hundreds of regulatory interventions and estimates their costs and life-saving benefits. The chapter assesses the opportunity costs of the current activity and determines an "optimal portfolio" of regulatory activity that could save more lives at less cost.

In chapter nine John D. Graham describes a "syndrome of paranoia and neglect," in which society focuses its attention on minor risks to life and health while neglecting the far more serious—and often obvious—risks. He proposes new omnibus legislation that would require risk assessment as part of regulatory activity and, among other things, would force the government to make periodic rankings of risk, from the most serious to the trivial, to help establish sensible regulatory priorities.

My final chapter provides a new and comprehensive analysis of the benefits and costs of virtually all environmental, health, and safety regulations issued by federal agencies since 1990. The data are from the government agencies themselves. I find that estimates of net benefits to government regulation are substantially overstated and that about half the regulations would not pass a cost-benefit test.

Taken together, the chapters in this book, and the new and updated information and conclusions they contain, provide an indispensable guide to current thinking about environmental, health, and safety regulation.

Chapter 2

THE CAUSES AND PREVENTION OF CANCER
Gaining Perspectives on the Management of Risk

Bruce N. Ames and Lois Swirsky Gold

OVERVIEW

Epidemiological studies have identified several factors that are likely to have a major effect on reducing rates of cancer: reduction of smoking, increased consumption of fruits and vegetables, and control of infections. Other factors include avoidance of intense sun exposure, increased physical activity, and reduced consumption of alcohol and possibly red meat. Humans can already reduce risks of many forms of cancer, and the potential for further reductions is great. In the United States cancer death rates for all cancers combined are decreasing if lung cancer—90 percent of which is due to smoking—is excluded from the analysis. In this chapter we review the latest research on the causes of cancer, show why much cancer is preventable, and offer a scientific perspective on the management of risk.

The idea that traces of synthetic chemicals such as DDT are major contributors to human cancer is not supported by the evidence. Pollution appears to account for less than 1 percent of human cancer; yet public concern and resource allocation for chemical pollution are very high, in good part because standard risk assessment uses limited data from high-dose animal cancer tests. Scientists do those tests at the maximum tolerated dose of a substance, and the tests are typically misinterpreted to mean that low doses of synthetic chemicals and industrial pollutants are relevant to human cancer. About half the chemicals tested, whether synthetic or natural, are carcinogenic to rodents at such high doses. One early series of mouse studies by Innes

4

et al. (1969) has frequently been cited as evidence that the true proportion of rodent carcinogens is low; however, the Innes test did not meet current standards. Among those Innes chemicals that have subsequently been retested, our analysis indicates that about half are positive. A plausible explanation for the high frequency of positive results in rodent bioassays is that testing at the maximum tolerated dose frequently can cause chronic cell killing and consequent cell replacement—a risk factor for cancer that can be limited to high doses. Ignoring the effects of high-dose risks greatly exaggerates estimates of low-dose risks. Scientists must determine mechanisms of carcinogenesis for each substance and revise acceptable dose levels as understanding advances.

Almost all chemicals in the human diet are natural. For example, 99.99 percent of the pesticides we eat are naturally present in plants to ward off insects and other predators. Half of the natural pesticides that scientists have tested at the maximum tolerated dose are rodent carcinogens. Reducing exposure to the .01 percent of pesticides that are synthetic will not reduce cancer rates. On the contrary, although fruits and vegetables contain a wide variety of naturally occurring chemicals that are rodent carcinogens, epidemiology indicates that inadequate consumption of fruits and vegetables doubles the risk for most types of cancer. If reducing the use of synthetic pesticides increases the cost of fruits and vegetables, then the incidence of cancer is likely to increase because of reduced consumption. Cooking food produces large numbers of natural dietary chemicals. Chemists have found more than a thousand chemicals in roasted coffee: more than half of those tested—nineteen of twenty-six—are rodent carcinogens. By weight, there are more rodent carcinogens in a single cup of coffee than there are potentially carcinogenic pesticide residues in the average American diet in a year, and a thousand chemicals in roasted coffee are still untested. That does not mean that coffee is dangerous, but rather that animal cancer tests and worst-case risk assessment build in enormous safety factors and should not be considered true risks.

Humans, like other animals, can eat the tremendous variety of natural chemicals that are "rodent carcinogens" because we are extremely well protected by many general defense enzymes, and most of them are inducible: whenever a defense enzyme is in use, the body produces more of it. Since the defense enzymes are equally effective against natural and synthetic chemicals, we neither expect nor find a general difference between synthetic and natural chemicals in the frequency of positive results in high-dose rodent tests.

There is no epidemiological evidence that exposure to traces of synthetic industrial chemicals has increased human cancer. Indeed, if lung cancer is excluded, death rates from all other cancers combined have declined 14 percent in the past forty years. In addition, life expectancy in the developed countries is steadily rising. Linear extrapolation from the maximum tolerated dose in rodents to low-level exposure in humans has led to grossly exaggerated forecasts of mortality. Epidemiology cannot verify such extrapolations. Furthermore, relying on such extrapolations to assess the risk of synthetic chemicals while ignoring the enormous natural background leads to an imbalanced perception of hazard and the misallocation of resources. The perception of hazard is also greater now because major advances in analytical techniques allow chemists to detect extremely low concentrations of chemicals, often a million times lower than they could detect thirty years ago. Moreover, low levels of rodent carcinogens of natural origin are ubiquitous in the environment. Thus, it is impossible for people to be totally free of exposure to rodent carcinogens or to background radiation. The progress of scientific research and technology will continue to lengthen human life expectancy.

Society must distinguish between significant and trivial cancer risks. Regulating trivial risks or exposure to substances erroneously inferred to cause cancer at low doses can harm health by diverting resources from programs that could be effective in protecting public health. Moreover, wealth creates health: poor people have a shorter life expectancy than wealthy people. When government policy results in wasting money and resources on trivial problems, it reduces society's wealth and hence harms health.

Cancer Trends

According to the National Cancer Institute's 1993 Surveillance, Epidemiology, and End-Results Program (Miller et al. 1993), cancer caused 23 percent of the person-years of premature loss of life and about 530,000 deaths in the United States in 1993. Four major cancers—lung, colon-rectum, breast, and prostate—accounted for 55 percent of the deaths. Cancer death rates in the United States are decreasing, after adjusting for age and excluding lung cancer. The age-adjusted mortality rate for all cancers combined (excluding lung and bronchus) declined 14 percent from 1950 to 1990. The mortality rates for all individual age groups declined except for those aged over eighty-five, who show a 6 percent increase in cancer deaths. The decline ranged from 71 percent in the group under four years old to 8 percent in the group aged seventy-four to eighty-five years old. One plausible explanation for the increase in those over eighty-five is that autopsies of the very old were less common in former years. Smoking, in addition to causing 90 percent of lung cancer, contributes to other malignancies such as cancers of the mouth, esophagus, pancreas, bladder, and possibly colon; if those were taken into account, the decline would be greater. Figure 2-1 shows U.S. cancer death rates by site from 1930 through 1992.

Cancer mortality (including lung cancer) has decreased more than 25 percent for each age group under forty-five and has increased for age groups over fifty-five. The decreases in cancer deaths during this period have been primarily from stomach, cervical, uterine, and rectal cancer. The increases have been primarily from lung cancer, which is due to smoking—as is about one-third of all U.S. cancer deaths—and from non-Hodgkin's lymphoma. Reasons for the increase in non-Hodgkin's lymphoma are not clear, but smoking and sun exposure may possibly contribute (Brown et al. 1992; Linet et al. 1992; Adami et al. 1995), and human immunodeficiency virus is a small but increasing cause.

Professor Peto (Peto et al. 1994) has come to the same conclusion:

> The common belief that there is an epidemic of death from cancer in developed countries is a myth, except for the effects of tobacco. In many countries cancer deaths from tobacco are going up, and in some they are at last coming down. But, if we take away the cancer deaths that are attributed to smoking, then the cancer death rates that remain are, if anything, declining. This is reassuringly true in Western Europe, Eastern Europe and North America, and in the "West," the death rates from other diseases are falling rapidly. For most nonsmokers, the health benefits of modern society outweigh the new hazards. Apart from tobacco (and

Figure 2-1   Cancer Death Rates by Site, 1930–1992

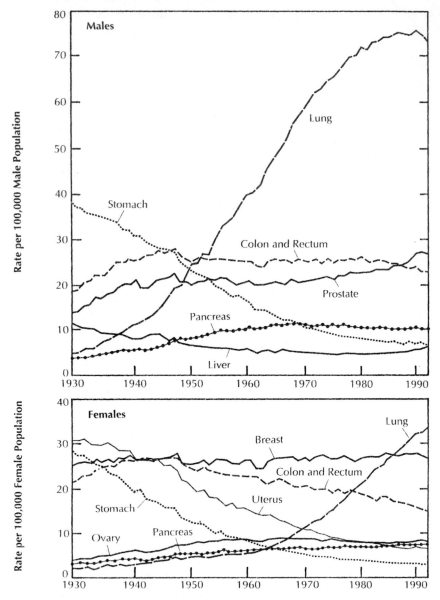

Note: Rates are per 100,000 and are age-adjusted to the 1970 U.S. census population.
Source: American Cancer Society, *Cancer Facts and Figures—1996* (Atlanta: ACS, 1996).

in places, HIV), the Western world is a remarkably healthy place to live.

Figure 2-2 shows cancer mortality in the United States attributed to smoking and not attributed to smoking for individuals aged thirty-five to sixty-nine from 1955 through 1990.

Lung cancer continues to increase in the United States despite the decline in the number of smokers because of decades of delay between the time a person begins smoking and the onset of the disease. The rate of lung cancer among American men appears to have peaked, while the rate is still increasing for American women, who started smoking more recently than men. See figure 2-1 for lung cancer and figure 2-2 for cancer deaths attributed to smoking.

The number of people newly diagnosed with cancer—the incidence rate—has been increasing for some types of cancer. To interpret changes in mortality rates, we must consider changes in both incidence rates and the effects of treatment. In their comprehensive study on the causes of cancer, Doll and Peto (1981) of Oxford University, two of the world's leading epidemiologists, point out that incidence rates should not be taken in isolation, because reported incidence rates for a disease might reflect increases in the registration of cases and improvements in diagnosis. The reported rise in cancer incidence rates among men born in the 1940s compared with rates among those born in the 1890s (Davis, Dinse, and Hoel 1994) may be due to such artifacts. For example, the rapid increase in the incidence of age-adjusted prostate cancer without any major increases in mortality is almost certainly due largely to increased screening and incidental detection during transurethral resection of the prostate for benign prostatic hypertrophy.

Major Contributors to Risk of Cancer

Tobacco

Tobacco is the most important global cause of cancer. Smoking contributes to about one-third of cancer, about one-quarter of heart disease, and about 400,000 premature deaths per year in the United States (Peto et al. 1992). Tobacco is a known cause of cancer of the lung, bladder, mouth, pharynx, pancreas, stomach, larynx, esophagus (Peto et al. 1994), and possibly colon (Fielding 1994; Giovannucci et al. 1994a; Giovannucci et al. 1994b). Tobacco causes even more

Figure 2-2   Total Cancer Mortality in the United States, 1930–1991

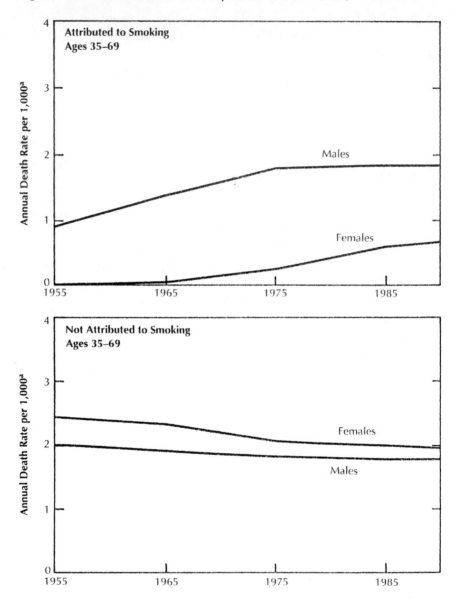

a. Mean of seven age-specific rates, ages 35–69; annual death rate/1,000.
Source: Peto et al. (1994).

deaths by diseases other than cancer. Tobacco is causing about three million deaths per year worldwide in the 1990s and will, if present rates of smoking continue, cause about ten million deaths per year a few decades from now (Peto et al. 1992). Indeed, Peto et al. (1994) note, "Over the whole of the second half of this century (1950–2000) the total number of deaths caused by smoking in developed countries will be about 60 million." The evidence for environmental tobacco smoke as a cause of cancer is much weaker. Studies have estimated that environmental tobacco smoke causes up to 3,000 additional cases of cancer (Environmental Protection Agency 1992; Fontham et al. 1994), although some researchers have disputed that estimate (Huber, Brockie, and Mahajan 1993).

The carcinogenic mechanisms of tobacco smoking are not well understood. Smoke contains a wide variety of mutagens and rodent carcinogens, and smoking is a severe oxidative stress and causes inflammation in the lungs. The oxidants in cigarette smoke—mainly nitrogen oxides—deplete the body's antioxidants. Thus, smokers must ingest two to three times more ascorbate than nonsmokers to achieve the same level of ascorbate in blood, but they rarely do (Bui et al. 1991; Duthie, Arthur, and James 1991; Schectman, Byrd, and Hoffmann 1991). Men who have inadequate diets or smoke may damage both their somatic DNA and the DNA of their sperm. When the level of dietary ascorbate is insufficient to keep seminal fluid ascorbate at an adequate level, the oxidative lesions in sperm DNA increase 2.5 times (Fraga et al. 1991). An inadequate intake of ascorbate is more common among single males, the poor, and smokers (Patterson and Block 1991). Paternal smoking may plausibly increase the risk of birth defects and childhood cancer in offspring (Ames et al. 1994).

Diet

Doll and Peto (1981) and other scientists (Ames, Gold, and Willett 1995) estimate that diet accounts for about one-third of cancer risk, and current research is slowly clarifying specific factors. In our brief overview of the field we shall emphasize the major contribution of fruit and vegetable consumption in preventing cancer.

Cancer prevention by calorie or protein restriction. In rodents a calorie-restricted diet compared with ad libitum feeding markedly decreases tumor incidence and increases life span (Boutwell and Pariza 1987; Roe 1989; Roe et al. 1991) but decreases reproduction. Protein restriction appears to have a similar effect on rodents as calorie restriction, although research is less extensive on protein restriction (Youngman, Park, and Ames 1992). An understanding of mechanisms for the marked effect of dietary restriction on aging and cancer is becoming clearer. That beneficial effect may, in good part, be due to reduced oxidative damage and reduced rates of cell division. Although epidemiological evidence on restriction in humans is sparse, epidemiologic studies indicating higher rates of breast and other cancers among taller persons (Swanson et al. 1988; Hunter and Willett 1993) support the possible importance of restricting growth to reduce the incidence of human cancer. Japanese women, who are now taller and menstruate earlier, have increased breast cancer rates. Also, many of the variations in breast cancer rates among countries and trends over time within countries are compatible with changes in growth rates and attained adult height (Willett and Stampfer 1990).

Cancer prevention by dietary fruits and vegetables. Adequate consumption of fruits and vegetables is associated with a lowered risk of degenerative diseases such as cancer, cardiovascular disease, cataracts, and brain and immune dysfunction (Ames, Shigenaga, and Hagen 1993). Nearly 200 studies in the epidemiological literature have been reviewed. With great consistency those studies relate the lack of adequate consumption of fruits and vegetables to cancer incidence (Steinmetz and Potter 1991a; Block, Patterson, and Subar 1992; Hill, Giacosa, and Caygill 1994). The quarter of the population with the lowest dietary intake of fruits and vegetables has roughly twice the cancer rate for most types of cancer (lung, larynx, oral cavity, esophagus, stomach, colon and rectum, bladder, pancreas, cervix, and ovary) compared with the quarter with the highest consumption of those foods. The protective effect of consuming fruits and vegetables is weaker and less consistent for hormonally related cancers: for breast cancer the protective effect appears to be about 30 percent (Howe, Hirohata, and Hislop 1990; Block et al. 1992; Hunter and Willett 1993). Two servings of fruits plus three of vegetables per day is the intake recommended by the National Cancer Institute and the National Research Council (Patterson et al. 1990; Block 1992). Laboratory studies suggest that antioxidants such as vitamins C and E and carotenoids in fruits and vegetables account for a good part of their beneficial effect (Ames et al. 1993); however, epidemiologists have difficulty disentangling the effects of dietary intakes of the antioxidants ascorbate, tocopherol, and carotenoids from other important vitamins and ingredients in fruits and vegetables (Steinmetz and Potter 1991b; Block 1992).

A wide array of compounds in fruits and vegetables in addition to antioxidants may contribute to the reduction of cancer. Folic acid may be particularly important. Low folic acid intake causes chromosome breaks in rodents (MacGregor et al. 1990) and in humans (Everson et al. 1988; Blount 1994) and increases tumor incidence in some rodent models (Bendich and Butterworth 1991). Folic acid is essential for the synthesis of DNA. Scientists have found that low folate intake is associated with several neoplasms including adenomas and cancers of the colon (Freudenheim et al. 1991; Giovannucci et al. 1993; Glynn and Albanes 1994). Maternal deficiency is associated with neural tube birth defects (Rush 1994). Deficient intake of folic acid is common in U.S. diets. About 15 percent of the U.S. population (Senti and Pilch 1985) and about half of low-income black children (Bailey et al. 1982) or black elderly (Bailey et al. 1979) have a folate level at which chromosome breaks are seen (Blount 1994). Dietary fiber, obtained only from foods of plant origin, may contribute to lower risk of colon cancer (Trock, Lanza, and Greenwald 1990). Plant foods also contain a wide variety of weak estrogens that may act as antiestrogens by competing with estrogenic hormones (Steinmetz and Potter 1991a; Steinmetz and Potter 1991b; Safe 1994).

Other aspects of diet. Although epidemiologic studies most clearly support the benefits of fruits and vegetables in the prevention of cancer, strong international correlations suggest that animal (but not vegetable) fat and red meat may increase the incidence of cancers of the breast, colon, and prostate (Armstrong and Doll 1975). Large prospective studies, however, have consistently shown either a weak association or a lack of association between fat intake and breast cancer (Hunter and Willett 1993). Consumption of animal fat and consumption of red meat have been associated with risk of colon cancer in many case-control and cohort studies; the association with meat consumption appears more consistent (Willett et al. 1990; Giovannucci et al. 1994c; Goldbohm et al. 1994). Consumption of animal fat and red meat has also been associated with risk of prostate cancer (Giovannucci et al. 1994c; Le Marchand et al. 1994). Mechanisms for those associations are not clear, but they may include the effects of dietary fats on endogenous hormone levels (Henderson, Ross, and Pike 1991), the local effects of bile acids on the colonic mucosa, the effects of carcinogens produced in the cooking of meat, and excessive iron intake. Excess iron absorption, particularly heme iron from meat, is a plausible, though unproven, contributor to the production of oxygen radicals (Ames et al. 1993). Some of the large geographical differences in colon cancer rates that have been attributed to dietary factors are probably due to differences in physical activity, which is inversely related to colon cancer risk in many studies (Gerhardsson, Floderus, and Norell 1988; Slattery et al. 1988; Thun et al. 1992).

Alcoholic beverages cause inflammation and cirrhosis of the liver and liver cancer (International Agency for Research on Cancer 1988). Alcohol is an important cause of oral and esophageal cancer, is synergistic with smoking (International Agency for Research on Cancer 1988), and possibly contributes to colorectal cancer (Freudenheim et al. 1991; Giovannucci et al. 1995). Breast cancer is also associated with alcohol consumption.

Cooking food is plausible as a contributor to cancer (Sugimura et al. 1986). Cooking forms a wide variety of chemicals. Four groups of chemicals that cause tumors in rodents have attracted attention because of mutagenicity, potency, or concentration: nitrosamines, heterocyclic amines, polycyclic hydrocarbons, and furfural and similar furans. Epidemiological studies on cooking are difficult and so far are inadequate to evaluate a carcinogenic effect in humans (International Agency for Research on Cancer 1993).

Oxidative Damage Causing the Degenerative Diseases of Aging

Oxidant byproducts of normal metabolism cause extensive damage to DNA, protein, and lipid. Metabolism, like other aspects of life, involves trade-offs. We argue that this oxidative damage is a major contributor to aging and to degenerative diseases of aging such as cancer, heart disease, cataracts, and brain dysfunction (Ames, Shigenaga, and Hagen 1993). Antioxidant defenses against such damage include vitamins C and E and carotenoids. To the extent that the major external risk factors for cancer—smoking, unbalanced diet, and chronic inflammation—are diminished, cancer will appear at a later age, and the proportion of cancer that is caused by normal metabolic processes will increase.

Studies of carcinogenesis have found that there is significant metabolic oxidative damage to DNA despite elaborate defense and repair processes. The rate of cell division, which is influenced by hormones, growth, cell killing, and inflammation, is also key because it determines the probability of converting DNA lesions to mutations. These mechanisms are likely to underlie many epidemiologic observations, and together suggest practical interventions and areas for further research.

Aging and the degenerative diseases accompanying it appear to be due in good part to oxidative damage to DNA and other macromolecules that accumulate with age (Ames et al. 1993). Byproducts of normal metabolism—

To the extent that the major external risk factors for cancer— smoking, unbalanced diet, and chronic inflammation— are diminished, cancer will appear at a later age, and the proportion of cancer that is caused by normal metabolic processes will increase.

superoxide, hydrogen peroxide, and hydroxyl radical—are the same oxidative mutagens produced by radiation (Von Sonntag 1987). Oxidative lesions in DNA accumulate with age, so that by the time a rat is old (two years) it has about a million DNA lesions per cell, which is about twice that in a young rat (Ames et al. 1993). Mutations also accumulate with age. DNA is oxidized in normal metabolism because antioxidant defenses, though numerous, are not perfect.

Oxidants from metabolism damage proteins as well as DNA (Stadtman 1992). In two human diseases associated with premature aging, Werner's syndrome and progeria, oxidized proteins accumulate at a much higher rate than normal (Stadtman 1992). Cataracts, which also represent the accumulation of oxidized protein, are a common manifestation of oxidative stresses, such as ultraviolet radiation and smoking, as well as of insufficient antioxidant protection (Jacques et al. 1988; Hankinson et al. 1992b; Hankinson et al. 1992c; Ames et al. 1993).

Cancer from Inflammation Caused by Chronic Infection

White cells and other phagocytic cells of the immune system combat bacteria, parasites, and virus-infected cells by destroying them with potent, mutagenic oxidizing agents. While such oxidants protect humans from immediate death from infection, they also cause oxidative damage to DNA, mutation, and chronic cell killing with compensatory cell division (Yamashina, Miller, and Heppner 1986; Shacter et al. 1988) and thus contribute to the carcinogenic process. Antioxidants appear to inhibit some of the pathology of chronic inflammation (Ames et al. 1993).

Chronic infections contribute to about one-third of the world's cancer. Hepatitis B and C viruses are a major cause of chronic inflammation leading to liver cancer—one of the most common cancers in Asia and Africa (Beasley 1987; Yu et al. 1991a; Tabor and Kobayashi 1992). Hepatitis B and C viruses infect about 500 million people worldwide. Nearly half the world's liver cancer occurs in China (Parkin, Suernsward, and Muir 1984). Vaccinating babies at birth is potentially an effective method to reduce liver cancer and is routinely done for hepatitis B in Taiwan.

The mutagenic mold toxin, aflatoxin, which is found in moldy peanut and corn products, appears to interact with chronic hepatitis infection in liver cancer development (Qian et al. 1994). Biomarker measurements on populations in Africa and China confirm that those populations are chronically exposed to high levels of aflatoxin (Pons 1979; Groopman et al. 1992). Liver cancer is rare in the United States. Although hepatitis B and C viruses infect less than 1 percent of the U.S. population, hepatitis viruses can account for half of liver cancer cases among non-Asians (Yu et al. 1991b) and even higher percentages among Asians (Yeh et al. 1989).

Another major chronic infection is schistosomiasis, which is widespread in Egypt and Asia. In Egypt, the eggs of *Schistosoma haematobium*, deposited in the bladder, cause inflammation and bladder cancer (International Agency for Research on Cancer 1994a). In Asia, the eggs of *Schistosoma japonicum*, deposited in the colonic mucosa, cause inflammation, and there is limited epidemiological evidence for an association with colon cancer (International Agency for Research on Cancer 1994a). *Opisthorchis viverrini*, a liver fluke, infects millions of people in Thailand and Malaysia. The flukes lodge in bile ducts and increase the risk of cholangiocarcinoma (International Agency for Research on Cancer 1994a). *Chlonorchis sinensis* infects millions of people in China and increases the risk for biliary tract cancer (International Agency for Research on Cancer 1994a). *Helicobacter pylori* bacteria, which infect the stomachs of more than one-third of the world's population, are a major cause of stomach cancer, ulcers, and gastritis (International Agency for Research on Cancer 1994a). In wealthy countries the infection is often asymptomatic, which suggests that inflammation may be at least partially suppressed, possibly by adequate levels of dietary antioxidants (Howson, Hiyama, and Wynder 1986).

Human papilloma virus, a major risk factor for cervical cancer, does not appear to work through an inflammatory mechanism (Lowy, Kirnbauer, and Schiller 1994). It is spread by sexual contact, an effective way of transmitting viruses.

Chronic inflammation resulting from noninfectious sources can also lead to cancer. For example, asbestos exposure leading to chronic lung inflammation may be in good part the reason that asbestos is a significant risk factor for lung cancer (Marsh and Mossman 1991; Korkina et al. 1992).

Hormones

Henderson, Pike, and colleagues have reviewed the extensive literature on hormones and cancer, which indicates that sex hormones play a large role in cancer and possibly contribute to as much as one-third of all cancer (Henderson et al. 1991). Hormones are likely to act by causing cell division. Endometrial cancer appears most exquisitely sensitive to cumulative estrogen exposure; long-term use of exogenous estrogens elevates risks ten- to twentyfold (Jick et al. 1980). Estrogens increase the division of endometrial cells, but progestogens reduce division; thus, the addition of progestogens to estrogen therapy after menopause may reduce the risk of endometrial cancer (Henderson et al. 1991).

Ovarian cancer seems to be related to factors that increase the division of surface epithelial cells; for example, pregnancies substantially reduce the number of ovulations and the risk of the malignancy (Henderson et al. 1991). Oral contraceptives, which also block ovulation, decrease risk—by as much as 50 percent with five years of use (Hankinson et al. 1992a).

Factors that increase cumulative exposure to estrogens, such as early age at menarche, late menopause, and prolonged estrogen therapy after menopause, increase the risk of breast cancer (Henderson et al. 1991; Harris et al. 1992). Breast cancer cells also proliferate in the presence of estrogens, and progestogens also appear to enhance cell division (Henderson et al. 1991). Moreover, the addition of progestogens to estrogen therapy does not reduce, and may further increase, the risk of breast cancer (Colditz et al. 1992). Pregnancy has a complex relation with breast cancer; for one to two decades pregnancy increases risk—probably because it stimulates hormones—but pregnancy ultimately reduces the lifetime incidence of breast cancer (Rosner, Colditz, and Willett 1994), possibly because of a permanent differentiation of stem cells that results in less proliferation (Russo et al. 1993). Lactation modestly reduces the incidence of breast cancer (Byers et al. 1985; Newcomb et al. 1994). The evidence that hormones influence breast cancer suggests ways of reducing incidence. One proposal is to develop a hormonal contraceptive that mimics the effect of an early menopause; that might reduce breast cancer by half (Henderson, Ross, and Pike 1993). Exercise may lower the risk of breast cancer in young women, probably by influencing hormone levels (Bernstein et al. 1994). Alcohol consumption, which has been consistently associated with risk of breast cancer in large prospective studies and most case-control studies (Longnecker 1994), appears to increase endogenous estrogen levels (Dorgan et al. 1994). Thus, the reduced consumption of alcohol may decrease breast cancer risk.

Less Important Contributors to Risk of Cancer

Occupation

The International Agency for Research on Cancer of the World Health Organization evaluates potential cancer risks to humans from a range of chemical exposures (International Agency for Research on Cancer 1994b). Half of the sixty chemicals and chemical mixtures the agency has evaluated as having sufficient evidence of carcinogenicity in humans represent occupational exposures, which tend to be concentrated among small groups of people who have been chronically exposed at high levels. Those include workplace exposures such as in the rubber industry or in coke production, as well as exposure to specific aromatic amines, petrochemicals, and metals. How much cancer can be attributed to occupational exposure has been a controversial issue, but a few percent seems a reasonable estimate. Doll and Peto (1981) have discussed difficulties in making such estimates, including the lack of accurate data on the history of exposure and current exposures, as well as confounding factors such as socioeconomic status and smoking. Lung cancer was by far the largest contributor to Doll and Peto's estimate of the proportion of cancers due to occupation. The preeminence of smoking as a cause of lung cancer confounds the interpretation of rates in terms of particular workplace exposures to substances such as asbestos; asbestos appears to multiply rather than just add to the effect of smoking. In contrast, asbestos alone is a known risk factor for mesothelioma. Doll and Peto (1981) estimated that asbestos caused a high proportion of occupational cancers, but recent estimates for asbestos-related cancer are lower (Connelly et al. 1987; Reynolds 1992).

Exposures to substances in the workplace can be high in comparison with other chemical exposures in food, air, or water. We have argued (Ames and Gold 1990; Ames, Shigenaga, and Gold 1993) that increased cell division rates are important in causing mutation and cancer, and therefore, that one cannot extrapolate from the results of high-dose animal cancer tests to low-dose human exposures without considering the mechanism of carcinogenesis for the chemical. Past occupational exposures have often been high, however, and comparatively little quantitative extrapolation may be required from high-dose rodent tests to high-dose occupational exposures. Since occupational cancer is concentrated among small groups exposed at high levels, there is an opportunity to control or eliminate risks once they are identified. The Occupational Safety and Health Administration, however, unlike other federal agencies such as the Environmental Protection Agency, regulates few chemicals as potential human carcinogens. For seventy-five rodent carcinogens regulated by OSHA with permissible exposure limits, we recently ranked potential carcinogenic hazards on an index that compares the permitted dose-rate for workers with the carcinogenic dose for rodents (Gold, Garfinkel, and Slone 1994). We found that for nine chemicals the permitted exposures were within a factor of ten of the rodent carcinogenic dose and for seventeen they were between ten and a hundred times lower. Those values are high in comparison with hypothetical risks that other federal agencies regulated. An additional 120 rodent carcinogens had no OSHA permissible exposure limit, which suggests the need for further regulatory attention.

Sun Exposure

Exposure to the sun is the major cause of skin cancer, most important, melanoma. Exposure during the early decades of life appears to be the dominant factor, particularly when sufficient to cause burns (International Agency for Research on Cancer 1992). Prevention of skin cancer is feasible if fair-skinned people become aware of that fact and take protective measures.

Medical Interventions

Some cancer chemotherapeutic drugs, particularly alkylating agents, cause second malignancies, most commonly leukemias, lymphomas, and sarcomas (Ellis and Lisher 1993). Some formerly used drugs, such as phenacetin and diethylstilbesterol, were associated with increased cancer risk (International Agency for Research on Cancer 1987). Potent immunosuppressive agents such as cyclosporin also increase the risk of a variety of cancers (Ryffel 1992). Estrogen replacement therapy may increase the risk of endometrial and breast cancer. Diagnostic X-rays have also contributed to malignancies (Preston-Martin et al. 1989). Although such side effects should weigh in therapeutic decisions, medications and diagnostic procedures contribute little to cancer incidence.

Pollution

Much of the public fears synthetic pollutants as major causes of cancer, but that fear is based on a misconception. Even assuming that the Environmental Protection Agency's worst-case risk estimates for synthetic pollutants are true risks, the proportion of cancer that the EPA could prevent by regulation would be tiny (Gough 1990). Epidemiological studies, moreover, are difficult to conduct because of inadequacies in assessing exposure and failure to account for confounding factors such as smoking, diet, and geographic mobility of the population. Since the focus of this chapter is cancer causation, we shall not discuss other issues in environmental protection and health.

Air pollution. Indoor air is generally of greater concern than outside air because people spend 90 percent of their time indoors, and the concentrations of pollutants indoors tend to be higher than outdoors. Radon is likely to be the most important carcinogenic air pollutant. It occurs naturally as a radioactive gas, generated as a decay product of the radium present in trace quantities in the earth's crust. Radon primarily enters houses in air that is drawn from the underlying soil. On the basis of epidemiological studies of high exposures to underground miners, researchers have estimated that radon causes as many as 15,000 lung cancers per year in the United States, mostly among smokers because of the synergistic effect with smoking (Nero 1992; Lubin et al. 1994; Pershagen et al. 1994). Epidemiological studies of radon exposures in homes (Létourneau et al. 1994; Lubin 1994) have failed to demonstrate convincingly an excessive risk. About 50,000 to 100,000 of U.S. homes (.1 percent) are estimated to have annual average radon levels approximately twenty times the national average, and inhabitants receive annual radiation doses that exceed the current occupational standard for underground miners. Efforts to identify houses with high levels of radon indicate that they occur most frequently in concentrated geographic areas (Nero 1994). In areas with high levels of radon, individuals can perform a measurement in their homes for about $20, and if they find high levels, they can reduce them substantially—by using available contractors— for perhaps $1,500 (Nero 1992). With respect to outdoor air pollution, a recent large study has reported an association with lung cancer when sulfates are used as an index, but not when fine particles are used; the study did not control for diet (Pope et al. 1995).

Water pollution. Water pollution as a risk factor for cancer appears small. Among potential hazards that have been of concern, the most important are radon (exposure is small compared with air) and arsenate. Natural arsenate is a known human carcinogen at high doses (Bates, Smith, and Hopenhayn 1992; Smith et al. 1992), and further research is needed to determine mechanisms of carcinogenesis and the dose response in humans. Chlorination of water, an important public health intervention, produces large numbers of chlorine-containing chemicals as byproducts, some of which are rodent carcinogens. The International Agency for Research on Cancer

(1991) has judged that the evidence that chlorination of water increases cancer is inadequate. A recent case-control interview study did not confirm earlier associations with bladder cancer and colon cancer but did find an association with rectal cancer (Cantor, Lynch, and Hildesheim 1995).

Hereditary Factors

Inherited factors clearly contribute to some percentage of cancer, particularly childhood cancer and cancer in early adulthood. Generally, cancer increases exponentially with age except for a blip on the curve for childhood cancer, which may be due to inheriting a mutant cancer gene (Knudsen 1989; Ponder 1990). Heredity is likely to affect susceptibility to all cancers, but to what extent is not clear, although it is obvious that skin color plays a large role in sun-associated cancers such as melanoma. With the rapid progress of molecular biology, scientists will soon understand more about the genetic factors. Factors other than heredity play the dominant causative role for most major cancers, as indicated by the large differences in cancer rates among countries, the observation that migrants adopt cancer rates close to those of their host populations, and the large temporal changes in the rates of many cancers.

Distractions: Animal Cancer Tests and the Rachel Carson Fallacy

Neither toxicology nor epidemiology supports the idea that synthetic industrial chemicals are causing an epidemic of human cancer. Although some epidemiologic studies find an association between cancer and low levels of industrial pollutants, the associations are usually weak, the results are usually conflicting, and the studies do not correct for diet, which is a potentially large confounding factor. Moreover, the levels of synthetic pollutants are low and rarely seem plausible as a causal factor when compared with the background of natural chemicals that are rodent carcinogens (Gold et al. 1992).

Rachel Carson's fundamental misconception was: "For the first time in the history of the world, every human being is now subjected to contact with dangerous chemicals, from the moment of conception until death" (Carson 1962). She was wrong. The vast bulk of the chemicals to which humans are exposed are natural, and for every chemical some amount is dangerous. Carson thus lacked perspective about the wide variety of naturally occurring chemicals to which all people are exposed and did not address the fact that, outside the workplace, exposures to synthetic pollutants are extremely low relative to the natural background.

Animal cancer tests are conducted on synthetic chemicals at the maximum tolerated dose of the chemical, and regulatory agencies use the results to predict

Neither toxicology nor epidemiology supports the idea that synthetic industrial chemicals are causing an epidemic of human cancer. Policy makers are misinterpreting results of animal cancer tests to mean that low doses of synthetic chemicals and industrial pollutants are relevant to human cancer.

human risk at low levels of exposure. Since the vast proportion of human exposures are to naturally occurring chemicals, while the vast proportion of chemicals tested for carcinogenicity are synthetic, there is an imbalance in data and perception about chemicals and cancer. Policy makers are misinterpreting results of animal cancer tests to mean that low doses of synthetic chemicals and industrial pollutants are relevant to human cancer. Under the usual experimental conditions about half of the chemicals tested are carcinogenic to rats or mice at the high doses administered, and that proportion is similar for the natural chemicals and synthetic chemicals that have been tested (Ames and Gold 1990; Gold et al. 1993a). A plausible explanation for the high proportion of positive results is that testing at the maximum tolerated dose frequently can cause chronic cell killing and consequent cell replacement—a risk factor for cancer that can be limited to high doses (Ames and Gold 1990; Ames et al. 1993).

To the extent that increases in tumor incidence in rodent studies are due to the secondary effects of inducing cell division at the maximum tolerated dose, then any chemical is a likely rodent carcinogen, and carcinogenic effects at low doses are likely to be much lower than what would be predicted by the linear model that regulatory agencies use. The true risk might often be zero. Data from standard rodent bioassays are not sufficient to estimate low dose risks; the predicted regulatory one-in-a-million risk estimate can, in fact, be obtained simply by dividing the high dose given in a bioassay by 740,000 (Gaylor and Gold 1995). The high proportion of positive chemicals among those tested and the limited information from animal cancer tests emphasize the need for data on the mechanism of carcinogenesis for each chemical when trying to estimate low-dose risk.

Because regulatory agencies routinely use results of high-dose rodent tests to identify a chemical as a possible cancer hazard to humans, it is important to try to understand how representative the 50 percent positivity rate might be of all the untested chemicals. If half of all chemicals, both natural and synthetic, to which humans are exposed would be positive if tested, then the utility of a test to identify a chemical as a "potential human carcinogen" is questionable. To determine the true proportion of rodent carcinogens among chemicals would require comparing a random group of synthetic chemicals with a random group of natural chemicals. Such an analysis has not been done. We have found that the high positivity rate is consistent for all chemicals tested: synthetic chemicals, natural chemicals, natural pesticides, and the chemicals in roasted coffee (Gold et al. 1993a). Additionally, Davies and Monro (1995) have reported that half the drugs in the *Physician's Desk Reference* that report animal cancer test results are carcinogenic.

It has been argued that the high positivity rate is due to selecting more suspicious chemicals to test for carcinogenicity. For example, researchers may select chemicals structurally similar to known carcinogens or chemicals that have been shown to be mutagens more often than other substances. That is a likely bias since cancer testing is both expensive and time-consuming, and it is prudent to test suspicious compounds. On the other hand, chemicals are selected for testing for several reasons, including the extent of human exposure, level of production, and scientific questions about carcinogenesis. Moreover, while some chemical classes are more often carcinogenic in rodent bioassays than others—for example, nitroso compounds, aromatic amines, nitroaromatics, and chlorinated compounds—predictive capability is still imperfect. In addition, although mutagens are positive in rodent bioassays about twice as frequently as nonmutagens, the proportion of tested chemicals that are mutagenic is about the same as nonmutagenic, which suggests that the prediction of positivity may often not be the basis for selecting a chemical to test.

One large series of mouse experiments by Innes et al. (1969) has been frequently cited (National Cancer Institute 1986) as evidence that the true proportion of rodent carcinogens is actually low among tested substances; however, our analysis of the Innes experiments comes to the opposite conclusion. In the Innes study, among 119 chemicals tested—primarily the most widely used pesticides at that time and some industrial chemicals—only eleven (9 percent) were judged as carcinogens. We note that those early experiments lacked power to detect an effect because they were conducted only in mice (not in rats), they included only eighteen animals in a group (compared with the usual fifty), the animals were tested for only eighteen months (compared with the usual twenty-four months), and the Innes dose was usually lower than the highest dose in subsequent mouse tests of the same chemical.

To assess whether the low proportion of positive chemicals may have been due to the design of the experiments, we used results in our Carcinogenic Potency Database to examine the results of subsequent bioassays on the Innes chemicals that had not been evaluated as positive. Among thirty-four such chemicals that were subsequently retested, sixteen had a subsequent positive evaluation of carcinogenicity (47 percent), which is similar to the proportion among all chemicals in our database. Of the sixteen new positives, six were carcinogenic in mice and twelve in rats. Innes et al. had recommended further evaluation of some chemicals with inconclusive results in their study. If they were the chemicals that were subsequently retested, then one might argue that they would be the most likely to be positive. Our analysis does not support that view, however. We found that the positivity rate among the chemicals the Innes study said needed further evaluation was six of sixteen (38 percent) when retested, compared with ten of eighteen (56 percent) among the chemicals that Innes et al. evaluated as negative.

In a bioassay, pathologists examine about thirty tissues. The risk assessment is usually based on the most sensitive tissue in the experiment with the most potent result. Thus, classification of carcinogenicity is based on the response at the most sensitive site, and extrapolations from rodent to human and from high dose to low dose are based on the potency at that site. Rodent carcinogens, however, often increase the tumor rate at some target sites, while decreasing the rate at other sites—even in the same experiment (that is, for sites at which control animals develop tumors). Risk assessment ignores that effect. In evaluating carcinogenic effects of a chemical in rodent studies, it would be desirable to consider chemically induced decreases of tumors, which occur frequently (Davies and Monro 1994; Haseman and Johnson 1995). Those results emphasize the importance of further investigating mechanisms of carcinogenesis for each chemical.

Correlation between cell division and cancer. Many studies on rodent carcinogenicity show a correlation between cell division at the maximum tolerated dose and cancer. Cunningham has analyzed fifteen chemicals at that dose; eight mutagens and seven nonmutagens, including several pairs of mutagenic isomers, one of which is a carcinogen and one of which is not (Cunningham, Foley, et al. 1991; Cunningham and Matthews 1991; Yarbrough, Cunningham, et al. 1991; Thottassery, Winberg, et al. 1992; Cunningham, Elwell, et al. 1993; Cunningham, Elwell, et al. 1994; Cunningham, Maronpot, et al., 1994; Cunningham, Pippin, et al. 1995; Hayward, Shane, et al. 1995). He found a perfect correlation between cancer causation and cell division in the target tissue: the nine chemicals causing cancer caused cell division in the target tissue, and the six chemicals not causing cancer did not. A similar result has been found in the analysis of Mirsalis (Mirsalis, Provost, et al. 1993). For example, both dimethyl nitrosamine (DMN) and methyl methane sulfonate (MMS) methylate liver DNA and cause unscheduled DNA synthesis, but DMN causes both cell division and liver tumors, while MMS does neither. A recent study on the mutagenic dose response of the carcinogen ethylnitrosourea concludes that cell division is a key factor in its mutagenesis and carcinogenesis (Shaver-Walker, Urlando, et al. 1995). Chloroform at high doses induces liver cancer by chronic cell division (Larson, Wolf, et al. 1994). Extensive reviews on rodent studies (Ames and Gold 1990; Cohen and Ellwein 1991; Ames, Shigenaga, et al. 1993; Cohen 1995; Cohen and Lawson 1995; Counts and Goodman 1995) document that chronic cell division can induce cancer. There is also a large epidemiological literature reviewed by Preston-Martin, Henderson, and colleagues (Preston-Martin, Pike, et al. 1990; Preston-Martin, Monroe, et al. 1995) that shows that increased cell division by hormones and other agents can increase human cancer.

The great bulk of chemicals ingested by humans is natural, by both weight and number. As we pointed out, 99.99 percent of the pesticides in the diet are naturally present in plants to ward off insects and other predators (Ames, Profet, and Gold 1990a). Half the natural pesticides tested—thirty-one of sixty-one—are rodent carcinogens (Gold et al. 1992; Gold et al. 1993a; Gold et al. 1995). Reducing exposure to the .01 percent of pesticides that are synthetic, either individual chemicals or mixtures, will not appreciably reduce cancer rates. On the contrary, fruits and vegetables are important for reducing cancer; making them more expensive by reducing the use of synthetic pesticides is likely to increase the incidence of cancer. People with low incomes eat fewer fruits and vegetables (Patterson and Block 1988) and spend a higher percentage of their income on food.

Humans also ingest large numbers of natural chemicals from cooking food. Of the more than one thousand chemicals identified in roasted coffee, over half of those tested—nineteen of twenty-six—are rodent carcinogens (Gold et al. 1992). In table 2-1 we classify the carcinogenicity status of natural chemicals in roasted coffee. A single cup of coffee has more natural "rodent carcinogens" by weight than the average U.S. diet has of potentially carcinogenic synthetic pesticide residues in a year. A thousand known chemicals in roasted coffee still have not been tested. That does not necessarily mean that coffee is dangerous, but that high-dose animal cancer tests and worst-case risk assessments build in enormous safety factors and should not be considered true risks at the low dose of most human exposures.

Because of their unusual lipophilicity and long environmental persistence, a small group of polychlorinated synthetic chemicals such as DDT and PCBs has caused particular concern. There is no convincing epidemiological evidence (Key and Reeves 1994), nor is there much toxicological plausibility (Gold et al. 1992), that the levels normally found in the environment are likely to contribute significantly to cancer. TCDD, which is produced naturally by burning when chloride ion is present, for example in forest fires, and as an industrial byproduct, is an unusually potent rodent carcinogen but seems unlikely to be a significant human carcinogen at the levels to which the general population is exposed.

The reason humans can eat the tremendous variety of "rodent carcinogens" is that, like other animals, we are extremely well protected by many general defense enzymes, most of which are inducible (Ames, Profet, and Gold 1990b). Defense enzymes are effective against both natural and synthetic chemicals, including potentially

Table 2-1   Carcinogenicity Status of Natural Chemicals in Roasted Coffee

Positive	Not Positive	Yet to Test
Acetaldehyde	Acrolein	~1,000 chemicals
Benzaldehyde	Biphenyl	
Benzene	Eugenol	
Benzofuran	Nicotinic acid	
Benzo(a)pyrene	Phenol	
Caffeic Acid	Piperidine	
Catechol	[Uncertain: caffeine]	
1,2,5,6-Dibenzanthracene		
Ethanol		
Ethylbenzene		
Formaldehyde		
Furan		
Furfural		
Hydrogen Peroxide		
Hydroquinone		
Limonene		
MeIQ		
Styrene		
Toluene		

Source: Gold et al. (1992).

mutagenic reactive chemicals. One does not expect, nor does one find, a general difference between synthetic and natural chemicals in their ability to cause cancer in high-dose rodent tests (Ames and Gold 1990; Gold et al. 1992; Gold et al. 1993a).

We have ranked possible carcinogenic hazards from known rodent carcinogens by using an index (HERP) that relates human exposure to carcinogenic potency in rodents (Gold et al. 1992; Gold et al. 1993b; Gold et al. 1994). In table 2-2 we report an updated HERP ranking. Our ranking does not estimate risks because current science does not have the ability to do so. Instead, we put possible hazards of synthetic chemicals into perspective against the background of naturally occurring rodent carcinogens in typical portions of common foods. The residues of synthetic pesticides or environmen-

Table 2-2   Ranking Possible Carcinogenic Hazards from Natural and Synthetic Chemicals

Possible Hazard: HERP (%)	Daily Human Exposure	Human Dose of Rodent Carcinogen
140	EDB: workers' daily intake (high exposure)	EDB, 150 mg (before 1977)
17	Clofibrate (average daily dose)	Clofibrate, 2 g
16	Phenobarbital, 1 sleeping pill	Phenobarbital, 60 mg
[14]	Isoniazid pill (prophylactic dose)	Isoniazid, 300 mg
6.2	Comfrey-pepsin tablets, 9 daily	Comfrey root, 2.7 g
[5.6]	Metronidazole (therapeutic dose)	Metronidazole, 2 g
4.7	Wine (250 ml)	Ethyl alcohol, 30 ml
4.0	Formaldehyde: workers' average daily intake	Formaldehyde, 6.1 mg
2.8	Beer (12 oz; 354 ml)	Ethyl alcohol, 18 ml
1.4	Mobile home air (14 hr/day)	Formaldehyde, 2.2 mg
1.3	Comfrey-pepsin tablets, 9 daily	Symphytine, 1.8 mg
0.4	Conventional home air (14 hr/day)	Formaldehyde, 598 µg
[0.3]	Phenacetin pill (average dose)	Phenacetin, 300 mg
0.3	Lettuce, 1/8 head (125 g)	Caffeic acid, 66.3 mg
0.2	Natural root beer (12 oz; 354 ml)	Safrole, 6.6 mg (banned)
0.1	Apple, 1 whole (230 g)	Caffeic acid, 24.4 mg
0.1	Mushroom, 1 (15 g)	Mix of hydrazines, etc.
0.1	Basil (1 g of dried leaf)	Estragole, 3.8 mg
0.07	Mango, 1 whole (245 g; pitted)	d-Limonene, 9.8 mg
0.07	Pear, 1 whole (200 g)	Caffeic acid, 14.6 mg
0.07	Brown mustard (5 g)	Allyl isothiocyanate, 4.6 mg
0.06	Diet cola (12 oz; 354 ml)	Saccharin, 95 mg
0.06	Parsnip, 1/4 (40 g)	8-Methoxypsoralen, 1.28 mg
0.04	Orange juice (6 oz; 177 ml)	d-Limonene, 5.49 mg
0.04	Coffee, 1 cup (from 4 g)	Caffeic acid, 7.2 mg
0.03	Plum, 1 whole (50 g)	Caffeic acid, 6.9 mg
0.03	Safrole: U.S. average from spices	Safrole, 1.2 mg
0.03	Peanut butter (32 g; 1 sandwich)	Aflatoxin, 64 ng
0.03	Comfrey herb tea (1.5 g)	Symphytine, 38 µg
0.03	Celery, 1 stalk (50 g)	Caffeic acid, 5.4 mg
0.03	Carrot, 1 whole (100 g)	Caffeic acid, 5.16 mg

(Table continues)

Table 2-2   (continued)

Possible Hazard: HERP (%)	Daily Human Exposure	Human Dose of Rodent Carcinogen
0.03	Pepper, black: U.S. average (446 mg)	d-Limonene, 3.57 mg
0.02	Potato, 1 (225 g; peeled)	Caffeic acid, 3.56 mg
0.008	Swimming pool, 1 hour (for child)	Chloroform, 250 µg
0.008	Beer, before 1979 (12 oz; 354 ml)	Dimethylnitrosamine, 1 µg
0.006	Bacon, cooked (100 g)	Diethylnitrosamine, 0.1 µg
0.006	Well water, 1 liter contaminated (worst in Silicon Valley, Calif.)	Trichloroethylene, 2.8 mg
0.005	Coffee, 1 cup (from 4 g)	Furfural, 630 µg
0.004	Bacon, pan fried (100 g)	N-nitrosopyrrolidine, 1.7 µg
0.003	Nutmeg: U.S. average (27.4 mg)	d-Limonene, 466 g
0.003	Mushroom, 1 (15 g)	Glutamyl p-hydrazinobenzoate, 630 µg
0.003	Conventional home air (14 hr/day)	Benzene, 155 µg
0.003	Sake (250 ml)	Urethane, 43 µg
0.003	Bacon, cooked (100 g)	Dimethylnitrosamine, 300 ng
0.002	White bread, 2 slices (45 g)	Furfural, 333 µg
0.002	Apple juice (6 oz; 177 ml)	UDMH, 5.89 µg (from Alar, 1988)
0.002	Coffee, 1 cup (from 4 g)	Hydroquinone, 100 µg
0.002	Coffee, 1 cup (from 4 g)	Catechol, 400 µg
0.002	DDT: daily dietary average	DDT, 13.8 µg (before 1972 ban)
0.001	Celery, 1 stalk (50 g)	8-Methoxypsoralen, 30.5 µg
0.001	Tap water, 1 liter	Chloroform, 83 µg (U.S. average, 1976)
0.001	Heated sesame oil (15 g)	Sesamol, 1.13 mg
0.0008	DDE: daily dietary average	DDE, 6.91 µg (before 1972 ban)
0.0006	Well water, 1 liter contaminated (Woburn, Mass.)	Trichloroethylene, 267 µg
0.0005	Mushroom, 1 (15 g)	p-Hydrazinobenzoate, 165 µg
0.0005	Jasmine tea, 1 cup (2 g)	Benzyl acetate, 460 µg
0.0004	EDB: Daily dietary average	EDB, 420 ng (from grain; before 1984 ban)
0.0004	Beer (12 oz; 354 ml)	Furfural, 54.9 µg
0.0004	Tap water, 1 liter	Chloroform, 25 µg (U.S. average, 1987–92)

Table 2-2   (continued)

0.0003	Well water, 1 liter contaminated (Woburn, Mass.)	Tetrachloroethylene, 21 µg
0.0003	Carbaryl: daily dietary average	Carbaryl, 2.6 µg (1990)[a]
0.0002	Apple, 1 whole (230 g)	UDMH, 598 ng (from Alar, 1988)
0.0002	**Parsley, fresh (1 g)**	**8-Methoxypsoralen, 3.6 µg**
0.0002	Toxaphene: daily dietary average	Toxaphene, 595 ng (1990)[a]
0.0001	**Salmon steak, baked (3 oz; 85 g)**	**PhIP, 306 ng**
0.00008	**Salmon steak, baked (3 oz; 85 g)**	**MeIQx, 111 ng**
0.00008	DDE/DDT: daily dietary average	DDE, 659 ng (1990)[a]
0.00006	**Hamburger, pan fried (3 oz; 85 g)**	**PhIP, 176 ng**
0.00003	**Whole wheat toast, 2 slices (45 g)**	**Urethane, 540 ng**
0.00003	**Hamburger, pan fried (3 oz; 85 g)**	**MeIQx, 38.1 ng**
0.00002	Dicofol: daily dietary average	Dicofol, 544 ng (1990)[a]
0.00002	**Cocoa (4 g)**	**α-Methylbenzyl alcohol, 5.2 µg**
0.00001	**Lager beer (12 oz; 354 ml)**	**Urethane, 159 ng**
0.000005	**Hamburger, pan fried (3 oz; 85 g)**	**IQ, 6.38 ng**
0.000001	Lindane: daily dietary average	Lindane, 32 ng (1990)[a]
0.0000004	PCNB: daily dietary average	PCNB (Quintozene), 19.2 ng (1990)[a]
0.0000001	Chlorobenzilate: daily dietary average	Chlorobenzilate, 6.4 ng (1989)[a]
<0.00000001	Chlorothalonil: daily dietary average	Chlorothalonil, < 6.4 ng (1990)[a]
0.000000008	Folpet: daily dietary average	Folpet, 12.8 ng (1990)[a]
0.000000006	Captan: daily dietary average	Captan, 11.5 ng (1990)[a]

Notes: Natural chemicals are in boldface type.

Daily human exposure: Reasonable daily intakes are used to facilitate comparisons. The calculations assume a daily dose for a lifetime. Where drugs are normally taken for only a short period, we have bracketed the human exposure/rodent potency (HERP) index.

Possible hazard: The human dose of rodent carcinogen is divided by 70 kg to give an mg/kg of human exposure, and this dose is given as the percentage of the daily lifetime dose rate estimated to halve the proportion of tumor-free animals by the end of a standard lifetime. Those values in our Carcinogenic Potency Database span a ten-millionfold range. In the HERP calculation those values are averages calculated by

(table continues)

tal pollutants rank low in comparison with the background of naturally occurring rodent carcinogens, despite the fact that such a comparison gives a minimal view of hypothetical background hazards because
so few chemicals in the natural world have been tested for carcinogenicity in rodents. Our results indicate that many ordinary foods
would not pass the regulatory criteria used for synthetic chemicals.
Our analysis does not necessarily indicate that coffee consumption,
for example, is a significant risk factor for human cancer, even though
chemicals in coffee have a HERP value of more than a thousand
times the HERP equivalent to the one-in-a-million worst-case risk
estimate that the EPA uses (Gold et al. 1992). Adequate risk assessment from animal cancer tests requires more information about many
aspects of toxicology, such as effects on cell division, induction of
defense and repair systems, and species differences.

Linear extrapolation from the maximum tolerated dose in rodents
to low-level exposure in humans for synthetic chemicals, while ignoring the enormous background of natural chemicals, has led to exaggerated estimates of cancer risk and to an imbalance in the perception of
hazard and the allocation of resources. If the costs were minor, the
issue of putting hypothetical risks into perspective would not be so
important, but the costs are huge (Crandall 1992; Bartlett 1994).
Costs escalate as cleanliness approaches perfection. Most attempts to
deal with pollutants do not adequately deal with trade-offs; instead,
policy makers assume that upper-bound risk assessment to one in a million protects the public. Reports by the Office of Management and
Budget (OMB 1993) and the Harvard Center for Risk Analysis (Tengs
et al. 1995) compared costs of risk reduction among government agencies and concluded that the money the EPA spent to save a life is often
orders of magnitude higher than what many other government agencies

taking the harmonic mean of the positive tests in that species from the Carcinogenic
Potency Database. Average values have been calculated separately for rats and mice,
and the more sensitive species is used for calculating possible hazard.
a. Estimate is based on average daily dietary intake for 60–65-year-old females, the
only adult group reported for 1990. Because of the agricultural usage of those chemicals and the prominence of fruits and vegetables in the diet of older Americans, the
residues are generally slightly higher than for other adult age groups.
Sources: Gold et al. (1992) TD_{50} values and references are reported in Gold et al.
(1993b, 1994). Chloroform in tap water data are from the American Waterworks
Association's *Disinfectant/Disinfection By-Products Database for the Negotiated
Regulation* (Washington, D.C., October 1993).

spent. EPA risk estimates are based on "risk assessment"—default, worst-case, linear extrapolations to one-in-a-million risk from hypothetical maximum exposures—so that the actual discrepancy between the EPA and many other agencies is even greater. Many scholars have pointed out that expensive regulations intended to save lives may actually lead to increased deaths (Keeney 1990), in part because they divert resources from important health risks and in part because higher incomes are associated with lower mortality (Wildavsky 1988; Viscusi 1992). Worst-case assumptions in risk assessment represent a policy decision, not a scientific one; they confuse attempts to allocate money effectively for risk abatement. Regulating trivial risks impedes effective risk management (Breyer 1993).

Conclusion

Epidemiological evidence in humans is sufficient to identify several broad categories of cancer causation for which the evidence is strong and plausible. Since many of those risks are avoidable, it is possible to reduce the incidence rates of many types of cancer. In a monumental 1981 review of avoidable risks of cancer in the United States, Doll and Peto (1981) attributed 30 percent of cancer deaths to tobacco and 35 percent to

In general, new data on diet and cancer have most strongly emphasized the inadequate consumption of protective factors rather than the excessive intake of harmful factors.

dietary factors, although the plausible contribution of diet ranged from 10 to 70 percent. Doll and Peto judged other factors to contribute far less. Since that time the contribution of smoking appears to have increased to about 35 percent—even though the prevalence of smoking in adults has decreased—because the relative risk due to smoking has greatly increased for almost all cancers as well as for cardiovascular disease (Peto et al. 1992). That result is probably due both to a declining risk of cancer death in nonsmokers and to the fact that the lifetime impact of smoking since adolescence is being experienced only now. Available data on diet and cancer have increased manyfold since 1981, and they generally support the earlier estimate; a slightly narrower estimated range of 20 to 40 percent seems most plausible

(Willett 1995). In general, new data have most strongly emphasized the inadequate consumption of protective factors rather than the excessive intake of harmful factors. The estimate for diet is revised slightly downward largely because the large international contrasts in colon cancer rates are probably due to differences in physical activity as well as diet. The Doll and Peto estimate for the dietary contribution to breast cancer of 50 percent is still plausible, although that may not be avoidable in a practical sense if rapid growth rates are the most important underlying nutritional factor. The estimate for alcoholic beverages can be increased slightly from 3 percent plus or minus 1 percent, to 5 percent plus or minus 1 percent, as many new studies have supported associations with breast and colon cancer. Data subsequent to 1981 have not provided a basis to alter appreciably the earlier estimates for other causes of cancer.

One approach to estimating the impact on the population of adopting major lifestyle factors associated with low cancer risk is to compare cancer incidence and mortality rates of the general population with those of Seventh-Day Adventists—who generally do not smoke, drink heavily, or eat much meat but do eat a diet rich in fruits and vegetables (Phillips et al. 1980; Mills et al. 1994). Seventh-Day Adventists experience substantially lower mortality rates of lung, bladder, and colon cancers. Total cancer mortality is about half that of the general U.S. population. While such a comparison has limitations—better use of medical services may contribute to reduced mortality, and imperfect compliance with recommendations may underestimate the impact of lifestyle—the results strongly suggest that people can avoid a large portion of cancer deaths by using knowledge at hand. Incidence rates rather than mortality rates provide a similar picture, although the differences are somewhat less. For breast cancer, the healthy behavior of Seventh-Day Adventists was not sufficient to have a major effect on risk.

Decreases in physical activity and increases in smoking, obesity, and recreational sun exposure have contributed importantly to increases in some cancers in the modern industrial world, whereas improvements in hygiene have reduced other cancers related to infection. There is no good reason to believe that synthetic chemicals underlie the major changes in incidence of some cancers. In the United States and other industrial countries, life expectancy is steadily increasing and will increase even faster as smoking declines.

NOTES

This chapter has been adapted in part from Bruce N. Ames and Lois S. Gold, "The Causes and Prevention of Cancer: The Role of Environment," in Ronald Bailey, ed., *The True State of the Planet* (New York: Free Press, 1995), pp. 141–75, and from Bruce N. Ames, Lois S. Gold, and Walter C. Willett, "The Causes and Prevention of Cancer," *Proceedings of the National Academy of Sciences, USA* 92 (1995): 5258–65. We are indebted to Walter C. Willett for his help and to Thomas H. Slone for work on updating our section on animal cancer tests.

This work was supported by the National Institute of Environmental Health Sciences Center Grant ESO1896; by the National Cancer Institute Outstanding Investigator Grant CA39910 to Bruce N. Ames; and by the director, Office of Energy Research, Office of Health and Environmental Research of the U.S. Department of Energy under contract DE-AC03-76SF00098 to Lois S. Gold.

REFERENCES

Adami, J., M. Frisch, J. Yuen, B. Glimelius, and M. Melbye. "Evidence of an Association between Non-Hodgkin's Lymphoma and Skin Cancer." *British Medical Journal* 310 (1995): 1491–95.

American Cancer Society. *Cancer Facts and Figures—1996.* Atlanta: American Cancer Society, 1996.

Ames, Bruce N., and Lois S. Gold. "Chemical Carcinogenesis: Too Many Rodent Carcinogens." *Proceedings of the National Academy of Sciences, USA* 87 (1990): 7772–76.

Ames, Bruce N., Lois S. Gold, and Walter C. Willett. "The Causes and Prevention of Cancer." *Proceedings of the National Academy of Sciences, USA* 92 (1995): 5258–65.

Ames, Bruce N., P. A. Motchnik, C. G. Fraga, M. K. Shigenaga, and T. M. Hagen. "Antioxidant Prevention of Birth Defects and Cancer," in D. R. Mattison and A. Olshan, eds., *Male-Mediated Developmental Toxicity.* New York: Plenum Publishing Corporation, 1994.

Ames, Bruce N., M. Profet, and Lois S. Gold. "Dietary Pesticides (99.99% All Natural)." *Proceedings of the National Academy of Sciences, USA* 87 (1990a): 7777–81.

———. "Nature's Chemicals and Synthetic Chemicals: Comparative Toxicology." *Proceedings of the National Academy of Sciences, USA* 87 (1990b): 7782–86.

Ames, Bruce N., M. K. Shigenaga, and L. S. Gold. "DNA Lesions, Inducible DNA Repair, and Cell Division: Three Key Factors in Mutagenesis and Carcinogenesis." *Environmental Health Perspectives* 101 (supp. 5) (1993): 35–44.

Ames, Bruce N., M. K. Shigenaga, and T. M. Hagen. "Oxidants, Antioxidants, and the Degenerative Diseases of Aging." *Proceedings of the National Academy of Sciences, USA* 90 (1993): 7915–22.

Armstrong, B., and R. Doll. "Environmental Factors and Cancer Incidence and Mortality in Different Countries, with Special Reference to Dietary Practices."

International Journal of Cancer 15 (1975): 617–31.

Bailey, L. B., P. A. Wagner, G. J. Christakis, P. E. Araujo, H. Appledorf, C. G. Davis, et al. "Folacin and Iron Status and Hematological Findings in Predominately Black Elderly Persons from Urban Low-Income Households." *American Journal of Clinical Nutrition* 32 (1979): 2346–53.

Bailey, L. B., P. A. Wagner, G. J. Christakis, C. G. Davis, H. Appledorf, P. E. Araujo, et al. "Folacin and Iron Status and Hematological Findings in Black and Spanish-American Adolescents from Urban Low-Income Households." *American Journal of Clinical Nutrition* 35 (1982): 1023–32.

Bartlett, B. "The High Cost of Turning Green." *Wall Street Journal* (1994).

Bates, M. N., A. H. Smith, and R. C. Hopenhayn. "Arsenic Ingestion and Internal Cancers: A Review." *American Journal of Epidemiology* 135 (1992): 462–76.

Beasley, R. P. "Hepatitis B Virus." *Cancer* 61 (1987): 1942–56.

Bendich, A., and C. E. Butterworth, Jr., eds. *Micronutrients in Health and in Disease Prevention.* New York: Marcel Dekker, Inc., 1991.

Bernstein, L., B. E. Henderson, R. Hanisch, J. Sullivan-Halley, and R. K. Ross. "Physical Exercise and Reduced Risk of Breast Cancer in Young Women." *Journal of the National Cancer Institute* 86 (1994): 1403–8.

Block, G. "The Data Support a Role for Antioxidants in Reducing Cancer Risk." *Nutrition Reviews* 50 (1992): 207–13.

———, B. Patterson, and A. Subar. "Fruit, Vegetables and Cancer Prevention: A Review of the Epidemiologic Evidence." *Nutrition and Cancer* 18 (1992): 1–29.

Blount, B. C. "Detection of DNA Damage Caused by Folate Deficiency and Chronic Inflammation." University of California, Berkeley, 1994.

Boutwell, R. K., and M. W. Pariza. "Historical Perspectives: Calories and Energy Expenditure in Carcinogenesis." *American Journal of Clinical Nutrition* 45 (supp.) (1987): 151–56.

Breyer, Stephen G. *Breaking the Vicious Circle: Toward Effective Risk Regulation.* Cambridge: Harvard University Press, 1993.

Brown, L. M., G. D. Everett, R. Gibson, L. F. Burmeister, L. M. Schuman, and A. Blair. "Smoking and Risk of Non-Hodgkin's Lymphoma and Multiple Myeloma." *Cancer Causes and Control* 3 (1992): 49–55.

Bui, M. H., A. Sauty, F. Collet, and P. Leuenberger. "Dietary Vitamin C Intake and Concentrations in the Body Fluids and Cells of Male Smokers and Nonsmokers." *Journal of Nutrition* 122 (1991): 312–16.

Byers, T., S. Graham, T. Rzepka, and J. Marshall. "Lactation and Breast Cancer: Evidence for a Negative Association in Premenopausal Women." *American Journal of Epidemiology* 121: 664–74.

Cantor, K. P., C. F. Lynch, and M. Hildesheim. "Chlorinated Drinking Water and Risk of Bladder, Colon, and Rectal Cancers: A Case-Control Study in Iowa, USA." *Epidemiology* 6 (1995): S30.

Carson, Rachel. *Silent Spring.* Boston: Houghton-Mifflin, 1962.

Cohen, S. "Human Relevance of Animal Carcinogenicity Studies." *Regulatory Toxicology and Pharmacology* 21 (1995): 75–80.

Cohen, S., and T. Lawson. "Rodent Bladder Tumors Do Not Always Predict for Humans." *Cancer Letters* 93 (1995): 9–16.

Cohen, S. M., and L. B. Ellwein. "Genetic Errors, Cell Proliferation, and Carcinogensis." *Cancer Research* 51 (1991): 6493–505.

Colditz, G. A., M. J. Stampfer, Walter C. Willett, D. J. Hunter, J. E. Manson, C. H. Hennekens, et al. "Type of Postmenopausal Hormone Use and Risk of Breast Cancer: 12-Year Follow-up from the Nurses' Health Study." *Cancer Causes and Control* 3(5) (1992): 433–39.

Connelly, R. R., R. Spirtas, M. H. Myers, C. L. Percy, and J. F. Fraumeni, Jr. "Demographic Patterns for Mesothelioma in the United States." *Journal of the National Cancer Institute* 78 (1987): 1053–60.

Counts, J., and J. Goodman. "Principles Underlying Dose Selection for, and Extrapolation from, the Carcinogen Bioassay: Dose Influence Mechanism." *Regulatory Toxicology and Pharmacology* 21 (1995): 418–21.

Crandall, Robert W. *Why Is the Cost of Environmental Regulation So High?* St. Louis: Center for the Study of American Business, 1992.

Cunningham, M. L., and H. B. Matthews. "Relationship of Hepatocarcinogenicity and Hepatocellular Proliferation Induced by Mutagenic Noncarcinogens vs. Carcinogens. II. 1- vs. 2-Nitropropane." *Toxicology and Applied Pharmacology* 110 (1991): 505–13.

Cunningham, M. L., M. R. Elwell, et al. "Relationship of Carcinogenity and Cellular Proliferation Induced by Mutagenic Noncarcinogens vs. Carcinogens." *Fundamental Applied Toxicology* 23 (1994): 363–69.

Cunningham, M. L., M. R. Elwell, et al. "Site-Specific Cell Proliferation in Renal Tubular Cells by the Renal Tubular Carcinogen *tris* (2,3-Dibromopropyl)phosphate." *Environmental Health Perspectives* 101 (supp. 5) (1993): 253–58.

Cunningham, M. L., J. Foley, et al. "Correlation of Hepatocellular Proliferation with Hepatocarcinogenicity Induced by the Mutagenic Noncarcinogen: Carcinogen Pair—2,6- and 2,4-Diaminotoluene." *Toxicology and Applied Pharmacology* 107(1991): 562–67.

Cunningham, M. L., R. R. Maronpot, et al. "Early Responses of the Liver of B6C3F1 Mice to the Hepatocarcinogen Oxazepam." *Toxicology and Applied Pharmacology* 124 (1994): 31–38.

Cunningham, M. L., L. L. Pippin, et al. "The Hepatocarcinogen Methapyrilene But Not the Analog Pyrilamine Induces Sustained Hepatocellular Replication and Protein Alterations in F344 Rats in a 13-Week Feed Study." *Toxicology and Applied Pharmacology* 131 (1995): 216–23.

Davies, T. S., and A. Monro. "The Rodent Carcinogenicity Bioassay Produces a Similar Frequency of Tumor Increases and Decreases: Implications for Risk Assessment." *Regulatory Toxicology and Pharmacology* 20 (1994): 281–301.

Davis, D. L., G. E. Dinse, and D. G. Hoel. "Decreasing Cardiovascular Disease and Increasing Cancer among Whites in the United States from 1973 through 1987." *Journal of the American Medical Association* 271 (1994): 431–37.

Doll, R., and R. Peto. "The Causes of Cancer: Quantitative Estimates of Avoidable Risks of Cancer in the United States Today." *Journal of the National Cancer Institute* 66 (1981): 1191–1308.

Dorgan, J. F., M. E. Reichman, J. T. Judd, C. Brown, C. Longcope, A. Schatzkin, et al. "The Relation of Reported Alcohol Ingestion to Plasma Levels of Estrogens and Androgens in Premenopausal Women (Maryland, United States)." *Cancer Causes and Control* 5 (1994): 53–60.

Duthie, G. G., J. R. Arthur, and W. P. T. James. "Effects of Smoking and Vitamin E on Blood Antioxidant Status." *American Journal of Clinical Nutrition* 53 (1991): 1061S–63S.

Ellis, M., and M. Lisher. "Second Malignancies Following Treatment in Non-Hodgkin's Lymphoma." *Leukemia and Lymphoma* 9 (1993): 337–42.

Environmental Protection Agency. *Respiratory Health Effects of Passive Smoking: Lung Cancer and Other Disorders.* Washington, D.C.: Office of Health and Environmental Assessment, Office of Research and Development, 1992.

Everson, R. B., C. M. Wehr, G. L. Erexson, and J. T. MacGregor. "Association of Marginal Folate Depletion with Increased Human Chromosomal Damage *in Vivo*: Demonstration by Analysis of Micronucleated Erythrocytes." *Journal of the National Cancer Institute* 80 (1988): 525–29.

Fielding, J. E. "Preventing Colon Cancer: Yet Another Reason Not to Smoke." *Journal of the National Cancer Institute* 86 (1994): 162–64.

Fontham, E. T. H., P. Correa, P. Reynolds, A. Wu-Williams, P. A. Buffler, R. S. Greenberg, et al. "Environmental Tobacco Smoke and Lung Cancer in Non-smoking Women." *Journal of the American Medical Association* 271 (1994): 1752–59.

Fraga, C. G., P. A. Motchnik, M. K. Shigenaga, H. J. Helbock, R. A. Jacob, and Bruce N. Ames. "Ascorbic Acid Protects against Endogenous Oxidative Damage in Human Sperm." *Proceedings of the National Academy of Sciences, USA* 88 (1991): 11003–6.

Freudenheim, J. L., S. Graham, J. R. Marshall, B. P. Haughey, S. Cholewinski, and G. Wilkinson. "Folate Intake and Carcinogenesis of the Colon and Rectum." *International Journal of Epidemiology* 20 (1991): 368–74.

Gaylor, D. W., and Lois S. Gold. "Quick Estimate of the Regulatory Virtually Safe Dose Based on the Maximum Tolerated Dose for Rodent Bioassays." *Regulatory Toxicology and Pharmacology* 22 (1995): 57–63.

Gerhardsson, M., B. Floderus, and S. E. Norell. "Physical Activity and Colon Cancer Risk." *International Journal of Epidemiology* 17(4) (1988): 743–46.

Giovannucci, E., G. A. Colditz, M. J. Stampfer, D. Hunter, B. A. Rosner, Walter C. Willett, et al. "A Prospective Study of Cigarette Smoking and Risk of Colorectal Adenoma and Colorectal Cancer in U.S. Women." *Journal of the National Cancer Institute* 86 (1994a): 192–99.

Giovannucci, E., E. B. Rimm, A. Ascherio, M. J. Stampfer, G. A. Colditz, and Walter C. Willett. "Alcohol, Methyl-Deficient Diets and Risk of Colon Cancer in Men." *Cancer Research* 87 (1995): 265–73.

Giovannucci, E., E. B. Rimm, M. J. Stampfer, G. A. Colditz, A. Ascherio, J. Kearney, et al. "A Prospective Study of Cigarette Smoking and Risk of Colorectal Adenoma and Colorectal Cancer in U.S. Men." *Journal of the National Cancer Institute* 86 (1994b): 183–91.

Giovannucci, E., E. B. Rimm, M. J. Stampfer, G. A. Colditz, A. Ascherio, and Walter C. Willett. "Intake of Fat, Meat, and Fiber in Relation to Risk of Colon Cancer in Men." *Cancer Research* 54 (1994c): 2390–97.

Giovannucci, E., M. J. Stampfer, G. A. Colditz, E. B. Rimm, D. Trichopoulos, B. A. Rosner, et al. "Folate, Methionine, and Alcohol Intake and Risk of Colorectal Adenoma." *Journal of the National Cancer Institute* 85 (1993): 875–84.

Glynn, S. A., and D. Albanes. "Folate and Cancer: A Review of the Literature." *Nutrition and Cancer* 22 (1994): 101–19.

Gold, Lois S., G. B. Garfinkel, and T. H. Slone. "Setting Priorities among Possible Carcinogenic Hazards in the Workplace," in C. M. Smith, D. C. Christiani, et al., eds., *Chemical Risk Assessment and Occupational Health: Current Applications, Limitations, and Future Prospects.* Westport, Conn.: Greenwood Publishing Group, 1994.

Gold, Lois S., N. B. Manley, T. H. Slone, G. B. Garfinkel, Bruce N. Ames, K. Chow, et al. "The Sixth Plot of the Carcinogenic Potency Database: Results of Animal Bioassays Published in the General Literature 1989–1990 and by the National Toxicology Program 1990–1993." *Environmental Health Perspectives Supplements* 103(8) (1995): 1–123.

Gold, Lois S., N. B. Manley, T. H. Slone, G. B. Garfinkel, L. Rohrbach, and Bruce N. Ames. "The Fifth Plot of the Carcinogenic Potency Database: Results of Animal Bioassays Published in the General Literature through 1988 and by the National Toxicology Program through 1989." *Environmental Health Perspectives* 100 (1993a): 65–135.

Gold, Lois S., T. H. Slone, N. B. Manley, and Bruce N. Ames. "Heterocyclic Amines Formed by Cooking Food: Comparison of Bioassay Results with Other Chemicals in the Carcinogenic Potency Database." *Cancer Letters* 83 (1994): 21–29.

Gold, Lois S., T. H. Slone, B. R. Stern, N. B. Manley, and Bruce N. Ames. "Rodent Carcinogens: Setting Priorities." *Science* 258 (1992): 261–65.

Gold, Lois S., T. H. Slone, B. R. Stern, N. B. Manley, and Bruce N. Ames. "Possible Carcinogenic Hazards from Natural and Synthetic Chemicals: Setting Priorities," in C. R. Cothern, ed., *Comparative Environmental Risk Assessment.* Boca Raton, Fla.: Lewis Publishers, 1993b.

Goldbohm, R. A., P. A. van der Brandt, P. van 't Veer, H. A. M. Brants, E. Dorant, F. Sturmans, et al. "A Prospective Cohort Study on the Relation between Meat Consumption and the Risk of Colon Cancer." *Cancer Research* 54 (1994): 718–23.

Gough, Michael. "How Much Cancer Can EPA Regulate Anyway?" *Risk Analysis* 10 (1990): 1–6.

Groopman, J. D., J. Zhu, P. R. Donahue, A. Pikul, L.-S. Zhang, J. S. Chen, et al. "Molecular Dosimetry of Urinary Aflatoxin DNA Adducts in People Living in Guangxi Autonomous Region, People's Republic of China." *Cancer Research* 52 (1992): 45–51.

Hankinson, S. E., G. A. Colditz, D. J. Hunter, T. L. Spencer, B. Rosner, and M. J. Stampfer. "A Quantitative Assessment of Oral Contraceptive Use and Risk of Ovarian Cancer." *Obstetrics and Gynecology* 80 (1992a): 708–14.

Hankinson, S. E., M. J. Stampfer, J. M. Seddon, G. A. Colditz, B. Rosner, F. E. Speizer, et al. "Nutrient Intake and Cataract Extraction in Women: A Prospective Study." *British Medical Journal* 305 (1992b): 335–39.

Hankinson, S. E., Walter C. Willett, G. A. Colditz, J. M. Seddon, B. Rosner, F. E.

Speizer, et al. "A Prospective Study of Cigarette Smoking and Risk of Cataract Surgery in Women." *Journal of the American Medical Association* 268 (1992c): 994–98.

Harris, J. R., M. E. Lippman, U. Veronesi, and Walter C. Willett. "Breast Cancer." *New England Journal of Medicine* 327 (1992): 319–28.

Haseman, J. K., and F. M. Johnson. "Analysis of Rodent NTP Bioassay Data for Anticarcinogenic Effects." *Mutation Research* (1995).

Hayward, J., B. Shane, et al. "Differential *in vivo* Mutagenicity of the Carcinogen/ Noncarcinogen Pair 2,4- and 2,6-Diaminotoluene." *Carcinogensis* 16 (1995): 2429–33.

Henderson, B. E., R. K. Ross, and M. C. Pike. "Hormonal Chemoprevention of Cancer in Women." *Science* 259 (1993): 633–38.

———. "Toward the Primary Prevention of Cancer." *Science* 254 (1991): 1131–38.

Hill, M. J., A. Giacosa, and C. P. J. Caygill, eds. *Epidemiology of Diet and Cancer.* West Sussex, England: Ellis Horwood Limited, 1994.

Howe, G. R., T. Hirohata, and T. G. Hislop. "Dietary Factors and Risk of Breast Cancer: Combined Analysis of 12 Case-Control Studies." *Journal of the National Cancer Institute* 82 (1990): 561–69.

Howson, C., T. Hiyama, and E. Wynder. "The Decline in Gastric Cancer: Epidemiology of an Unplanned Triumph." *Epidemiology Review* 8 (1986): 1–27.

Huber, G., R. Brockie, and V. Mahajan. "Smoke and Mirrors: The EPA's Flawed Study of Environmental Tobacco Smoke and Lung Cancer." *Regulation* 16 (1993): 44–54.

Hunter, D. J., and Walter C. Willett. "Diet, Body Size, and Breast Cancer. *Epidemiology Review* 15 (1993): 110–32.

Innes, J. R. M., B. M. Ulland, M. G. Valerio, L. Petrucelli, L. Fishbein, E. R. Hart, et al. "Bioassay of Pesticides and Industrial Chemicals for Tumorigenicity in Mice: A Preliminary Note." *Journal of the National Cancer Institute* 42 (1969): 1101–14.

International Agency for Research on Cancer. *Alcohol Drinking.* Lyon, France: International Agency for Research on Cancer, 1988.

———. *Chlorinated Drinking-Water; Chlorination By-products.* Lyon, France: International Agency for Research on Cancer, 1991.

———. *Overall Evaluations of Carcinogenicity: An Updating of IARC Monographs Volumes 1 to 42.* Supp. 7. Lyon, France: International Agency for Research on Cancer, 1987.

———. *Schistosomes, Liver Flukes and Helicobacter Pylori.* Lyon, France: International Agency for Research on Cancer, 1994a.

———. *Solar and Ultraviolet Radiation.* Lyon, France. International Agency for Research on Cancer, 1992.

———. *Some Industrial Chemicals.* Lyon, France: International Agency for Research on Cancer, 1994b.

———. *Some Naturally Occurring Substances: Food Items and Constituents, Heterocyclic Aromatic Amines and Nycotoxins.* Lyon, France: International Agency for Research on Cancer, 1993.

Jacques, P. F., S. C. Hartz, L. T. J. Chylack, R. B. McGandy, and J. A. Sadowski. "Nutritional Status in Persons with and without Senile Cataract: Blood Vitamin and Mineral Levels." *American Journal of Clinical Nutrition* 48 (1988): 152–58.

Jick, H., A. M. Walker, R. N. Watkins, D. C. D'Ewart, J. R. Hunter, A. Danford, et al. "Replacement Estrogens and Breast Cancer." *American Journal of Epidemiology* 112 (1980): 586–94.

Keeney, Ralph L. "Mortality Risks Induced by Economic Expenditures." *Risk Analysis* 10 (1990): 147–59.

Key, T., and G. Reeves. "Organochlorines in the Environment and Breast Cancer." *British Medical Journal* 308 (1994): 1520–21.

Knudsen, A. "Hereditary Cancers: Clues to Mechanisms of Carcinogenesis." *British Journal of Cancer* 59 (1989): 661–66.

Korkina, L. G., A. D. Durnev, T. B. Suslova, Z. P. Cheremisina, N. O. Daugel-Dauge, and I. B. Afanas'ev. "Oxygen Radical-Mediated Mutagenic Effect of Asbestos on Human Lymphocytes: Suppression by Oxygen Radical Scavengers." *Mutation Research* 265 (1992): 245–53.

Larson, J., D. Wolf, et al. "Induced Cytotoxicity and Cell Proliferation in the Hepatocarcinogenicity of Chloroform in Female B6C3F1 Mice: Comparison of Administration by Gavage in Corn Oil vs. ad Libitum in Drinking Water." *Fundamental and Applied Toxicology* 22 (1994): 90–102.

Le Marchand, L., L. N. Kolonel, L. R. Wilkens, B. C. Myers, and T. Hirohata. "Animal Fat Consumption and Prostate Cancer: A Prospective Study in Hawaii." *Epidemiology* 5 (1994): 276–82.

Létourneau, E. G., D. Krewski, N. W. Choi, M. J. Goddard, R. G. McGregor, J. M. Zielinski, et al. "Case-Control Study of Residential Radon and Lung Cancer in Winnipeg, Manitoba, Canada." *American Journal of Epidemiology* 140 (1994): 310–22.

Linet, M. S., J. K. McLaughlin, A. W. Hsing, S. Wacholder, H. T. Co Chien, L. M. Schuman, et al. "Is Cigarette Smoking a Risk Factor for Non-Hodgkin's Lymphoma or Multiple Myeloma? Results from the Lutheran Brotherhood Cohort Study." *Leukemia Research* 16 (1992): 621–24.

Longnecker, M. P. "Alcoholic Beverage Consumption in Relation to Risk of Breast Cancer: Meta-analysis and Review." *Cancer Causes and Control* 5 (1994): 73–82.

Lowy, D. R., R. Kirnbauer, and J. T. Schiller. "Genital Human Papillomavirus Infection." *Proceedings of the National Academy of Sciences, USA* 91 (1994): 2436–40.

Lubin, J. H. "Invited Commentary: Lung Cancer and Exposure to Residential Radon." *American Journal of Epidemiology* 140 (1994): 323–32.

Lubin, J. H., J. D. Boice, Jr., C. Elding, R. W. Hornint, G. Howe, E. Kunz, et al. *Radon and Lung Cancer Risk: A Joint Analysis of 11 Underground Miner Studies.* Washington, D.C.: U.S. Department of Health and Human Services, 1994.

MacGregor, J. T., R. Schlegel, C. M. Wehr, P. Alperin, and Bruce N. Ames. "Cytogenetic Damage Induced by Folate Deficiency in Mice Is Enhanced by Caffeine." *Proceedings of the National Academy of Sciences, USA* 87 (1990): 9962–65.

Marsh, J. P., and Brooke T. Mossman. "Role of Asbestos and Active Oxygen Species in Activation and Expression of Ornithine Decarboxylase in Hamster Tracheal Epithelial Cells." *Cancer Research* 51 (1991): 167–73.

Miller, B. A., L. A. G. Ries, B. F. Hankey, C. L. Kosary, A. Harras, S. S. Devesa, et al. *SEER Cancer Statistics Review: 1973–1990.* Bethesda, Md.: National Cancer Institute, 1993.

Mills, P. K., W. L. Beeson, R. L. Phillips, and G. E. Fraser. "Cancer Incidence among California Seventh-Day Adventists." *American Journal of Clinical Nutrition* 59 (1994): 1136S–42S.

Mirsalis, J. C., G. S. Provost, C. D. Matthews, R. T. Hamner, J. E. Schindler, K. G. O'Loughlin, J. T. MacGregor, and J. M. Short. "Induction of Hepatic Mutations in *LacI* Transgenic Mice." *Mutagenesis* 8 (1993): 265–71.

National Cancer Institute. *Everything Doesn't Cause Cancer: But How Can We Tell Which Things Cause Cancer and Which Don't?* Bethesda, Md.: National Institutes of Health, 1986.

Nero, A. V. "Developing a Methodology for Identifying High-Radon Areas." *Center for Building Science News* (Lawrence Berkeley Laboratory) 1(3) (1994): 4–5.

———. "A National Strategy for Indoor Radon." *Issues in Science and Technology* 9 (1992): 33–40.

Newcomb, P. A., B. E. Storer, M. P. Longnecker, R. Mittendorf, E. R. Greenberg, R. W. Clapp, et al. "Lactation and a Reduced Risk of Premenopausal Breast Cancer." *New England Journal of Medicine* 330 (1994): 81–87.

Office of Management and Budget. *Office of Management and Budget Regulatory Program of the United States Government, April 1, 1991–March 31, 1992.* Washington, D.C.: Office of Management and Budget, 1993.

Parkin, D. M., J. Suernsward, and C. S. Muir. "Estimates of the Worldwide Frequency of Twelve Major Cancers." *Bulletin of the World Health Organization* 62 (1984): 163–82.

Patterson, B. H., and G. Block. "Food Choices and the Cancer Guidelines." *American Journal of Public Health* 78 (1988): 282–86.

———. "Fruit and Vegetable Consumption: National Survey Data," in A. Bendich and C. E. J. Butterworth, eds., *Micronutrients in Health and in Disease Prevention.* New York: Marcel Dekker, Inc., 1991.

Patterson, B. H., G. Block, W. F. Rosenberger, D. Pee, and L. L. Kahle. "Fruit and Vegetables in the American Diet: Data from the NHANES II Survey." *American Journal of Public Health* 80 (1990): 1443–49.

Pershagen, G., G. Akerblom, O. Axelson, B. Clavensjo, L. Damber, G. Desai, et al. "Residential Radon Exposure and Lung Cancer in Sweden." *New England Journal of Medicine* 330 (1994): 159–64.

Peto, R., A. D. Lopez, J. Boreham, M. Thun, and C. Heath, Jr. *Mortality from Smoking in Developed Countries 1950–2000.* New York: Oxford University Press, 1994.

———. "Mortality from Tobacco in Developed Countries: Indirect Estimation from National Vital Statistics." *Lancet* 339 (1992): 1268–78.

Phillips, R. L., L. Garfinkel, J. W. Kuzma, W. L. Beeson, T. Lotz, and B. Brin. "Mortality among California Seventh-Day Adventists for Selected Cancer Sites." *Journal of the National Cancer Institute* 65 (1980): 1097–1107.

Ponder, B. "Inherited Predisposition to Cancer." *Trends in Genetics* 6 (1990): 213–18.

Pons, W. A. "High Pressure Liquid Chromatography Determinations of Aflatoxins in Corn." *Journal of the Association of Official Analytical Chemists* 62 (1979): 584–86.

Pope, C. A., M. J. Thun, M. M. Namboodiri, D. W. Dockery, J. S. Evans, F. E. Speizer, et al. "Particulate Air Pollution as a Predictor of Mortality in a Prospective Study of U.S. Adults." *American Journal of Respiratory and Critical Care Medicine* 151 (1995): 669–74.

Preston-Martin, S., K. Monroe, et al. "Spinal Meningiomas in Women in Los Angeles County: Investigation of an Etiological Hypothesis." *Cancer Epidemiology, Biomarkers and Prevention* 4 (1995): 333–39.

Preston-Martin, S., M. C. Pike, et al. "Increased Cell Division as a Cause of Human Cancer." *Cancer Research* 50 (1990): 7415–21.

Preston-Martin, S., D. C. Thomas, M. C. Yu, and B. E. Henderson. "Diagnostic Radiography as a Risk Factor for Chronic Myeloid and Monocytic Leukaemia (CMML)." *British Journal of Cancer* 59 (1989): 639–44.

Qian, G.-S., R. K. Ross, M. C. Yu, J.-M. Yuan, Y.-T. Gao, B. E. Henderson, et al. "A Follow-up Study of Urinary Markers of Aflatoxin Exposure and Liver Cancer Risk in Shanghai, People's Republic of China." *Cancer Epidemiology, Biomarkers and Prevention* 3 (1994): 3–10.

Reynolds, T. "Asbestos-Linked Cancer Rates up Less Than Predicted." *Journal of the National Cancer Institute* 84 (1992): 560–62.

Roe, F. J. C. "Nongenotoxic Carcinogenesis: Implications for Testing Extrapolation to Man." *Mutagenesis* 4 (1989): 407–11.

Roe, F. J. C., P. N. Lee, G. Conybeare, G. Tobin, D. Kelly, D. Prentice, et al. "Risks of Premature Death and Cancer Predicted by Body Weight in Early Adult Life." *Human Exposure Toxicology* 10 (1991): 285–88.

Rosner, B., G. Colditz, and Walter C. Willett. "Reproductive Risk Factors in a Prospective Study of Breast Cancer: The Nurses' Health Study." *American Journal of Epidemiology* 139 (1994): 819–35.

Rush, D. "Periconceptional Folate and Neural Tube Defect." *American Journal of Clinical Nutrition* 59 (1994): 511S–16S.

Russo, J., G. Calaf, N. Sohi, Q. Tahin, P. L. Zhang, M. E. Alvarado, et al. "Critical Steps in Breast Carcinogenesis." *Annals of the New York Academy of Sciences* 698 (1993): 1–20.

Ryffel, B. "The Carcinogenicity of Cyclosporin." *Toxicology* 73 (1992): 1–22.

Safe, S. H. "Dietary and Environmental Estrogens and Antiestrogens and Their Possible Role in Human Disease." *Environmental Science and Pollution Research* 1 (1994): 29–33.

Schectman, G., J. C. Byrd, and R. Hoffmann. "Ascorbic Acid Requirements for Smokers: Analysis of a Population Survey." *American Journal of Clinical Nutrition* 53 (1991): 1466–70.

Senti, F. R., and S. M. Pilch. "Analysis of Folate Data from the Second National Health and Nutrition Examination Survey (NHANES II)." *Journal of Nutrition* 115 (1985): 1398–1402.

Shacter, E., E. J. Beecham, J. M. Covey, K. W. Kohn, and M. Potter. "Activated Neutrophils Induce Prolonged DNA Damage in Neighboring Cells." *Carcinogenesis* 9 (1988): 2297–2304. (Published erratum appears in *Carcinogenesis* 10 (1989): 628.)

Shaver-Walker, P., C. Urlando, et al. "Enhanced Somatic Mutation Rates Induced in Stem Cells of Mice by Low Chronic Exposures." *Proceedings of the National Academy of Sciences, USA* 92 (1995): 11470–74.

Slattery, M. L., M. C. Schumacher, K. R. Smith, D. W. West, and N. Abd-Eghany. "Physical Activity, Diet, and Risk of Colon Cancer in Utah." *American Journal of Epidemiology* 128 (1988): 989–99.

Smith, A. H., R. C. Hopenhayn, M. N. Bates, H. M. Goeden, P. I. Hertz, H. M. Duggan, et al. "Cancer Risks from Arsenic in Drinking Water." *Environmental Health Perspectives* 97 (1992): 259–67.

Stadtman, E. R. "Protein Oxidation and Aging." *Science* 257 (1992): 1220–24.

Steinmetz, K. A., and J. D. Potter. "Vegetables, Fruit, and Cancer. I. Epidemiology." *Cancer Causes and Control* 2 (1991a): 325–57.

Steinmetz, K. A., and J. D. Potter. "Vegetables, Fruit, and Cancer. II. Mechanisms." *Cancer Causes and Control* 2 (1991b): 427–42.

Sugimura, T., S. Sato, H. Ohgaki, S. Takayama, M. Nagao, and K. Wakabayashi. *Genetic Toxicology of the Diet.* New York: Alan R. Liss, 1986.

Swanson, C. A., D. Y. Jones, A. Schatzkin, L. A. Brinton, and R. G. Ziegler. "Breast Cancer Risk Assessed by Anthropometry in the NHANES I Epidemiological Follow-up Study." *Cancer Research* 48 (1988): 5363–67.

Tabor, E., and K. Kobayashi. "Hepatitis C Virus, a Causative Infectious Agent of Non-A, Non-B Hepatitis: Prevalence and Structure. Summary of a Conference on Hepatitis C Virus as a Cause of Hepatocellular Carcinoma." *Journal of the National Cancer Institute* 84 (1992): 86–90.

Tengs, Tammy O., M. E. Adams, J. S. Pliskin, D. G. Safran, Joanna E. Siegel, M. C. Weinstein, et al. "Five-Hundred Life-Saving Interventions and Their Cost-Effectiveness." *Risk Analysis* 15 (1995): 369–90.

Thottassery, J., L. Winberg, et al. "Regulation of Perfluorooctanoic Acid—Induced Peroxisomal Enzyme Activities and Hepatocellular Growth by Adrenal Hormones." *Hepatology* 15 (1992): 316–22.

Thun, M. J., E. E. Calle, M. M. Namboodiri, W. D. Flanders, R. J. Coates, T. Byers, et al. "Risk Factors for Fatal Colon Cancer in a Large Prospective Study." *Journal of the National Cancer Institute* 84 (1992): 1491–1500.

Trock, B., E. Lanza, and P. Greenwald. "Dietary Fiber, Vegetables, and Colon Cancer: Critical Review and Metaanalyses of the Epidemiologic Evidence." *Journal of the National Cancer Institute* 82 (1990): 650–61.

Viscusi, W. Kip. *Fatal Tradeoffs: Public and Private Responsibilities for Risk.* New York: Oxford University Press, 1992.

Von Sonntag, C. *The Chemical Basis of Radiation Biology.* London: Taylor & Francis, 1987.

Wildavsky, Aaron. *Searching for Safety.* New Brunswick, N.J.: Transaction Press, 1988.

Willett, Walter C. "Diet, Nutrition and Avoidable Cancer." *Environmental Health Perspectives* 103 (supp. 8) (1995): 165–70.

———, and M. J. Stampfer. "Dietary Fat and Cancer: Another View." *Cancer Causes and Control* 1 (1990): 103–9.

Willett, Walter C., M. J. Stampfer, G. A. Colditz, B. A. Rosner, and F. E. Speizer. "Relation of Meat, Fat, and Fiber Intake to the Risk of Colon Cancer in a Prospective Study among Women." *New England Journal of Medicine* 323 (1990): 1664–72.

Yamashina, K., B. E. Miller, and G. H. Heppner. "Macrophage-Mediated Induction of Drug-Resistant Variants in a Mouse Mammary Tumor Cell Line." *Cancer Research* 46 (1986): 2396–401.

Yarbrough, J., M. Cunningham, et al. "Carbohydrate and Oxygen Metabolism During Hepatocellular Proliferation: A Study in Perfused Livers from Mirex-Treated Rats." *Hepatology* 13 (1991): 1129–34.

Yeh, F.-S., M. C. Yu, C.-C. Mo, S. Luo, M. J. Tong, and B. E. Henderson. "Hepatitis B Virus, Aflatoxins, and Hepatocellular Carcinoma in Southern Guangxi, China." *Cancer Research* 49 (1989): 2506–9.

Youngman, L. D., J.-Y. K. Park, and Bruce N. Ames. "Protein Oxidation Associated with Aging Is Reduced by Dietary Restriction of Protein or Calories." *Proceedings of the National Academy of Sciences, USA* 89 (1992): 9112–16.

Yu, M.-W., S.-L. You, A.-S. Chang, S.-N. Lu, Y.-F. Liaw, and C.-J. Chen. "Association between Hepatitis C Virus Antibodies and Hepatocellular Carcinoma in Taiwan." *Cancer Research* 51 (1991a): 5621–25.

Yu, M. C., M. J. Tong, S. Govindarajan, and B. E. Henderson. "Nonviral Risk Factors for Hepatocellular Carcinoma in a Low-Risk Population, the Non-Asians of Los Angeles County, California." *Journal of the National Cancer Institute* 83 (1991b): 1820–26.

Chapter 3

MODELING RISK AT LOW LEVELS OF EXPOSURE

William R. Hendee

OVERVIEW

This chapter considers the case of ionizing radiation as an example of the evolution of risk assessment and its consequences. Ionizing radiation—from X-rays, from nuclear explosions, from uranium mines—can cause cancer at high doses. That is clear from the Japanese populations exposed to the atomic bomb explosions in 1945. But it is another question altogether whether far lower doses are damaging. The answer to that question has great consequences.

The chapter explores the history of scientific efforts to assess the risk of radiation and the gradual emergence of a "no-threshold model." This says, in effect, that there may be danger in even very small doses of radiation. The danger is inferred by a straight-line, or linear, extrapolation from the evident risks at high doses. The consequences of the no-threshold model are high-cost efforts to limit radiation (for example, the hugely costly cleanup of U.S. government nuclear weapons facilities) and the forgoing of some medical and other potential benefits from low-level radiation.

Yet we do not know, and probably cannot know with certainty, whether low doses cause any damage at all. Numerous studies of humans exposed to low doses of radiation have failed to show any statistically significant adverse health effects.

The question is raised whether the no-threshold model, now the paradigm for assessing radiation risk, may be like other once-universal but now abandoned paradigms such as the belief that the earth was the center of the solar system. This chapter does not explicitly reject the linear, no-threshold model but suggests that it may be mistaken and its disadvantages may far outweigh its advantages.

This volume has much discussion about the regulation of health risks, and how public policy needs to reflect some modicum of balance between risks to individuals and benefits to society. But we must answer two underlying questions in achieving that balance: What is a health risk, and how do we identify, measure, and quantify it? This chapter addresses those questions by using the hazard of exposure to ionizing radiation as a model for assessing risk in general.

We can think of radiation as energy in transit from one location to another. Ionizing radiation is radiation that produces the ejection of electrons from atoms that constitute the matter in the path of the radiation. Ionizing radiation includes X-rays from X-ray machines and particle accelerators, as well as alpha, beta, and gamma rays from atoms that spontaneously undergo radioactive decay. The ionization of atoms causes radiation to be biologically destructive in two ways. First, it can induce changes in the composition and bonding of important molecules in cells—for example, DNA and RNA—and thus cause the cells to become dysfunctional. Second, the ionization can produce intermediate chemical compounds in the cell, which in turn affect the composition and bonding of important molecules. Those two effects are respectively the *direct* effect and the *indirect* effect of exposure to radiation. The two effects together constitute the biological basis of risk associated with exposure to radiation.

To assess the response to exposure to radiation, we must identify the nature of the conditions under which exposure may place individuals at risk and quantify the degree of risk as a function of exposure. That process usually involves using a model of exposure/response that is based on experimental data acquired preferably on humans, but often with animals. In many situations researchers need an estimate of the response at exposure levels well beyond the range of experimental data. In those situations they must estimate the response by extrapolating the model beyond the range of experimental data. The uncertainty of the estimate grows with increasing displacement from the measured data. For example, exposure to ionizing radiation is thought to cause cancer in humans, but actual data supporting that hypothesis are available only at relatively high levels of exposure. The largest and most extensively studied population of exposed individuals is the Japanese atomic bomb survivors. That group revealed a clear elevation of leukemia incidence that peaked five to six years after exposure and an elevated incidence of various solid tumors that is correlated with the magnitude of exposure (Kato and Shimizu 1990). To estimate the response to radiation at low exposures, the exposure/response model must be extrapolated through orders of magnitude of exposure.

The No-Threshold Model

In the 1950s researchers began to use a linear, no-threshold model of radiation injury to establish guidelines for radiation protection. That model assumed that the long-term effects of radiation exposure increase linearly with increasing exposure to radiation and that a threshold exposure does not exist below which long-term effects do not occur.

Figure 3-1 shows example models of radiation-induced injury as a function of radiation exposure, extrapolated to low levels of radiation exposure from relatively high levels where data (denoted by •) are available. Model A, the linear, no-threshold model, suggests that risk increases in a straight-line fashion with increasing exposure, with no threshold exposure below which the risk is zero. Model B is the nonlinear, no-threshold model in which the risk at low exposures is relatively small but still greater than zero. Model C is the linear threshold model depicting a threshold exposure below which no risk of injury exists.

Müller (1928) and others suggested for several years that the linear, no-threshold model best describes the genetic effects of exposure to radiation. The model provided an upper bound for estimating radiation risk in the low-exposure region. Its acceptance was in part a response to concerns about the growing numbers of persons exposed to radiation in peacetime nuclear industries and from worldwide fallout released during atmospheric tests of nuclear weapons.

The no-threshold model of radiation risk was seductive in its mathematical simplicity and universal applicability. It did not, however, reflect any new data related to the occurrence of cancer or other somatic effects at low levels of radiation. Those effects were demonstrable primarily at relatively high doses in the Japanese survivors of the atomic bomb. The no-threshold model implied, without experimental verification, that we could estimate the risk of such effects at low exposures by extrapolating from high-exposure regions.

Figure 3-1   Radiation-Induced Injury as a Function of Exposure

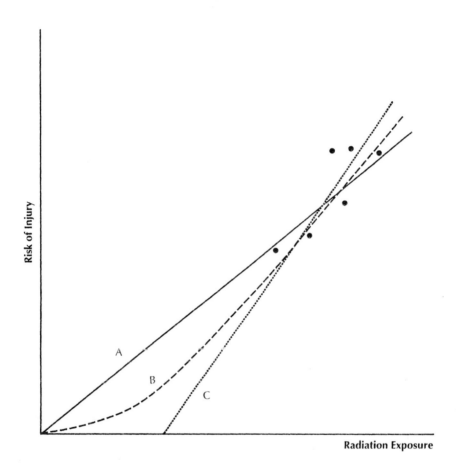

Implicit in the no-threshold model is the idea that the true risk of adverse health effects in the low-exposure region would lie somewhere between zero and an upper limit defined by extrapolation, usually by extending a straight line from a relatively high exposure to zero exposure. The model does not eliminate the possibility of a threshold exposure. Instead it includes that threshold in the estimate of low-exposure health risks that ranged from zero to a maximum value obtained by extrapolation. Over the years, however, researchers have largely forgotten the concept of a range of health-risk values, and the extrapolated upper limit has assumed an unintended prominence as a quantified measure of health risk related to low-level radiation exposure. That assumption lacks support by evidence of somatic or hereditary effects in human populations exposed to ionizing radiation at low levels. Indeed, numerous studies of large populations of humans have failed to demonstrate with statistical significance any adverse health effects at low radiation exposures. Despite those limitations, the no-threshold model has become widely adopted as the "preferred model" not only for estimating radiation risk, but also for quantifying the number of potentially injured persons in a population exposed to ionizing radiation. Such interpretations of the model go far beyond the intentions of those initially responsible for developing it.

The use of the no-threshold model of radiation risk to predict radiation injury in exposed populations occurred relatively rapidly after its introduction in the late 1940s. In 1954 the National Council on Radiation Protection and Measurements issued new guidance on radiation protection in which it replaced the tolerance dose—the level of radiation exposure that a person could receive on a continuous basis without demonstrable ill effect—by a new concept, the maximum permissible dose (NCRP 1954). The maximum permissible dose implicitly rejected the concept of tolerance dose and established the idea of "acceptable risk" at low levels of exposure. In 1958 the United Nations Scientific Committee on the Effects of Atomic Radiation issued its first report on the effects of radiation exposure in humans (UNSCEAR 1958). That report estimated the risk of adverse effects of low-level radiation exposure using both a no-threshold and a threshold (that is, a tolerance dose) model of radiation risk. The committee also issued the following statement, which is as relevant today as it was in 1958:

> Present knowledge concerning long-term effects and their correlation with the amount of radiation received does not permit us to evaluate with any precision the possible consequence to man of exposure to low radiation levels. Many effects of radiation are delayed; often they cannot be distinguished from other agents; many will develop once a threshold dose has been exceeded; some may be cumulative and others not; and individuals in large populations or particular groups such as children and foetuses may have special sensitivity. These facts render it very difficult to accumulate reli-

able information about the correlation between small doses and their effects either in individuals or in large populations. (UNSCEAR 1958, 42)

With respect to radiation-induced leukemia identified in the Japanese populations exposed to atomic radiation well above the low-exposure limit, the UNSCEAR concluded that the threshold and no-threshold models of radiation injury have equal validity. The Committee on Pathologic Effects of Atomic Radiation of the National Academy of Sciences-National Research Council (NAS-NRC) contested that conclusion. The committee stated unequivocally that "a considerable body of experimental evidence" favored non-linearity—and hence presumably a threshold—and urged that nonlinear relationships between dose and effect be given greater attention (NAS-NRC 1959). The following year, the short-lived U.S. Federal Radiation Council observed that the linear, no-threshold model merely presented an extrapolated upper limit of radiation risk for low exposure levels (FRC 1960). In UNSCEAR reports in the 1960s the committee emphasized that extrapolation of the no-threshold curve provided an upper limit to the risk of low-level exposures (UNSCEAR 1962, 1964). The International Commission on Radiological Protection (ICRP 1966) endorsed that position.

In the late 1950s the congressional Joint Committee on Atomic Energy conducted hearings on the potential long-term effects of exposure to low levels of ionizing radiation. Those hearings had a major influence on the thinking of both the scientific community and the public with regard to radiation hazards. The hearings began in 1957 with an inquiry into the nature of radioactive fallout from weapons testing and its possible effects on humans (JCAE 1957). Testimony from scientific experts led the committee to conclude that atmospheric testing of nuclear weapons constituted a hazard, but left unresolved the issue of the most appropriate model to estimate the degree of risk at low exposure levels. The JCAE addressed that issue again in its 1959 hearings (JCAE 1959) and again left it unresolved. The committee's report (JCAE 1960, 59) included testimony by E. B. Lewis, who strongly supported the linear, no-threshold hypothesis as a model for radiation protection standards. Lewis conceptually proposed the protection philosophy of "as low as reasonably achievable" (ALARA) (JCAE 1960, 404–7). In subsequent hearings on the hazards of uranium mining and fallout exposure, and in considerations of standards for protecting and compensating radiation workers, the JCAE moved slowly to the no-threshold model of radiation risk over the course of the 1960s.

Concern over long-term effects of low-level radiation exposure continued during the 1960s despite the cessation of atmospheric testing of nuclear weapons. In 1964 the National Academy of Sciences-National Research Council responded to an inquiry from the Federal Radiation Council by establishing an advisory committee on the Biological Effects of Atomic Radiation (BEAR) to examine issues related to radiation protection, including the shape of the dose-response curve at low exposures. The BEAR committee introduced the concept of regulating doses to the population, as well as to radiation workers, as a way to limit effects of radiation on future generations. The BEAR committee, renamed the National Academy of Sciences-National Research Council committee on the Biological Effects of Ionizing Radiation (BEIR), issued its first report in 1972 (NAS-NRC 1972). That report reviewed the literature on the effects of radiation at low exposure levels. The report sidestepped the issue of the shape of the dose-response curve. It did, however, provide estimates of cancer risk at low exposures on the basis of a linear extrapolation from cancer-mortality data at high exposures in Japanese survivors and other exposed groups. Those estimates implied that radiation-induced cancer does not exhibit a threshold exposure, despite the absence of confirmatory experimental data. Also in 1972, the U.S. Atomic Energy Commission, the forerunner of the U.S. Nuclear Regulatory Commission, introduced the concept of ALARA—then known as "as low as practicable" (ALAP)—in Appendix I to Title 10, Part 50, of the Code of Federal Regulations. The implication of ALARA is that no threshold exists for radiation bioeffects, and that any dose, no matter how small, is potentially injurious to exposed individuals. Those actions of the National Academy of Sciences-National Research Council and the Atomic Energy Commission completed a major transition in the conceptualization of radiation risk at low exposures and provided a foundation for the evolution of the discipline of health physics as a major industry devoted to the protection of workers and the public against small exposures to ionizing radiation.

In 1977 the International Commission on Radiological Protection announced its risk-based approach to establishing standards for radiation protection (ICRP 1977). That approach radically departed from traditional exposure-based standards and defined the concept of acceptable risk from radiation exposure of workers in terms of the fatal accident rate in so-called safe industries. In taking that approach the commission compared real and measurable fatalities in other industries with hypothetical and unidentifiable deaths from radiation-induced cancers predicted by extrapolation of the linear, no-threshold model to low exposures. The commission also introduced a number of tissue-weighting factors to compute a new unit of radiation quantity—the effective dose equivalent—that expressed the risk of partial-body irradiation in terms of the equivalent risk of whole-body exposure. The commission (ICRP 1990, 1991), the National Council on Radiation Protection (NCRP 1987), and several U.S. regulatory agencies, including the Environmental Protection Agency (EPA 1987), Department of Energy (DOE 1988), and Nuclear Regulatory Commission (NRC 1991), refined and expanded the risk-based approach to standards of radiation protection.

In 1979 the BEIR committee released a new report (the BEIR III report) on the risks of exposure to ionizing radiation. Several committee members characterized the release of that report as premature, and it was subsequently withdrawn. When finally published in 1980, the report was accompanied by two "minority opinions" of members who objected to the linear-quadratic, no-threshold model of radiation-induced cancer that the majority of the committee supported (NAS-NRC 1980). One minority opinion supported a linear, no-threshold model, and the other endorsed a purely quadratic model of cancer induction. That dispute depicted general disagreement within the scientific community about the most appropriate way to characterize radiation risk at low exposures. It also reflected concern over the growing practice of using dose-response models to estimate hypothetical cancer risks at exposures substantially below levels where epidemiological studies have confirmed injury.

The BEIR III report offered several important observations. It noted that whether exposure rates on the order of one millisievert per year—those from background radiation—were detrimental to people was unknown and probably not determinable. The report concluded that data presented by Sternglass (1968) and others that purported to show an increased incidence of cancer in populations exposed to low levels of radiation were the result of flawed studies. The BEIR III committee recognized that different groups of people may exhibit different degrees of cancer risk for exposure to a specific amount of radiation and that developmental effects from radiation exposure in utero may exhibit a threshold exposure. Finally, the report suggested that the linear, no-threshold model of radiation risk provides the best estimate of genetic risk. The committee had to base that suggestion on observations of genetic effects in exposed animals, since no hereditary effects have been documented in human populations exposed to ionizing radiation.

Two additional BEIR reports have been issued since the 1980 report of the BEIR III committee. The BEIR IV report, published in 1988, addressed the health risks of radon and other internally deposited radionuclides (NAS-NRC 1988). The report offered several suggestions for further research that, collectively, called for intensified experimental efforts to characterize the shape of the dose-response curve for long-term health effects at low levels of exposure. The most recent report, BEIR V, once again considered the broad topic of adverse health effects from exposure to low levels of ionizing radiation (NAS-NRC 1990). As in previous reports, the committee noted the failure of epidemiological studies to demonstrate hereditary effects in humans exposed to low radiation levels. Nevertheless, the committee confirmed previous estimates of radiation-induced genetic risk in humans. There was, however, a significant change in the BEIR V estimates of cancer risk from radiation compared with earlier BEIR reports. The committee determined the new estimates by using the linear, no-threshold model and obtained a threefold increase in the risk of solid tumors and a fourfold increase for leukemia. Although the committee did not consider the rate of delivery of radiation in its estimates of cancer risk, it proposed a dose rate effectiveness factor that, if applied, would reduce the lifetime cancer risk by a factor of two or more if the radiation were delivered over a protracted period.

Discussion

The no-threshold model of radiation injury has had major consequences for human health and public policy in the United States and around the world. If the model were correct in portraying radiation risk at low levels of exposure, then its use in setting limits for radiation exposure of occupationally exposed persons and members of the public would certainly be justified. Furthermore, the model would support implementation of the ALARA concept of radiation exposure limitation, wherein exposures are reduced to the lowest possible levels consistent with economic and social considerations. On the other hand, if the no-threshold model is overly conservative, and if risks are less—or nonexistent—at low levels of exposure, then the costs of radiation protection may be higher than necessary, and the intrusiveness of regulations into the beneficial applications of radiation may be excessive. Furthermore, public policy decisions that incur large sums of taxpayer money or that deprive the public of beneficial applications of radiation would be unjustified. For example, the U.S. Department of Energy has embarked on a program of radiation cleanup at DOE facilities that is estimated to cost as much as $200 billion. Whether that immense expenditure will reduce the risk of the public to any measurable degree is highly debatable. As another example, no new repository for low-level radioactive waste has been sited anywhere in the country, and the one remaining site that has recently been reopened —to all states except North Carolina—is subject to closure at any time. That problem compromises the continued availability—at reasonable cost—of medical procedures using radioactive sources. Both of those issues exist because of the assumption that there is no threshold below which adverse effects of radiation exposure do not occur.

> **If the no-threshold model is overly conservative, and if risks are less— or nonexistent—at low levels of exposure, then the costs of radiation protection may be higher than necessary, and the intrusiveness of regulations into the beneficial applications of radiation may be excessive.**

The dilemma for public policy is that existing data are simply inadequate to establish the validity—or lack thereof—of the no-threshold model of radiation-induced injury. Furthermore, no reasonable experiment or epidemiological study of human exposures can be conceived that would answer the question. At low exposure levels, the numbers of persons required for both the exposed and control populations are simply too great to be attainable under any practical circumstances. What can be said is that the no-threshold model defines an upper limit for the response of humans to radiation exposure. What cannot be said is whether the actual response may be significantly lower than that upper limit—even zero, or perhaps less than zero if beneficial effects occur at low levels of exposure (radiation hormesis).

Replacing the concept of tolerance dose by the no-threshold model of radiation response, as described earlier in this chapter, reflects several influences that worked together after World War II to enhance the desirability of the no-threshold model. First, selected approaches to biological modeling of radiation injury at the cellular level support the no-threshold theory. Those approaches evolved from early studies of radiation-induced mutations in fruit flies in which Müller and others were unable to demonstrate an exposure threshold below which no effects were observed. The cellular model of radiation injury that grew from that work assumed that damage was caused by deposition of small, discrete amounts of energy ("hits") in sensitive "targets" within the cell. That hypothetical approach, known as the target theory of radiation injury (Lea 1947, 132), assumed that the hits occur randomly in the cell so that even the smallest dose would have a probability greater than zero of hitting a target and producing harm. The target theory suggests that even very low exposures might be harmful and supports the no-threshold model and the restriction of radiation exposures to the lowest practical level.

> **The dilemma for public policy is that existing data are simply inadequate to establish the validity—or lack thereof— of the no-threshold model of radiation-induced injury.**

In the 1950s it became apparent that mutations in somatic (body) cells, instead of in germ (sex) cells, may be responsible as the first step in the development of cancer in exposed individuals. As studies began to show an increased incidence of leukemia and, later, other forms of cancer in Japanese survivors, the target theory gained prominence as a model of cellular radiation injury that leads ultimately to cancer. Over the years, studies of Japanese survivors and other exposed populations have failed to reveal an increased incidence of genetic abnormalities in the offspring of members of the exposed population. At the same time, an increased incidence of a variety of cancers has been detected with varying levels of statistical significance. Today the induction of cancer, rather than genetic effects, is widely recognized as the major risk of radiation exposure. It is important, however, to emphasize that the populations that yield the increased incidence of cancer have all been exposed to relatively large amounts of radiation. For example, individuals in the Japanese populations that the Radiation Effects Research Foundation has studied all received doses of .5 sievert or more.

Sagan (1993) has suggested additional reasons why the no-threshold model of radiation response became the dominant explanation of radiation injury after World War II. When civil engineers design a structure such as a bridge or building for safety, they construct a plan that accommodates maximum loads and stresses and then add a relatively large safety factor—often a factor of two or more—for good measure. Such an approach results in a zero probability of the structure's failing if builders follow the design and use materials of high physical integrity. But in designing a nuclear facility such as a nuclear reactor, nuclear engineers reject the notions of absolute safety and risk thresholds. Instead, they assume that the risk of accidents is always finite. That assumption requires using backup safety systems to reduce the likelihood and the consequences of an accident to an acceptable minimum that may approach but never reach zero. The no-threshold model of accident probability has served the public well in several instances, the most notable of which was the Three Mile Island accident. But the model also sends the message that accidents can always occur and that radiation and radiation-producing facilities are never without some level of risk, no matter how many safety features are built into their design.

Sagan also believes that the "new environmentalism" movement introduced in the late 1950s has exerted a major influence on the emergence of the no-threshold model of injury resulting from exposure to a wide spectrum of toxic agents. A turning point in that movement was the widespread popularity of Rachel Carson's *Silent Spring* (1962). Carson not only depicted the ecological consequences of environmental exploitation but also suggested that trace quantities of a variety of chemicals in the environment are capable of causing cancer in humans. At about the same time, there was intense public debate about the possible health effects of radioactive fallout from atmospheric tests of nuclear weapons. Opponents of weapons testing emphasized the possible health effects of fallout at very low concentrations, even though no data existed to substantiate those effects. Although more political than scientific, those statements largely went unchallenged by the scientific community and added to the public's concern that exposure to even the smallest amounts of toxins such as ionizing radiation could lead to significant adverse effects on health.

No-Threshold Model as an Operational Paradigm

I have described several reasons to explain why the no-threshold model has become the operational model for estimating the risk of exposure to low levels of radiation as well as to other potentially toxic agents. Those reasons, all rather hypothetical, have foundations in science (target theory and susceptible biological molecules), engineering (finite risks of disastrous consequences), and social policy (elimination of environmental contaminants by governmental action). There may be other reasons as well, some of which may reflect innate biases, preferred judgments, and social values of the principals who endorse the use of the no-threshold model.

The widely accepted philosophy in public health circles is that protection standards to control risks to individuals and populations should always err on the conservative side. That is, if one is uncertain about the magnitude of risk, then one should estimate the risk in such a manner that if the estimate is wrong, it is so because it overestimates the risk. Thus, agencies can establish protection standards and procedures that reflect a cautious, perhaps even overcautious, approach to protecting people against toxic agents.

While it is one thing to use a conservative model to estimate the magnitude of risk at low levels of exposure, it is something else to use that estimate to project the number of persons affected in a population exposed to low levels of a toxic agent, and then to assign significance to that number as if the effects actually exist. For example, suppose that a researcher uses linear extrapolation to estimate an upper limit of lifetime risk of cancer of one in 10,000 per unit exposure for a toxic agent—for example, ionizing radiation—thought to induce cancer at high levels of exposure. Now assume that each person in a population of 250 million, such as the U.S. population, receives on the average one unit of exposure over a lifetime. By multiplying the risk times the population size, the researcher computes the number 25,000. Not infrequently, researchers inappropriately use such an approach to determine the number of hypothetical cancers induced in the population as a result of exposure to the toxic agent. Almost as frequently, the public media report that number without *hypothetical* as a qualifying adjective. This attempt to estimate numbers of persons affected is disingenuous, and grossly perverts the efforts of scientists to establish an upper limit for purposes of estimating risk and setting standards.

It is interesting to speculate on why, until recently, so few scientific challenges have been directed against accepting the no-threshold model of injury following low-level exposure to various toxic agents, including radiation. Probably there are many reasons, including the notion that the no-threshold model suits the purposes of many people. For example, the model plays to the paranoia of many who fear the "dark side" of technologies that they do not fully understand. The professional community of protection experts benefits from that fear because it enhances job opportunities and security. Researchers benefit from the continued flow of funds to identify and quantify the degree of risk associated with exposure to toxic agents. Attorneys benefit from increased litigation resulting from the public's conviction that low levels of exposure cause cancers and other forms of illness and abnormality. Regulators have their budgets and authorities enhanced through legislative actions taken in response to the public's fear of exposures.

Whether the public truly benefits from those responses to the fear of low-level exposures is questionable, especially in light of the observation that we cannot prove whether an actual risk exists. The responses are developed at significant financial expense and at the further cost of reinforcing the public's fear of the unknown. Money spent to address those suspected but unproven risks is not available to prevent or correct problems such as industrial and domestic accidents, personal violence, tobacco use, alcohol abuse, and other known threats to human health. Those costs are the unfortunate consequences of misplaced fears and misused public funds. Although there is no good way to quantify their consequences, the social implications of such actions are enormous.

Values in Science

There is considerable uncertainty about the relevance of the no-threshold model to estimate the risk of low-level exposure to toxic agents such as ionizing radiation. Yet that model has become widely accepted as the preferred paradigm for risk estimation at low exposures. I have described some of the reasons for acceptance of the model. But there is yet another reason that may override all the others in explaining why the no-threshold model has been adopted with such universality. The reason is that the model is consistent with the expectations of society that scientists, and the designers of public policies and governmental regulations, should provide a "safe" margin of error in situations where risk cannot be quantified. Those expectations coincide with the values of the scientific community that is looked to for leadership in cases where risk is uncertain.

The concept of values in the formulation of scientific guidance may seem paradoxical. Many—perhaps most—persons assume that science functions as a value-free enterprise, and they perceive scientists as searching for "truth" in a value-free universe. As Sagan (1993) suggests, scientists are thought of as trained to "observe the world dispassionately and collect data in a scrupulously objective fashion, which they then dutifully report in peer-reviewed journals. These reports then become the substance of an ever-expanding knowledge."

But in fact, scientists are subject, just as everyone else, to value judgments in everything that they do, including constructing hypotheses for scientific experiments, selecting approaches and materials for testing hypotheses, acquiring data from experiments, and interpreting the data according to one or more prevailing paradigms that are intrinsic to the hypotheses. Those paradigms influence the way scientists think about their work and the results that it produces. It is probably true that science is more objective than some other courses of study that are not so verifiable through experimental protocols and rigid methods of statistical analysis. But it is anything but value-free.

In *The Structure of Scientific Revolutions*, Kuhn (1970) suggests that scientific thinking is guided by the use of accepted models of truth that he describes as scientific paradigms. Those models are developed to explain natural phenomena, and they gradually become so ingrained into scientific thinking that they achieve a state of unquestioned acceptance. In that condition the underlying assumptions and universal applicability of the paradigms are seldom challenged. When persons raise questions about the paradigms, they are likely to be labeled as "quacks" or "pseudoscientists" by other scientists, journal editors, and committees of peers empowered to recommend research funding (Lindzen 1992). Usually, those individuals ignore experimental evidence that is not consistent with a scientific paradigm because they consider it outside the bounds of conventional knowledge. Such evidence may be censored as heretical, at least until it becomes so overwhelming that a new model that encompasses it arises as a replacement. The acceptance of that new model represents, in Kuhn's terms, a "paradigm shift" in scientific thinking.

Kuhn emphasizes that scientific thinking often progresses not so much through gradual unidirectional evolution, but instead by infrequent but dramatic paradigm shifts that most often are driven by persons outside of the "scientific establishment." Major paradigm shifts have occurred throughout the history of science. Examples include the transition from the earth to the sun as the acknowledged center of the solar system, the replacement of Newtonian mechanics by quantum physics as the preferred model to explain physical phenomena at the atomic level, and the model of natural selection as a paradigm of biological evolution. But not all paradigm shifts withstand scientific scrutiny over the course of time. An example of a paradigm shift that ultimately proved to be fraudulent is Lysenkoism, a theory widely accepted in the Soviet Union that inherited characteristics of individuals are not mediated by physical properties of chromosomes and that acquired behaviors of individuals can be passed on to future generations. In the field of radiation biology and protection, the transition after World War II from the concept of tolerance dose to the no-threshold model of radiation injury represents a paradigm shift in scientific thinking. Whether the new model of radiation injury will hold up over time remains to be seen. It currently is receiving intense scrutiny (Health Physics Newsletter 1995).

The scientific understanding of the causes of cancer has advanced well beyond the rather simplistic model of cellular changes resulting exclusively from a single exposure to a mutagenic agent (Hendee 1995). Ames, once an outspoken critic of environmental pollution, has challenged the prevailing notion that industrial contaminants in the environment are a major cause of mutations leading to increased cancers in exposed populations (Ames and Gold 1990, 1996). The challenge is not that some of the contaminants are not theoretically capable of producing somatic mutations leading to cancer, but that their concentrations are very low compared with mutagenic agents that occur naturally in the environment. For example, all plant materials contain naturally occurring pesticides that are at least as mutagenic as industrial contaminants. Ames estimates that the average person daily consumes about 1,500 milligrams of natural pesticides that overwhelm the small amount (less than 0.1 milligram) of synthetic pesticides that finds its way into the human diet. Many seasonings and spices, such as pepper, curry, and cinnamon, are mutagenic, and cooking, including frying and baking, adds to the concentration of dietary mutagens. Charred meats and toasted bread yield plentiful concentrations of mutagenic agents, as do coffee, tea, and many soft drinks.

Today it is accepted that cells in the body are exposed each day to thousands of potentially damaging events, and that those events do not yield disastrous consequences because the body has elegant processes to repair the damage they may cause. It also is understood that the effectiveness of those repair mechanisms declines with age, with the decrease occurring more rapidly in some individuals than in others. In all persons it is probably true that the integrity of repair processes, rather than the exposure to mutagenic agents, is the more significant influence on the susceptibility of individuals to cancer and many other diseases.

> **The scientific understanding of the causes of cancer has advanced well beyond the rather simplistic model of cellular changes resulting exclusively from a single exposure to a mutagenic agent.**

For the no-threshold paradigm of radiation injury, several observations justify its reexamination as the preferred model for estimating health risks of exposure to low levels of radiation.

- There are little data available concerning actual effects in human or animal populations following exposure to low levels of radiation, and the data that do exist are contradictory, with some suggesting an adverse consequence and some yielding a beneficial effect (radiation hormesis). Evidence supporting the latter effect has been compiled by Luckey (1991) in a book entitled *Radiation Hormesis.*

- The concept of a beneficial effect at low exposures is not unique to radiation. Many agents that are toxic at high concentrations are known, or at least thought, to be beneficial at low concentrations. Examples are aspirin, wine, and even water, as well as a variety of other chemicals (Calabrese, McCarthy, and Kenyon 1987).

- Each person is exposed daily to amounts of naturally occurring mutagenic agents that overwhelm the small amounts introduced by synthetic chemical agents and by radiation in exposed individuals.

- The current understanding of the action of mutagenic agents suggests that past models of cancer induction are overly simplistic and that repair mechanisms at the cellular level play a dominant role in determining the susceptibility of individuals to cancer, including that possibly induced by radiation.

- The no-threshold model of radiation injury has been widely adopted by the press and politicians and has led to a number of very costly social policies and governmental regulations to protect radiation workers and the public from even minute amounts of radiation exposure.

The disadvantages of the no-threshold model of radiation injury may outweigh the advantages by a substantial margin.

- Those policies and regulations have increased the cost and decreased the availability of beneficial uses of radiation in a wide spectrum of applications, including medicine and electricity generation.

Those observations suggest that the disadvantages of the no-threshold model of radiation injury may outweigh the advantages by a substantial margin. They also suggest that reexamination of the merits of that model may be appropriate. But reexamination will not be easy. As Alan Barker (1988) has emphasized:

New paradigms put everyone practicing the old paradigm at great risk. And, the higher one's position, the greater the risk. The better you are at your paradigm, the more you have invested in it. To change your mind is to lose that investment.

NOTE

The work of two individuals has contributed substantially to the ideas presented in this chapter. Those individuals are Ronald Kathren of Washington State University at Tri-Cities in Richland, Washington, and Leonard Sagan, recently retired from the Electric Power Research Institute in Palo Alto, California.

REFERENCES

Ames, Bruce N., and Lois S. Gold. "The Causes and Prevention of Cancer: Gaining Perspectives on Management of Risk," in Robert W. Hahn, ed., *Risks, Costs, and Lives Saved: Getting Better Results from Regulation*. New York and Washington, D.C.: Oxford University Press and AEI Press, 1996.
————. "Chemical Carcinogenesis: Too Many Rodents." *Proceedings of the National Academy of Sciences* 87 (1990): 7772.
Barker, J. A. *Discovering the Future: The Business of Paradigms*. St. Paul: Illinois Press, 1988.
Calabrese, E. J., M. E. McCarthy, and E. Kenyon. "The Occurrence of Chemically Induced Hormesis." *Health Physics* 52 (1987): 531.
Carson, Rachel L. *Silent Spring*. Boston: Houghton Mifflin, 1962.
Department of Energy. *Radiation Protection of Occupational Workers*. Order 5480.11. Washington, D.C.: Department of Energy, December 21, 1988.
Environmental Protection Agency. "Radiation Protection Guidance to Federal Agencies for Occupational Exposure." *Federal Register* 52 (January 27, 1987): 2822–34.
Federal Radiation Council. *Background Material for the Development of Radiation Protection Standards*. Report No. 1. Washington, D.C.: Federal Radiation Council, 1960.
Hendee, William R. "Radiation Carcinogenesis," in William R. Hendee and F. M. Edwards, eds., *Health Effects of Exposure to Low-Level Ionizing Radiation*, 2nd ed. London: Institute of Physics, 1995.
International Commission on Radiological Protection. *The Evaluation of Risks from Radiation*. ICRP Publication 8. Oxford: Pergamon, 1966.
————. *Recommendations of the International Commission on Radiological Protection*. ICRP Publication 26. Oxford: Pergamon, 1977.
Joint Committee on Atomic Energy of the Congress of the United States. *Hearings on Fallout from Nuclear Weapons Tests*, May 5–8 (3 vols. and summary). Washington, D.C.: Government Printing Office, 1959.
————. *Hearings on the Nature of Radioactive Fallout and Its Effects on Man*, May 27–29

and June 3–7 (2 vols.). Washington, D.C.: Government Printing Office, 1957.

———. *Selected Materials on Radiation Protection Criteria and Standards: Their Basis and Use.* Washington, D.C.: Government Printing Office, May 1960.

Kato, H., and Y. Shimizu. "Cancer Mortality Risk among A-Bomb Survivors," in *Health Effects of Atomic Radiation: Proceedings of Japan-USSR Symposium on Radiation Effects Research.* Tokyo: June 25–29, 1990.

Kuhn, Thomas. *The Structure of Scientific Revolutions,* 2nd ed. Chicago: University of Chicago Press, 1970.

Lea, D. A. *Actions of Radiation on Living Cells.* New York: Macmillan, 1947.

Lindzen, Richard S. "Global Warming: The Origin and Nature of the Alleged Scientific Consensus." *Regulation* 15 (Spring 1992): 87–98.

Luckey, T. D. *Radiation Hormesis.* Boca Raton, Fla.: CRC Press, 1991.

Müller, H. J. "Artificial Transmutation of the Gene." *Science* 66 (1928): 84–87.

National Academy of Sciences-National Research Council. *The Effects on Populations of Exposure to Low Levels of Ionizing Radiation.* Washington, D.C.: National Academy Press, 1972.

———. *The Effects on Populations of Exposure to Low Levels of Ionizing Radiation: BEIR III.* Washington, D.C.: National Academy Press, 1980.

———. *Health Effects of Exposure to Low Levels of Ionizing Radiation: BEIR V.* Washington, D.C.: National Academy Press, 1990.

National Academy of Sciences-National Research Council Committee on the Biological Effects of Ionizing Radiation (BEIR IV). *Health Effects of Radon and Other Internally Deposited Alpha-Emitters.* Washington, D.C.: National Academy Press, 1988.

National Academy of Sciences-National Research Council Committee on Pathologic Effects of Atomic Radiation. *A Commentary on the Report of the United Nations Scientific Committee on the Effects of Atomic Radiation.* NAS-NRC Publication 647. Washington, D.C.: National Academy of Sciences/National Research Council, 1959.

National Council on Radiation Protection and Measurements. *Permissible Dose from External Sources of Ionizing Radiation.* NCRP Report No. 17. Washington, D.C.: Department of Commerce, National Bureau of Standards Handbook 50, September 24, 1954.

———. *Recommendations on Limits for Exposure to Ionizing Radiation.* NCRP Report No. 93. Bethesda, Md.: National Council on Radiation Protection and Measurements, 1987.

Nuclear Regulatory Commission. "Standards for Protection against Radiation: Final Rule." *Federal Register* 56 (May 21, 1991): 23360–474.

Sagan, Leonard. "A Brief History and Critique of the Low Dose Effects Paradigm." *BELLE Newsletter* 2(2) (1993): 1–7.

Sternglass, E. J. "Evidence for Leukemogenic Effects in Man at Low Dose Rates." *Health Physics* 15 (1968): 202.

United Nations Scientific Committee on the Effects of Atomic Radiation. *Report of the United Nations Scientific Committee on the Effects of Atomic Radiation.* General Assembly Official Records: Thirteenth Session Supplement No. 17 (A/3838). New York: United Nations, 1958.

————. *Report of the United Nations Scientific Committee on the Effects of Atomic Radiation.* General Assembly Official Records: Seventeenth Session Supplement No. 16 (A/5216). New York: United Nations, 1962.

————. *Report of the United Nations Scientific Committee on the Effects of Atomic Radiation.* General Assembly Official Records: Nineteenth Session Supplement No. 14 (A/5814). New York: United Nations, 1964.

Chapter 4

RISK ASSESSMENT AS AN INDICATOR FOR DECISION MAKING

Bernard D. Goldstein

OVERVIEW

This chapter seeks to bring the art of risk assessment into perspective. Risk assessment is neither a sure-fire scientific means of reaching correct regulatory decisions, nor a technique so seriously plagued by data imperfections and personal bias as to be useless. Risk assessment can be very valuable if its limitations are realized and it is not asked to do too much.

Both critics and practitioners of risk assessment often present it as an abstruse cabalistic exercise of incredible complexity. Risk assessment is in fact a reasonably straightforward attempt to apply scientific principles to estimate endpoints of concern to policy makers and the public. As such, the tool is similar to commonly used economic indicators such as the unemployment level or the gross domestic product. Those economic indicators are not presented as absolutely true—in fact, they are frequently revised without any presentation of error bounds or other estimates of uncertainty. Rather they are measures that inform policy makers and the public, allow priority setting to occur, and provide the basis for an informed debate on policy matters. Any indicator that is to be used for decisions on complex issues must be performed according to guidelines that lay out a standard estimation approach so that the numbers are understandable in context and not open to partisan distortion by altering the estimation process.

The first step is to establish generic guidelines based on both the objectives of the policy process and the scientific knowledge underlying the assessment. Of course, differences between risk assessment and common governmental economic indicators exist. Those differences include the facts that risk assessment is primarily an indicator of adverse impact, that health is a visceral concern, that extrapolation for risk assessment is almost always beyond the bounds of the available data, that the weight-of-evidence approach required for hazard identification is an inherent source of controversy, and that risk assessment is often a tool for developing a research agenda. To maximize the value of risk assessment as a helpful indicator, it is important to distinguish among the different goals for which it is used and to assign an appropriate objective for data quality that is consistent with the needs of the decision maker and the limitations of risk science for each assessment.

This chapter contends that risk assessment is just another one of the many government indicators that are part of the information flow characterizing complex modern societies. Like economic indicators, it is valuable in making and anticipating social decisions but is not in itself the sole determinant of those decisions. For example, in decisions related to environmental protection, risk assessment has a very useful but also limited role.

Unfortunately, we do not clearly understand the extent to which risk assessment provides information of value to decision makers and the public. Perhaps the biggest problem is that risk assessment appears to be all things to all people. Scientists often focus on the methodology of risk assessment; they insist that it must retain the purity of science and remain completely free of any policy aspects. Not surprisingly, risk scientists ask that risk methodology be advanced to whatever level is scientifically feasible, irrespective of whether an additional decimal point contributes to the decision process.

In contrast to the scientist's focus on methodology, policy makers tend to focus on the product, the risk probability number; they want risk assessment to provide absolute truth, and they recoil in horror if it is not accurate down to the last decimal point. At its best, however, risk assessment cannot exactly depict actual risk to one in a million plus a decimal place. Nor should risk assessment be a vague guess whose dimension primarily reflects the political view of whoever is in charge of the process.

The usefulness of risk assessment would be greatly improved if we had a greater understanding of the relation between the ability of the process to provide information and the information actually needed for the decision under consideration. This chapter recommends that we recognize different goals for which risk assessment may be of value; each of those goals may well call for a different data quality objective.

The risk manager needs to specify in advance the data quality objective for a risk assessment. The risk assessor then needs to state whether such an objective is attainable. If it is not attainable, then risk assessment should not be used as a tool for that purpose. If it is attainable, then the risk assessor needs to limit the depth and complexity of the risk assessment to those consistent with the data quality objective. For example, one does not need accuracy to one in a billion when scoping out priorities for a research budget.

Conversely, the risk manager must avoid the unfortunately common practice of using screening risk assessments as if they had achieved a data quality objective capable of being used to decide precisely whether, for example, a toxic chemical producer falls on one side or the other of the "bright line" in the 1990 Clean Air Act Amendments.

Risk Assessment as a Governmental Indicator

At least four attributes of common governmental indicators are pertinent when we consider the role of risk assessment. Two appear to be sufficiently uncontroversial and warrant no further discussion. First, governmental indicators, although inexact estimates, should be reasonably reproducible by others using the same methodology. Second, the primary value of government indicators to decision makers is to allow both reasonable comparisons over time or space and the setting of priorities. As I shall discuss, policy makers do not always recognize that risk assessment is far better as a means to set priorities for situations in which pollution has already occurred than it is for prevention.

Two other similarities between risk assessment and common economic indicators are that their primary value to stakeholders is to assist in predicting the actions of decision makers, and that they must be calculated in such a way that there is no imputation of partisan political bias. For example, the unemployment figure should not inappropriately dip and the gross domestic product erroneously rise just before an incumbent president comes up for reelection. To make my point I shall discuss those two factors in more detail.

The Value of Indicators in Predicting Action

Indicators have the value of helping to predict the response of legislative and administrative governmental institutions. Thus, private enterprises and individuals can make orderly and cost-effective decisions before the fact. For example, money market managers and individual investors pay close attention to any of the indicators that might affect how the Federal Reserve will adjust interest rates, multinational corporations ponder the effect of international trade figures on governmental policy, and businessmen and investors are well aware that figures reflecting unemployment and domestic product are good indicators of whether Congress might be resorting to pump-priming measures.

Generic risk assessment can and does provide major industries with a similar predictive function. No corporation today would make a decision about which chemical or chemical process to use without accounting for the risks of the various chemicals involved, including the potential for exposure. Industry routinely uses risk assessment to decide which of many potential new products to develop for the market. Furthermore, industrial stakeholders and investors closely watch new scientific information that might impinge on how risks are calculated. For example, the market appears to be well aware of the effect of the dioxin risk assessment on the pulp and paper industry. As a corollary, a smart industry will invest in developing credible information needed to support accurate risk assessment.

For industry to take maximum advantage of knowing that the government will routinely use risk assessment to help make decisions, the risk assessment process must be transparent and understandable to all. That permits the appropriate prediction of the role of information in assessing risk. Note that simply knowing the numerical outcome of a risk assessment does not necessarily predict what action will be taken, nor should it. That is also analogous to other government indicators. Translating an economic indicator related to inflation into predicting the action of the Federal Reserve requires much more information than any one indicator.

Using Guidelines to Free Indicators of Partisan Political Bias

Guidelines are the means by which risk assessment tries to achieve reproducible estimates that are perceived to be free of political bias. The goal of the guideline is to establish a standardized estimation process. Guidelines are generic approaches to the process of performing a risk assessment. In recent years the Environmental Protection Agency has developed many risk assessment guidelines, including those for assessing the risk of cancer, for assessing exposure, for dealing with mixtures, and for measuring reproductive and developmental effects (Goldstein 1988a). With limited success, policy makers have attempted to develop governmentwide guidelines to obviate the ridiculous specter of the Environmental Protection Agency, the Food and Drug Administration, and the Centers for Disease Control and Prevention having different methodologies for assessing cancer risk, despite their starting with the same scientific database. It is important not to overstate those differences among, or even within, governmental agencies. They are often due to the laws and regulatory approaches that govern the goals and degree of conservatism that must be built into the risk assessment process, rather than the inability of the scientific community to agree on methodology.

It is important that the guidelines be sufficiently rigid to discourage risk managers from altering the process for a specific agent depending on whether they wish to encourage or discourage control. Yet there must be sufficient flexibility to incorporate newer scientific advances, or scientific information pertinent to default assumptions specific to the chemical or physical agent or to the situation under evaluation. The tension between the value of relatively rigid guidelines and the value of incorporating the rapidly evolving scientific base for risk assessment is in part responsible for controversies concerning risk assessment methodology. As long as a change in methodology can reduce the estimated risk of a regulated industry's product, the industry will focus on convincing regulators to adopt the change. The process of changing the guideline is, and ought to be, a relatively slow one, depending on the speed of the peer-review processes of the scientific community. It will always be difficult to demarcate the weight of evidence needed to change a guideline. Only recently did the Bureau of Labor Statistics change the technique for estimating unemployment to reflect the greatly increased number of women in the workplace, a phenomenon that should have been evident decades ago.

Risk Assessment and Uncertainty

Risk characterization, the final step of the risk assessment process, usually leads to a single numerical estimate of the probability of the risk, for example, one in a million in a lifetime. As in any estimation process, that number has an inherent degree of uncertainty. There have been many calls to state numerically the uncertainty in the risk estimate. They have come from groups as diverse as the Committee on Risk Assessment of Hazardous Air Pollutants of the National Academy of Sciences (NAS 1994) and the Republican Contract with America, the latter in part reflecting a concern that, on the basis of prudence, uncertainties tend to be resolved in favor of higher risk numbers.

Quantifying that uncertainty raises at least three problems: the difficulty in developing a consistent scientific approach to describing uncertainty, the reluctance of the regulator to deal with more than one number, and the public misunderstanding a range would cause. Presumably similar problems have led economists to provide single numbers for uncertain economic indicators. Although they are often modified, the government does not deem it necessary to confuse people by releasing error estimates for those indicators.

The scientific and technical problems of providing a numerical description of the uncertainty of a risk assessment are significant. Note that the NAS committee's report (NAS 1994) supporting the addition of uncertainty analysis only describes the sources of uncertainty: inherent biological variability, measurement errors, and that related to extrapolation. The committee did not suggest how those should be combined. Presumably that will require additional committees from the National Research Council and the EPA—and years of litigation.

The apparently greater concern about the uncertainties in risk assessment than about other governmental indicators is puzzling. Particularly puzzling is why economists, who blithely develop and use all sorts of governmental indicators without any expression of their inherent uncertainties, are among those demanding that risk assessment numbers be given with some form of an uncertainty estimate. For example, at a 1985 meeting at the EPA on whether and how to control evaporative emissions that occurred while refueling gasoline-powered automobiles, the two major approaches were to improve gasoline delivery nozzles at gasoline stations—so-called stage 2 controls—and to require on-board controls that would require changes in the automobile. Those alternatives pitted the automobile industry, which wanted changes made at the gasoline station, against the petroleum industry, including local gas station owners, who insisted that it was preferable to make changes in the automobile. The data presented at the meeting included: the EPA's model of the amount of evaporative emissions caused while refueling, which was based on a minimum amount of data; the effect of those emissions on ozone levels nationally, a controversial subject to say the least; the extent of human exposure to benzene during the refueling process, which was based on a minimal amount of data; the resulting leukemia cases from that exposure, which was based on the estimate of the cancer potency of benzene; the efficacy of the various control options in reducing emissions; and the direct and indirect economic costs of the two control options. Despite the great uncertainties in every one of those parameters, including the expectedly widely differing analyses of cost and efficacy by the two industries involved, the meeting focused on the accuracy of the cancer potency number for benzene. Of course, the cancer potency of benzene is uncertain, but that is just one of the many uncertainties the decision maker encounters. In addition, researchers presented no error bounds for any of the other estimations.

> **Particularly puzzling is why economists, who blithely develop and use all sorts of governmental indicators without any expression of their inherent uncertainties, are among those demanding that risk assessment numbers be given with some form of an uncertainty estimate.**

There is a need to inform decision makers and the public about crucial uncertainties that have major impacts on a risk probability number. But adding a formal uncertainty analysis will only add to the complexities and the litigation potential of a process that is already too complex and too litigious (Goldstein 1989).

Differences between Risk Assessment and Common Government Indicators

Obviously, despite the many commonalities, risk assessment has attributes that distinguish it from usual governmental indicators. First, the implications of direct effects on health differ from those on economic activity. In addition, risk assessment usually concerns itself with endpoints that are inherently uncountable. Moreover, the hazard identification step of risk assessment inevitably causes controversy.

Finally, risk assessment has value as a research planning tool.

Health versus Wealth

Risk assessment inherently refers to a negative effect. There is nothing good about risk; there is nothing bad about a housing start. Even the unemployment figures can be turned around to be considered as employment levels. We respond more viscerally to a threat to human health than to a threat to economic well-being. Job loss or economic decline can be reversed; a death from cancer is final.

Risk Assessment and Countability

An often overlooked rationale for risk assessment is that it has been developed as a means to move environmental policy forward by counting the uncountable. We have little need for a formal estimation process to count the number who are injured or die in car accidents each year. Statistics can be kept, and the direct cause is obvious. The formal process of environmental risk assessment is required both because it is difficult to count adverse impacts directly due to specific environmental agents and because the levels of unacceptable risk enshrined in our regulatory approaches are well below any risk that can be counted by standard epidemiological approaches. The lack of scientific certainty inherent in counting the uncountable presents difficulties to the policy maker (Costanza and Cornwell 1992).

Risks due to environmental agents are often subtle. With rare exceptions, the environmental agent is only one of many causes, known or unknown, of a single countable endpoint, such as a disease. For example, there are many known causes of lung cancer, with smoking overwhelming all the others. Ionizing radiation, benzene, and various cancer chemotherapeutic agents can cause acute myelogenous leukemia, the adult form of acute leukemia, but for most cases the cause is unknown. For other diseases we know little about the cause of any specific case, only that the environment, in the broadest sense of the term, contributes to aggregate causality. That ignorance is compounded by only sketchy information about exposure, unless it has occurred at the workplace, and often by long lag times between the initial exposure and the eventual effect. We also know little about human susceptibility. Only now is science giving us a glimmer of hope that we can look at cancerous or other diseased tissue and tell something about the cause, that we can accurately determine the extent of human exposure, and that we can unravel the multifactorial basis of human susceptibility. Until then we must depend on an indirect estimate of the risk if we are to control environmental agents to the extent society now demands.

The demands of our society to be protected against environmental risk levels perhaps as low as one chance in a million also severely challenge any approach that depends on counting actual adverse events. Except in the rare situation where an endpoint is solely linked to a single environmental cause, such as mesothelioma caused by asbestos, it is almost impossible to use standard vital statistics to determine the risk resulting from an environmental agent. Were it not for the need to respond to laws requiring protection against those low levels of risk, we would have far less of a rationale for risk assessment. Critics who seemingly oppose risk assessment as a science because they consider it inappropriate to be concerned with such low-level risks should direct their criticism against the risk management decision that has required such concerns.

The requirement to count the uncountable also affects approaches to extrapolation and the provision of uncertainty factors. A major distinction between risk assessment and economic analysis is that extrapolation for risk assessment is almost always beyond the bounds of the available data, while there are usually good data points that straddle the estimation of many economic indicators. Economists have often asked for risk assessment to use the technique of the maximum likelihood estimate, which is valuable when one has a cloud of data and is looking for a midpoint, but risk is harder to estimate when extrapolating well beyond the range of the existing data.

Hazard Identification as an Inherent Source of Controversy

We have a relatively poor understanding of another difference between risk assessment and usual governmental indicators: the inherent controversy because, in identifying hazard, we must use a weight-of-evidence approach to establish categories for regulation.

Hazard identification, the first step in risk assessment, is a qualitative process that itself does not lead to a numerical statement. It is based on the second law of toxicology, the specificity of effects of chemical and physical agents. Controversy due to the hazard identification process is inevitable, even when scientists are in excellent agreement about the data. That is particularly true for potential chemical carcinogens. An example is a recent International Agency for Research on Cancer meeting in Lyon, France, that considered the evidence for human carcinogenicity of formaldehyde. The six epidemiologists in attendance agreed on the interpretation of the body of epidemiological studies concerning formaldehyde and cancer. Yet they had a major split, at least initially, about whether the evidence for human carcinogenicity was sufficient or only limited.

The apparent paradox of excellent scientific agreement, yet a closely split vote, is due to the process by which the weight of scientific evidence is translated into a discrete category. The inherent problem is that the weight of evidence for carcinogenicity is almost always a continuum, starting at the bottom with negative evidence, ranging upward through chemicals for which there might be some positive short-term assays, through chemicals with more or less clear-cut animal data supporting chemical carcinogenesis, through compounds with some extent of epidemiological evidence, to, at the top, a chemical or physical agent such as asbestos or ionizing radiation for which epidemiological evidence of human carcinogenesis is unequivocal. On this continuum the International Agency for Research on Cancer (1992) defines points that separate compounds into different categorical groups: carcinogenic to humans; probably carcinogenic to humans; possibly carcinogenic to humans; not classifiable; and probably not carcinogenic. The EPA has a similar listing, which it is considering changing. Separating the continuum of the weight of evidence for carcinogenicity into categories is not a scientific issue. Rather, the policies and definitions of the organization responsible for convening the scientific panel define the cutpoints in the continuum in advance. In essence, a continuum of evidence is converted into discrete boxes.

The reason that controversy is inevitable is that no matter where the cutpoint is placed, the weight of evidence for some chemical will be on or close to that point. Minor differences in the interpretation of the nuances of the data will inevitably be convertible into yes or no statements as to the category, and hence the regulation, of the chemical.

Risk Assessment as a Research Planning Tool

One other difference between risk assessment and the usual governmental indicator is the former's value as a research planning tool. The process of risk assessment can provide its own impetus to develop the research needed to improve risk assessment. This is so since risk assessment is a superb, but limited, research planning tool for an agency responsible for protecting the public against environmental risks. The goal of any scientific activity is to address crucial questions. To the basic scientist the crucial question is the one that, if answered properly, will advance the frontiers of knowledge. To the regulator the crucial question is that which, in the short or long term, provides information allowing for better decision making. If left to themselves, scientists can address and answer many questions concerning environmental pollutants that may be immaterial to present or future decisions. If left to themselves, regulators are usually unaware of what science can offer that is pertinent to their decisions. The process of risk assessment is one in which scientists and regulators come together to review both the available science and the regulatory needs. Just as it is a truism that scientists do a poor job of explaining what we know to the public, it is also true that regulators do a poor job of explaining their crucial uncertainties to scientists early enough in the decision process so that science can make a difference (Jasonoff 1993). Risk assessment helps to bridge that gap.

Problems and Limitations of Risk Assessment

Of the many limitations of risk assessment, the one we must always keep in mind is that, regardless of how good our assessments of current risks are, that activity should always have lesser priority than developing the information to prevent new risks. Our rapidly evolving technological society continually produces possibilities for significant adverse environmental consequences to ourselves and our planet. Primary prevention consists of avoiding those risks. Secondary prevention, of far lesser value, consists of accurately measuring how dirty we are so that we may more effectively clean up, but it would be better not to get dirty in the first place. Formal risk assessment is now much more effective as a tool to assess what is dirty than to lead us to primary prevention (Goldstein 1991).

One of the limitations of risk assessment is its complexity. Some of the formulas are well beyond the comprehension of an informed layman, and abstruse detail can be built in to defy understanding by anyone but the initiated. In many cases that complexity is unnecessary; it reflects both the lack of understanding of the data quality objective of risk assessment and the propensity, particularly at the EPA, to rely on highly complex mathematical models in preference to actual measurements of exposure or effect (Goldstein 1993a). We can and should streamline risk assessment to reflect the need to answer the questions being asked by the decision maker and by the general public in a way that is understandable. The complexity of risk assessment was one reason that seemingly simpler technology-based controls were preferred in the air toxics portion of the 1990 Clean Air Act Amendments (Lash 1994). As the EPA Office of Air and Radiation struggles to try to write complex technology-based controls for the many different sources of air toxics, however, that rationale has become less persuasive.

A particular problem with the current practice of risk assessment is that there is often a substantial gap between the decision maker's data quality objective and the degree of complexity of the assessment, with unnecessary analyses confusing and delaying response. Treating risk assessment as an arcane exercise fit only for the initiated robs regulatory agencies and the public of the opportunity to take full advantage of such a valuable tool. At its simplest, risk assessment can be useful in providing numbers to illustrate a point of view. For example, a simple risk assessment demonstrated the potential problem of removing asbestos from buildings and was instrumental in the EPA's eventual focus on training workers to remove asbestos from school buildings (Goldstein 1988). Assume that ten schools have risks of a hundred in a billion due to asbestos and that nine of those schools are remediated with 99 percent effectiveness. The putative saving of life is nine times ninety-nine in a billion, or 891 in a billion lives saved. Assume that in the tenth school unskilled workers botch the job and spread asbestos so that there is a tenfold increase in risk. Effectively remediating nine of ten schools for a 90 percent compliance rate would seem to be a highly desirable outcome. Yet simple arithmetic demonstrates that the increase in risk due to the one ineffective remediation outweighs the value of the nine successful remediations: the risk in the one problem school increases from 100 to 1,000, for a loss

> **Formal risk assessment is now much more effective as a tool to assess what is dirty than to lead us to primary prevention.**

of 900 in a billion putative lives versus the estimated gain of 891.

A mirror to the excess complexity caused by the risk assessor's fail-ure to understand the regulator's data quality objective is the regula-tor's unreasonable complacency in the face of a risk assessment per-formed with a database inadequate to the public health needs. We can find a current example in the significant change in the composition of automotive fuels, including the use of 15 percent oxygenated fuels to achieve compliance with the carbon monoxide standard.

We now have enough data to perform a standard risk assessment that seemingly permits us to be reassured that MTBE, the most com-monly used oxygenated additive, is unlikely to be harmful. But the data quality objective for a gasoline additive ought to extend beyond that of the routine risk assessment. The surest way to poison the most people through an air pollutant in America is to tinker with the auto-motive fuel to which we are all exposed. Months before researchers thoroughly reviewed standard laboratory animal cancer studies, fuel producers significantly increased MTBE levels to 15 percent during wintertime in much of the United States. The industy does not want to bother with studies for other oxygenates, such as ETBE or TAME, because the industry believes that such studies are unlikely to prove positive despite the fact that some cancers were seen with high-level exposures to MTBE.

As a toxicologist, I believe it unlikely that any one of the oxy-genated fuel additives will cause human cancer or chronic disease. There are, however, three problems with disposing of the issue so glibly. First, from a public health point of view, it is simply wrong to lose sight of the fact that the data quality objective for risk assessment must be greater if we are to so blithely expose more than 100 million Americans (Goldstein 1995). Second, we should be concerned that people are exposed to a mixture of an oxygenate in gasoline, not to the oxygenate alone. Therefore, the basic toxicological studies and the risk assessment should be on that mixture and its combustion products—something not really done for MTBE. Third, the toxico-logical database used for risk assessment is not capable of ruling out subtle neurobehavioral effects in a small subset of the population (Fiedler et al. 1994).[1]

The last point brings up the importance of comparative risk assessment as a means to set the data quality objective (Lash 1994; EPA 1987). Meeting the carbon monoxide standard was the driving force in raising the MTBE levels in wintertime gasoline to 15 percent. The major known impact of carbon monoxide is a reversible effect on a small subset of the population. If MTBE may also cause a reversible effect on a subset of the population—something not inconsistent with public complaints and not ruled out by the animal studies—it would seem unreasonable to trade off a known adverse effect for the potential of a similar but unstudied adverse effect. Note that this risk-risk comparison will differ to the extent that using oxygenated fuels cuts down on tropospheric ozone levels, because ambient ozone is potentially more harmful than carbon monoxide to a greater portion of the population.

A variant on the issue of failing to understand a realistic data quality objective for risk assessment is the propensity to make absolute decisions based on risks of literally one in ten million—the equivalent of a decimal point to the right of one in a million. That reflects the temptation for Congress and federal agencies to overuse the seeming scientific certainty of risk assessment as a means to avoid difficult political decisions (Graham 1988). Such a tendency also suggests that risk assessors have oversold the accuracy of their product by making it seem as if they have a laser micrometer, capable of accurately measuring to a thousandth of an inch, rather than a reasonably good yardstick.

An example is the "bright line" in the air toxics provision of the 1990 Clean Air Act Amendments. The new law seems to call for the use of risk assessment only after achieving maximum available control technology. At that point a bright line test would determine whether further regulatory effort was required. As the industrial facility involved would already have been subjected to "maximum" technological control, additional regulatory action would clearly contemplate closing the facility. The EPA seems to be coming up with definitions of *maximum* that will allow more technology to be used to control industries above the bright line while at the same time trying to fuzz over the bright line by approaches to assessing the risk to the maximally exposed individual that are more realistic than originally proposed.

One of the problems with many government indicators is that national or statewide figures may mask what is happening at the local level. A bleak local economic picture due to the failure of a single major enterprise may show up as nothing more than a rounding of a decimal place in the broader picture, yet it deeply affects the lives of an entire community. The classic faceless government bureaucrat uses risk assessment to help make national decisions, including prioritizing industrial sectors for control, driving regulatory attention and budget to higher risk areas, and deciding among technologies (Davies 1994). But risk assessments on local pollutant sources are as highly pertinent to the local community as are local economic indicators. One of the problems with risk assessment is that many of its nationally based practitioners have been slow to realize fully the impact of using the technique for local issues. Rounding off approaches that may be perfectly reasonable in making nationwide priority decisions can be intolerable to a local community. Particularly galling to the community are exposure assessment strategies that take no account of local conditions; for example, assuming average national fish consumption patterns for a community on a well-stocked trout lake is unacceptable. Communities are becoming more suspicious of risk probability numbers and more sophisticated in their ability to probe the risk assessment methodology. Policy makers must focus on the increasing need for community risk assessment and on the role of the community in the risk assessment and risk management processes (Goldstein 1993b; NAS 1994). The community may consist of groups with diverse interests and stakes in the outcome of the risk assessment. We need to develop a breed of risk assessors capable of listening first to the public before they crank up their computers.

Constraints on the Evolution of Risk Assessment

The evolution of risk assessment has a number of constraints. One is the increasingly paltry support for the research base needed to advance the field. Whether calculated as absolute dollars, dollars corrected for inflation, a percent of the EPA's budget, or, most important, a percent of the imposed environmental costs, research and development funding continues to decrease from past levels. Given the enormous costs and potential benefits of protecting the environment, it is important to understand whether what we are doing is based on the best available information and whether the action has the desired impact.

One of the most frustrating aspects of being a scientist dealing with environmental issues is that when it is easiest to find out whether an action has an impact, there is almost no regulatory interest in doing so. The scientific method is much more powerful in detecting cause and effect relationships when it records and analyzes the outcome of perturbing an observed system—for example, exposing rats to different levels of a pollutant. Most environmental regulation is based on presumptions as to what is happening to humans during a steady state, a much more difficult challenge to the scientist. Environmental regulations are almost exclusively responsible for perturbing human exposure in

> **One of the most frustrating aspects of being a scientist dealing with environmental issues is that when it is easiest to find out whether an action has an impact, there is almost no regulatory interest in doing so.**

the real world by changing pollutant levels in a planned way. The period following promulgation of a new regulatory control would be the optimal time to evaluate scientifically the predictions made from a risk assessment. Yet that is the period when regulators seem to have the least interest in scientifically evaluating the particular pollutant; they insist instead that the risk scientist focus on the next chemical on the regulatory timetable.

As a physician, I well understand the need to make decisions based on the available information at a time and place. But it would be malpractice if I were to use that as an excuse never to get the data despite the continued needs of my patient.

Regulators are also slow to incorporate new research findings or concepts into the risk assessment process. To some extent that appropriately reflects a natural conservatism before accepting new methodology to address regulatory issues. That is again consistent with the belated change in the approach for computing U.S. unemployment to reflect the role of women in the workplace. Impediments to changing risk assessment methodology reflect unnecessary brakes on the use of the tool. One is an institutional preference for mathematical models as compared with direct measurements that appears to pervade the EPA (Wallace 1993). That is particularly noticeable in the assessment of exposure, where many new and accurate tools—some developed by EPA scientists—are now available to measure the actual extent of human or ecosystem exposure to environmental agents. Yet the EPA continues to focus on mathematical models to estimate exposure, although those models were developed as stopgaps until the agency could develop ambient measurements, personal monitoring, or biological markers. The particular excitement in the field of biological markers—the use of biological fluids as an indicator of exposure, effect, or susceptibility to external chemical or physical agents—has led to a series of NAS committee documents recommending the use of biological markers (NRC 1989).

Another impediment to the evolution of risk assessment is understandable but more difficult to document. Risk managers are much more willing to embrace new approaches to risk assessment when they do not affect previous decisions. If a risk manager has already regulated ten chemicals, he is bound to be reluctant to change the approach for the eleventh chemical, even if there is complete scientific agreement about the new approach. Unfortunately, regulators rarely see beyond the eleventh chemical to the hundredth or more chemical that they will eventually regulate inappropriately to keep faith with the first ten.

Many of the approaches to evaluating the risk of noncancer endpoints suffer from that problem. The automatic use of "safety factors" for species extrapolation and human variability has a long history. Even with the more sophisticated information now available, regulators are reluctant to change any of the existing risk numbers derived from those safety factors. Perhaps the attention given to the use of noncancer endpoints in assessing the risk of dioxin may lead to a more reasonable approach to safety factors (EPA 1994).

NOTE

1. An old toxicological adage says rodents do not retch.

REFERENCES

Costanza, Robert, and Laura Cornwell. "The 4P Approach to Dealing with Scientific Uncertainty." *Environment* 34 (1992): 12–20.

Davies, Terrance. "Uses and Abuses of Risk Assessment." *Risk Policy Report* 1 (October 14, 1994).

Environmental Protection Agency. "Guidelines for Carcinogen Risk Assessment." *Federal Register* 51 (1986): 32992–4003 et seq.

———. "Guidelines for Developmental Toxicity Risk Assessment." *Federal Register* 56 (1991): 63798–826.

————. "Guidelines for Exposure Assessment." *Federal Register* 57 (1992): 22888–938.

————. *Health Assessment Document for 2,3,7,8-Tetrachlorodibenzo-p-dioxin (TCDD) and Related Compounds.* Review draft. EPA/600/BP-92/001a. Washington, D.C.: Government Printing Office, June 1994.

————. *Unfinished Business: A Comparative Assessment of Environmental Problems.* Washington, D.C.: Government Printing Office, 1987.

Fiedler, Nancy, Sandra Mohr, Kathy Kelly-McNeil, and Howard M. Kipen. "Response of Sensitive Groups to MTBE." *Inhalation Toxicology* 66 (1994): 539–52.

Goldstein, Bernard D. "Comment on Lance Wallace Perspective." *Risk Analysis* 13 (1993a): 141–42.

————. "EPA as a Public Health Agency." *Regulatory Toxicology and Pharmacology* 8 (1988b): 328–34.

————. "If Risk Management Is Broke, Why Fix Risk Assessment?" *EPA Journal* 19 (January–March 1993b): 37–38.

————. "The Need to Restore the Public Health Base for Environmental Control." *American Journal of Public Health* 85 (1995): 481–83.

————. "The Problem with the Margin of Safety: Toward the Concept of Protection." *Risk Analysis* 10 (1990): 7–10.

————. "Risk Assessment and the Interface between Science and Law." *Columbia Journal of Environmental Law* 14 (1989): 343–55.

————. "Risk Assessment/Risk Management Is a Three-Step Process: In Defense of EPA's Risk Assessment Guidelines." *Journal of the American College of Toxicology* 7 (1988a): 543–49.

————. "Should We Set Priorities Based on Risk Analysis?" *EPA Journal* 17 (March/ April 1991): 23.

Graham, John, L. C. Green, and Mark J. Roberts. *In Search of Safety: Chemicals and Cancer Risk.* Cambridge: Harvard University Press, 1988.

International Agency for Research on Cancer. *Monograph Evaluating Carcinogenic Risks to Humans* 54 (1992): 237.

Jasanoff, Sheila. "Bridging the Two Cultures of Risk Analysis." *Risk Analysis* 13 (1993): 123–29.

Lash, John. "Integrating Science, Values, and Democracy through Comparative Risk Assessment," in Adam M. Finkel and Dominic Golding, eds., *Worst Things First? The Debate over Risk-Based National Environmental Priorities.* Washington, D.C.: Resources for the Future, 1994.

National Academy of Sciences. *Building Consensus through Risk Assessment and Management of the Department of Energy's Environmental Remediation Program.* Washington, D.C.: National Academy Press, 1994.

National Research Council, Committee on Biological Markers. *Biological Markers in Reproductive Toxicology.* Washington, D.C.: National Academy Press, 1989.

Wallace, Lance. "A Decade of Studies of Human Exposure: What Have We Learned?" *Risk Analysis* 13 (1993): 135–39.

Chapter 5

SCIENCE AND POLITICS
Global Warming and Eugenics

Richard S. Lindzen

OVERVIEW

This chapter examines closely the uses and abuses of science in reaching essentially political decisions. It does so through two examples, one current and one nearly a century old—the global warming issue today, and the eugenics movement of the early twentieth century with its impact on immigration law.

Global warming has been one of the more confusing and misleading issues to be presented to the public. Despite the absence of a significant scientific basis for most predictions, the public has been led to believe that there is an overwhelming scientific consensus that the issue is a matter of immediate urgency requiring massive control of energy usage. The first part of this chapter will briefly describe that situation, including the mechanisms by which science, advocacy that is nominally based on science, and politics interact to produce an unscientific and possibly undesirable result.

The thought that scientists would allow such an abuse of science is difficult for most laymen to believe. But it is not unique to the case of global warming. The interaction noted above—together with the passiveness of scientists in not objecting to misuse of their work—has produced bad results in the past and presumably will do so in the future. A striking example, examined in some detail, was the mingling of genetics, eugenics, and public feelings about immigration in the United States in the first several decades of the twentieth century.

There is no evident solution to the problem posed by the ability of advocacy groups—often themselves quite well-meaning—to manipulate the political process by misusing science. It is, however, important for the informed public to understand what goes on.

Global Warming as a Public Issue

Temperature Change versus Warming

Global warming, as a public issue, is a semantic quagmire. First, there is confusion over the use of the expression *global warming*. At times the expression refers to observed global temperature change. Here there is widespread agreement that the globally averaged temperature of the earth has increased somewhere between .3 degree and .6 degree Celsius during the twentieth century, with a small but significant chance that the actual record might be outside that range. The change is also widely agreed to be within the range of natural variability.[1] Because of the existence of natural variability, it is possible to say that the observed record is "broadly consistent" with models predicting significant warming from the emissions of carbon dioxide resulting from man's activities. But the observations are comparably consistent with models predicting a small amount of cooling. We also know that there is poor correlation between regionally averaged temperatures—those that will affect actual people—and globally averaged temperatures. I have no argument with such a view of global warming. At other times, the expression *global warming* refers in the active sense to warming that might be due to increasing levels of carbon dioxide in the atmosphere. That is the issue concerning which there has been widespread argument for almost a century. There are many reasons to question the hypothesis. I shall briefly discuss the basic arguments.[2]

First, the basic greenhouse process is not simple. In particular, it is not merely a matter of the gases that absorb heat radiation—greenhouse gases—keeping the earth warm. If it were, the natural greenhouse would be about four times more effective than it actually is. In reality, the surface of the earth is cooled by evaporation and motion systems that bodily carry heat both upwards and polewards, thus bypassing much of the atmosphere's greenhouse absorption. The actual greenhouse effect depends on those motions as well as on the greenhouse gas concentrations above the levels where motions deposit heat and on the details of the temperature distribution at those levels. All of those are matters of significant basic uncertainty and involve errors in model behavior so large as to be discerned even in the uncertain data.

Second, the most important greenhouse gas in the atmosphere is water vapor, and percentage changes in that gas are comparably important at all levels of the atmosphere—at least below sixteen kilometers—despite the fact that the concentration of water vapor is thousands of times less at sixteen kilometers than at the surface of the earth. Roughly speaking, changes in relative humidity on the order of 1.3 to 4 percent are equivalent to the effect of doubling carbon dioxide. Our measurement uncertainty for trends in water vapor is in excess of 10 percent, and once again, model errors are known to substantially exceed measurement errors in a very systematic way.

Third, the direct impact of doubling carbon dioxide on the earth's temperature is rather small: on the order of .3 degree Celsius.[3] Larger predictions depend on positive feedbacks—primarily from upper atmosphere temperature and from water vapor—acting in such a manner as to greatly magnify the effect of carbon dioxide. Both those factors arise from models with errors in those factors, the importance of which greatly exceeds the effect of doubling carbon dioxide.

There is very little argument about the above points. They are, for the most part, textbook material showing that there are errors and uncertainties in physical processes central to model predictions that are an order of magnitude greater than the climate forcing due to a putative doubling of carbon dioxide. There is, nonetheless, argument over whether the above points mean that the predicted *significant* response to increased carbon dioxide is without meaningful basis. Here there is disagreement. Major users and developers of large models frequently defend model results regardless of the above. Theoreticians and data analysts are commonly more skeptical. The word *significant* should be emphasized. Global mean temperatures fluctuate by .25 degree Celsius and more without anyone's particularly noticing. It seems most peculiar that such disagreements should be described in terms of contrarians and consensuses. To understand that, one must turn to the next source of semantic confusion: the difference between a natural consensus arising in a field and a forged consensus. Note that a substantial body of both theoretical and observational analysis strongly suggests that the models have substantially exaggerated the effect of increasing carbon dioxide. For present purposes, however, it suffices to note that neither an observational basis for concerns nor a credible theoretical basis exists. Support for the popularly stated scenarios are, at this point, little more than statements of belief rather than science.

Natural versus Forged Consensus

The consensus concerning the behavior of the observed globally averaged temperature is pretty much a natural consensus. The consensus concerning the model response to increasing carbon dioxide is not. Boehmer-Christiansen (1994) describes the issue. Briefly, a number of groups in the early 1980s wanted to push increasing levels of carbon dioxide as a major environmental issue. They recognized, however, that this would be difficult to do in view of the degree of scientific disarray on the issue of anthropogenic global warming. The Intergovernmental Panel on Climate Change was created to forge a consensus on the scenario of significant warming—rather than to assess objectively the issue in terms of supporting and contradictory findings—so as to facilitate the development of international policy. Even so, such consensus as was forged was largely restricted to the Policymakers' Summaries of the panel's documents rather than included in the detailed texts. Moreover, the extent of the claimed consensus has steadily diminished in the panel's documents as one goes from the 1990 report through the 1992 update, to the 1994 report on warming potentials, and to the forthcoming 1995 report.[4] Clearly, the rapidity with which those reports are produced has little to do with the normal cycle of scientific research. Also, the effort involved in producing such a flurry of documents is largely incompatible with doing research. I would suggest that we are seeing a fairly harried effort to preserve whatever consensus has been forged until policy can be enacted.

> **Neither an observational nor a credible theoretical basis exists for concerns about global warming. The Intergovernmental Panel on Climate Change was created to forge a consensus on the scenario of significant warming—rather than to assess objectively the issue in terms of supporting and contradictory findings.**

Packing the Consensus

Of course, the whole issue has been further confused by the environmental advocates' largely successful attempt to mix natural with forged
consensus, natural climate fluctuations with anthropogenic warming,
insignificant warming with large warming, and the present relative
warmth with predictions of steadily increasing warmth. To that they
have added totally hypothetical claims of various consequences of putative global warming, and journalists have abetted them in all their
efforts. The whole disorderly exercise has been subsumed within a single
label, and universal scientific agreement has been claimed for the resulting confusion.[5] It feels most peculiar to be labeled a contrarian for recognizing the very weak foundations—if there are any foundations—of that
composite claim. To make matters worse, the exaggerated composite
claims have formed the basis for an international political process that
aims to control energy usage by controlling carbon emissions. The
enthusiasm for the political actions stems from a large variety of motiva-
tions. A few of the most obvious ones are the very large degree of
bureaucratic influence offered by energy control, competitive advantage
among different energy producers based on differing carbon emissions,
and the recycling of old efforts at energy policy that have been frustrated
by the decreasing prices of fossil fuels since the energy shock of 1973. To
the extent that curbs on fossil fuel consumption inhibit development in
the developing countries, we have the traditional attempt of the "haves"
to avoid sharing with the "have nots." There are also issues of vanity. It
has been claimed that Crispen Tickell—a British diplomat who published a small book on the need for an international response to global
cooling—convinced Margaret Thatcher to take up the cause of global
warming because with her background in chemistry she could assume
leadership among her fellow world leaders. Similarly, there is little doubt
that Vice President Gore's enthusiasm for environmental causes is part
of his self-image as a new-age futurist.

Scientific Acquiescence

At this point, the situation has moved vastly beyond what could be justified in any way by science. Rather, warming advocates have emphasized the fact that science cannot rule out global warming; they have
cynically ignored the fact that science is generally incapable of ruling

out anything. Nonetheless, the scientific community has raised surprisingly little objection, and such objection as has been made is typically confined to private exchanges and papers addressed purely to one's colleagues. A recent example was the report by the world's leading experts on hurricanes that there was no reason to suppose that, even were global warming to occur, it would have any particular effect on hurricanes (Lighthill et al. 1994). The scientists published the statement in the *Bulletin of the American Meteorological Society*, but their findings received no wider publicity. To be sure, that is how scientists normally communicate research results; going "public" is unusual. Although the absence of open scientific objection to the misuse of science seems surprising to the public, it is actually the norm. The public takes the absence of objection to constitute scientific support for the popular depiction of the science, and, indeed, there have been frequent efforts by advocacy groups to reinforce that view. Scientists outside the core area of climate change who wish to exploit the issue for their own benefit abet those advocates of global warming. Thus, the health sciences have been making a major pitch to examine the implications of the putative warming for epidemics (Stone 1995).

A naive public response to that situation has held that scientists, being governed by a selfless concern for the truth, would not support such an effort if it were not justified. Of course, there is enough cynicism abroad that would recognize that scientists might not be so pure, but it is interesting to examine what, exactly, is the mode by which scientists appear to accommodate such exploitation. The particular problems of global warming and other environmental issues stem, as far as I can tell, from the interaction of science, nominally science-based advocacy,[6] and politics. The credibility of the first is something the remaining two cannot resist exploiting, while the power and publicity wielded by the second pair are frequently irresistible to the first. The lack of clear definition of who is a relevant scientist complicates the situation. Advocacy groups characteristically use information to gain special influence over the political process. Their trophies, so to speak, are legislation, regulation, and treaties, and it would appear that their existence is an automatic feature of the political system. It is not at all clear that advocates have any specific political agenda. In many instances they may simply be eager to translate science in the interest of some perceived public good. Such perceptions are commonly political, however, and the fact that advocacy groups measure their success in terms of political effectiveness inevitably entrains them into the political process. Finally, both advocates and politicians tend to view science in terms of facts rather than process, and that leads to eventual conflict with scientists and science.

Human Heredity, Eugenics, and Immigration Law

Somewhat by accident, I came to realize that we have experienced such behavior before. Scholars have studied the interaction of genetics, eugenics, and the politics of immigration in the early 1920s at great length, primarily as an example of the misuse of science in the interests of racism. It was in this connection that a colleague gave me an article by Jon Beckwith (1993). Whatever the implications of that case for the responsible application of biology, however, it is also a remarkable example of the interaction of science, advocacy, and politics. Although I am neither a historian nor a social scientist, I find the history of that matter helpful in understanding contemporary environmental issues, and I would hope that those more capable than I am would examine it in a more professional manner. The following are my impressions of this issue. What I am discussing here is largely based on studies by Kevles (1985), Ludmerer (1972), Allen (1975), Provine (1973), and Beckwith (1993). I lay claim to no intensive searching of archives.

The primary actors in this story are a biology community that had embarked on the study of human genetics, an advocacy movement, eugenics, which was intent on applying human genetics immediately to the betterment of the human race, and a political configuration concerned with America's alarm over immigration. I shall focus on the American branch of this story, though the uglier example of a similar interaction in Germany is certainly better known. Briefly, segments of the biology community studying human heredity began, in the early 1900s, to consider the possibility that "feeblemindedness" might be a simple Mendelian genetic characteristic manifested by a single recessive gene. The eugenics movement seized on that as the basis for a variety of practical actions, including forced sterilization. During World War I, the U.S. Army administered primitive intelligence tests to army inductees. The results suggested rampant feeblemindedness in the population as a whole—47 percent of all Caucasians—and interpreters of the results claimed that immigrants from southern and eastern Europe were particularly affected. A general anti-immigration mood found support in the more noble notion of preserving America's genetic quality from foreign pollution, and the eugenics movement offered enthusiastic encouragement. Seizing the issue of genetics as an objective rationalization for restricting immigration, Congress passed the Immigration Restriction Act of 1924. Even then, most of the genetics community was beginning to understand that feeblemindedness was not a simple genetic characteristic. Observers were also beginning to recognize that the specific intelligence test and the way it was administered—in English—were deeply flawed. The scientific community even raised some public opposition to the premature application of uncertain science. The scientific opposition was mild, however, and thus was easily ignored or coopted. Today the archives show substantial private correspondence among prominent geneticists decrying the abuse of their science in connection with the passage of the immigration act. Generally, however, the most prominent geneticists were publicly silent on the issue, and many even continued to support the eugenics movement. Professional societies, as such, never objected to the abuse of genetic science, even after the particularly blatant abuse by the Nazis.

In addition, some individuals with scientific credentials endorsed the eugenic claims, and Congress designated one of those as the "leading expert" on the application of genetics to immigration law. That individual, Harry Laughlin, eventually received an honorary doctorate in 1936 from Heidelberg University.

In attempting to account for the passive, and even cooperative, behavior of the scientific community, one uncovers what I suspect is a fairly generic example of the interaction of science, nominally science-based advocacy, and politics. Certainly, relative to this earlier example, present examples offer little if anything anomalous. There are obvious analogies between fears of environmental degradation and fears of genetic degradation, the environmental movement and the eugenics movement, and environmental legislation and immigration legislation.[7]

In this chapter I sketch what appear to me to be characteristic features of that interaction.

The Assumption of High Moral Purpose by an Advocacy Movement

In the late nineteenth century in England, the study of human heredity and the study of eugenics were synonymous. Ignorant of Mendelian genetics, the British biometricians developed sophisticated mathematical tools to determine the role of heredity. Indeed, early British scientific eugenicists like Karl Pearson and Irving Fisher were also prominent among the founders of modern statistics. Almost immediately, the idea gained some popularity that the scientific findings should be immediately applied to the betterment of the human race, and advocacy groups developed with that aim. In 1891 Victoria Woodhull, author of *The Rapid Multiplication of the Unfit*, wrote, "The best minds of today have accepted the fact that if superior people are desired, they must be bred; and if imbeciles, criminals, paupers, and [the] otherwise unfit are undesirable citizens, they must not be bred." Alexander Graham Bell, Theodore Roosevelt, the Bishop of Ripon, George Bernard Shaw, Margaret Sanger, and Havelock Ellis were all enthusiastic eugenicists; thus, the claim concerning the "best minds" was not totally unjustified. While the specific views of those eminent eugenicists differed, they did succeed in gaining the attention of policy makers. Ludmerer (1972) notes:

> Eugenicists' strong feeling of moral purpose understandably contributed to their marked self-assuredness and sense of self-righteousness in discussing the eugenics program. . . . When [the eugenicists] campaigned for legislation, officials and other citizens could not help but heed the fervent, impassioned pleas of so many eminent persons.

Scientists themselves were not impervious to the moral fashion the advocates had established. Nor did they object to the public recognition given them and their field by the advocates. We shall return to this important influence later.[8] It is worth noting, however, that the publicly perceived exercise of "scientific responsibility" amounted to accepting the position of the eugenicists.

The power of self-righteousness can be illustrated by an example reported by Kevles (1985). In 1916 Esther Meyer, a non-English-speaking immigrant girl, was recommended for confinement in a custodial institution because of seeming low intelligence. Justice Goff, in rejecting the recommendation, admirably warned that "the votaries of science or pseudoscience" could too easily make prejudiced testimony of the tests. One might have hoped that Justice Goff would have been praised for his insight. The *New York Times*, however, decried Goff's decision. The paper contended, "The Binet-Simon tests, intelligently applied, are as trustworthy as the multiplication table."

Eugenics worked its way rapidly into college curricula and remained there long after much of its basis had been discredited. That is but one of the processes acting to rigidify public perceptions of science despite contradicting scientific developments. Such rigidity is at least partially associated with the tendency of advocacy groups to emphasize nominal facts over process. As noted by Kevles, the large majority of American colleges and universities—including Harvard, Columbia, Cornell, Brown, Wisconsin, Northwestern, and Berkeley—offered well-attended courses in eugenics, or genetics courses that incorporated eugenic material. As late as 1931, Harry Emerson Fosdick, the widely known pastor of the Riverside Church in New York, could argue that "few matters are more pressingly important than the application to our social problems of such well-established information in the realm of eugenics as we actually possess." In fact, eugenics remained in the curriculum even longer.

> **Apart from a sense of high moral purpose, popular acceptance of an issue seems to require a simplistic picture of the underlying science together with "events" that supply an immediacy to the resulting "understanding."**

Apart from a sense of high moral purpose, popular acceptance of an issue seems to require a simplistic picture of the underlying science together with "events" that supply an immediacy to the resulting "understanding."

Simple-Minded Pictures and Events

The popularity of the issue did not really take off until the rediscovery of Mendelian genetics in 1900. The simple mechanistic picture of single-gene inheritance had the immense appeal of making heredity "understandable," even though the picture proved to be frequently wrong and inadequate—especially for feeblemindedness. There is an important intellectual point here. It would appear that for a nominally science-based issue to catch on, there must be an almost trivial picture of the underlying scientific principle that can be widely "understood." Mendelian genetics satisfied that need; the sophisticated statistical analyses of the biometricians did not. A similar role exists in the global warming issue for the simplistic picture of the greenhouse effect where-in the increase in gases that absorb heat radiation—infrared radia-tion—must inevitably lead to warming. It is apparently irrelevant that the simple process described is not only very seriously incomplete—the actual greenhouse effect is only about 25 percent of what the illustrat-ed mechanism would produce—but leads, by itself, to very little warm-ing from projected increases in carbon dioxide.

Translating such "understanding" into legislation and policy ulti-mately requires popular support transcending the advocacy groups alone. It appears that "events" are the method of choice for achieving that goal. By *events* I mean some finding, relevant or not, true or not, which can dramatize the issue and generate, if possible, a degree of public hysteria. The hot summer of 1988 served that function in the global warming case. The finding of rampantly increasing feeblemind-edness served a similar function for the eugenics movement. The claim that southern and eastern Europeans were particularly affected was used to imply that immigrants were instrumental in the "epidem-ic" and that their continued admission into the United States was a threat to our future.

For the most part, "events" do not happen randomly. Enthusiasm within the environmental movement for control of carbon emissions arose during the early 1980s, but warming advocates quickly recog-nized that one would have to await an "event" to mobilize the public. In 1912 Irving Fisher, a professor of economics at Yale who was prominent in the eugenics movement, wrote to Charles Davenport, a prominent geneticist, "The stresses of immigration alone provided a golden opportunity to get people in general to talk eugenics." When immigration came to the fore of the political agenda, the eugenics movement was ready to provide the "scientific" foundation.

The final element in the brew appears to be the establishment of scientific credibility for the advocacy movement and the suppression of opposition. In the global warming issue, the Intergovernmental Panel on Climate Change and its forged consensus have been the dominant mechanism. The situation with eugenics was somewhat more primitive.

Achievement of Scientific Credibility

One of America's most important enthusiasts for Mendelian genetics was Charles Davenport, a member of the National Academy of Sciences and a scientific entrepreneur. He convinced the Carnegie Institution of Washington to set up the Cold Spring Harbor Laboratory for the experimental study of evolution in 1904. His approach to studying human heredity was to gather numerous pedigrees, which were to be studied to determine heritable characteristics. To carry out that effort on an appropriate scale, Mary Harriman, a noted progressive[9] and the sister of Averell Harriman, funded through the Carnegie Institution the creation of the Eugenics Records Office at Cold Spring Harbor. The office was headed by Harry Laughlin, who held a doctorate in biology from Princeton, but who was apparently not regarded as a significant scientist within the scientific community. The office employed hundreds of fieldworkers, most of them volunteers. Davenport was generally considered to be overenthusiastic and incautious in his science. He was convinced that numerous human characteristics including "feeblemindedness" were simple single-gene characteristics. His instructions (Davenport 1911) to fieldworkers displayed a painful lack of scientific objectivity:

> The fieldworker finds a person suffering from feeblemindedness, a descendant of two normal parents—by hypothesis both of these parents are simplex [heterozygous]; the fieldworker must understand that each parent will probably have somewhere in his or her ancestry a feebleminded person and it is the business of the fieldworker to make a special search for such a person or persons in the pedigree.

The focus on supporting rather than testing hypotheses is a noted characteristic of environmental studies as well and typifies the modus operandi of the Intergovernmental Panel on Climate Change; that focus is also antithetical to normative scientific methodology. Not surprisingly, Davenport's methodological directive produced ample material for the political aspirations of the eugenics movement. The eugenicists were hardly oblivious to the implications of the efforts of Cold Spring Harbor. Davenport did not involve himself in the application of eugenics to the politics of immigration. Rather, Congress's leading expert on this matter was his assistant, Laughlin of the Eugenics Records Office. Laughlin (1922) stated his position on the matter with admirable simplicity: "Making all logical allowances for environmental conditions, which may be unfavorable to the immigrant, the recent immigrants, as a whole, present a higher percentage of inborn socially inadequate qualities than do the older stocks." Congress, committed to establishing Laughlin's credibility, did so by allowing bald assertions by Laughlin in his own behalf with the reaffirmations of Chairman Alfred Johnson of the House Committee on Immigration and Naturalization and others. Kevles (1985) notes that Laughlin (1924) actually frequently "twisted the facts (often he had found proportionately more native- than foreign-born in asylums) and indulged in blatant prejudice (recent immigrants, he said, might themselves be healthy, but they carried bad recessive genes, which would sooner or later out)."

Although there were objections to what Laughlin was doing, according to Ludmerer (1972), Laughlin, "rather than answering objections to his work, . . . ridiculed his critics and bragged of his 'scientific authority.'" Laughlin told Congress, "The only criticism which I must take most seriously is that of Prof. H. S. Jennings of Johns Hopkins." Jennings had appeared before the House Committee to impugn Laughlin's conclusions. The other critics, as far as he was concerned, were merely bitter losers.[10] According to Ludmerer (1972, 109), Rep. Johnson reassured Laughlin: "Don't worry about criticism, Doctor Laughlin. You have developed a valuable research and demonstrated a most startling state of affairs. We shall pursue these biological studies further." The admiration was hardly one-sided. In 1923 Johnson was elected honorary president of the Eugenics Research Association.[11] Laughlin called him "the great American watchdog whose job it is to protect the blood of the American people from contamination and degeneracy."

The case of Jennings is not without interest. He was, indeed, regarded as one of the leading geneticists, and it was clearly advantageous for someone like Laughlin to pretend to some parity with Jennings. Jennings's (1925) objections were clear but typically turgid and unpointed:

> Knowledge has moved rapidly and has, indeed, changed fundamentally within the last ten years, altering the picture as to the relations of heredity and environment. What has gotten into popular consciousness as Mendelism—still presented in the conventional biological gospels—has become grotesquely inadequate and misleading.

We can infer the ineffectiveness of Jennings's objections from a November 24, 1923, letter to Jennings by Raymond Pearl, who was both a prominent geneticist at Columbia and a one-time enthusiast for eugenics. Pearl wrote that the Laughlin group was "likely to do a great deal of real harm," but "[f]rom what I hear, I judge that the opinions of Congressmen generally regarding this group [are] that it is the only one which has any scientific knowledge about immigration." Jennings's ineffectiveness may not have been totally unintentional, at least at the unconscious level. He, and other scientists, were clearly pleased by the public attention that eugenics and politics brought to them. Jennings, in his 1930 book, *The Biological Basis of Human Nature*, states:

> Gone are the days when the biologist . . . used to be pictured in the public prints as an absurd creature, his pockets bulging with snakes and newts. . . . The world . . . is to be operated on scientific principles. The conduct of life and society are to be based, as they should be, on sound biological maxims! . . . Biology has become popular![12]

The issue of scientific credibility is a more extensive problem than the above sketch may suggest. Outside any given specialty, there are few—including scientists—who can distinguish one scientist from another, and this leaves a great deal of latitude for advocates and politicians to invent their own "experts." Moreover, public recognition as such an "expert" seems to mute public criticism by colleagues. There are useful sanity checks for the general public. The *Citation Index* comes to mind, though it is hardly perfect. Even when scientific problems are acknowledged, there is the common demand that policy not wait on the resolution of those problems since the issue is of such urgency. This was as true in the case of immigration law as it is during the present concern with "global warming." In effect, once political action is anticipated, the supporting scientific position is given a certain status whereby objections are reckoned to represent mere uncertainty, while scientific expertise is strongly discounted.

Consequences

In any event, Congress passed the Immigration Restriction Act of 1924, and it remained the law of the land until the 1960s. America's doors were largely closed to the victims of Hitler's racism. It would, of course, be naive to suppose that Congress passed the act solely or

even primarily because of the "scientific" rationale. But such a rationale gave a general respectability and aura of objective necessity to
the political decision. Indeed, the activities of America's eugenics
movement lent a certain approbation even to the Nazi eugenics
movement. The latter movement did, however, provoke far more
widespread denunciation of the abuses of genetic science within the
scientific community, although one might question whether there
would have been comparable objections if racism had not been
involved. Note also that the whole field of human genetics fell into
disrepute during the 1930s, and the Carnegie Institution closed the
Eugenics Research
Office in 1940, thereby
forcing Laughlin's early
retirement. Spurred by
the concern over the
effect of radiation on
genes, the field was
essentially reborn in a
far healthier form in
the late 1940s.

> **Outside any given specialty, there are few—including scientists—who can distinguish one scientist from another, and this leaves a great deal of latitude for advocates and politicians to invent their own "experts." The advantages of advocacy groups over individual scientists in communicating with the public will inevitably give advocacy groups an opportunity to dominate the presentation of the science.**

    As we have seen
in this brief sketch, the
interactions of science,
advocacy, and politics
in both the global
warming and eugenics
cases share a number of characterisics:

- powerful advocacy groups claiming to represent both science and
  the public in the name of morality and superior wisdom
- simplistic depictions of the underlying science to facilitate widespread "understanding"
- "events," real or contrived, interpreted in such a manner as to
  promote a sense of urgency in the public at large
- scientists flattered by public attention and deferent to "political
  will" and popular assessment of virtue
- significant numbers of scientists eager to produce the science
  demanded by the "public."

Given the automatic tendency of our educated elites to form advocacy groups, the above interactions would appear to have a certain inevitability, and the advantages of advocacy groups over individual scientists in communicating with the public will inevitably give advocacy groups an opportunity to dominate the presentation of the science. This represents a fairly discouraging prognosis for the interaction of science and politics. Nevertheless, even in the case of human genetics and eugenics, the situation eventually self-corrected, though it involved a hiatus in human genetics for about a decade. Politicization generally involves its own mechanism for self-correction. Politicization causes decisions to come increasingly to depend on partisanship rather than science, and with the inevitable alternation of parties, there comes eventual deemphasis of the underlying issue. We can see this at the moment with respect to global warming. Whether a better approach to the problem of the interaction of science and politics can be devised is not obvious, but it is certainly a question worth examining.

Before ending, I should perhaps mention two aspects of scientists' attitudes toward nominally science-based issues. Scientists characteristically suppose that when science is claimed as the basis for political action, the action will be subject to frequent review as the science evolves. It is, therefore, worth repeating that the political "product," the Immigration Restriction Act of 1924, remained unchanged for forty years—well beyond the demise of the underlying "science." The point is that political actions are rarely simply a "product" of science; once science has served its supportive function, its political role is essentially over.

Also, although ideally science is independent of moral fashions, in practice there is undoubtedly an influence. Under the circumstances, it is reasonable to consider whether moral fashions are robust. In the case of eugenics, it is evident that the progressive moral fashion of one era later came to be regarded as morally repugnant. Whether the same fate awaits today's environmental ethos is impossible to predict, if only because of the ambiguities of the environmental ethos. To the extent, however, that the current environmental ethos calls for restricting the economic prospects of the world's poorer countries, it is by no means inconceivable that it too will come to be regarded as repugnant by future generations.

NOTES

1. There has recently been a good deal of publicity over the claim that warming over the past century exceeds natural variability, and thus *some* of it may be due to anthropogenic carbon dioxide (Stevens 1995). That weak claim, unfortunately, is based on the assumption that variability in models is the same as variability in nature. That is not widely believed. Although the scientific statement of that proposition included a caveat, Stevens's article did not. Stevens used as the basis for his article a draft of the 1995 report of the Intergovernmental Panel on Climate Change, which is still in review. On the basis of that draft, Stevens claimed a "consensus" for the new view—a claim vigorously endorsed by Michael Oppenheimer of the Environmental Defense Fund. What was remarkable about that claim was that it was accompanied by an admission that hitherto almost all climate scientists "refused to declare publicly that they can discern the signature of the greenhouse effect." Oddly enough, the scientists quoted continued to refuse.

2. A general review of the physics of climate may be found in Lindzen (1993).

3. The February 1995 issue of *Physics Today* has an exchange of correspondence on this matter.

4. There is a natural attempt to suggest in various summaries and press releases that progress is rendering the global warming scenario more certain. Scrutiny of the detailed statements reveals no evidence of that, however. Rather, one finds such odd contradictions as the 1990 and 1992 reports claiming broad consistency between model predictions and observations, while the 1994 and 1995 reports attempt to use the very uncertain and largely undocumented behavior of sulfate aerosols to account for the previously ignored discrepancies between predictions and observations.

5. Advocacy groups by their nature are far better equipped than individual scientists to communicate with the public. This undoubtedly contributes to their ability to coopt the scientists.

6. It is important to distinguish science- or issue-based advocacy groups from industry advocacy groups. The latter are clearly recognized as serving the special interests of business. The former are commonly thought to represent "public" interests, although one might sometimes argue that the business they represent is themselves.

7. There is, of course, one potentially major difference. Science today is heavily dependent on government support. That was not the case in the early 1900s. Thus, in the earlier case, there is relatively little reason to believe that concern for government funding was a major factor. Today that factor would be harder to rule out. We might, however, consider government funding as just another form of public recognition—a factor present in both cases.

8. Advocates generally extract a payment for that recognition by assuming the right to represent the science in the manner they wish. Ludmerer (1972) presents an interesting early example. In 1910 the Eugenics Laboratory, under the direction of Karl Pearson, published a report on the children of alcoholic parents in which

the investigators were unable to state that the children of alcoholics were less healthy than those of nonalcoholics by the time of school age. That prompted a reply published in the London *Times* by Montague Crackenthorpe, the chairman of the Eugenics Society, who termed the conclusion "contrary to general experience" without presenting a single piece of evidence in support of his view.

9. The reference to Mary Harriman's being a progressive is neither irrelevant nor capricious. As Ludmerer, remarking on the close relation of the eugenics and progressive movements, notes:

> Madison Grant, John C. Merriam, and Henry F. Osborn, all well-known eugenicists, were leading conservationists and friends of Theodore Roosevelt. Edward A. Ross, a staunch supporter of compulsory sterilization and birth control, and the author of the widely read plea for immigration restriction, *The Old World in the New* (1914), was part of Robert La Follette's University of Wisconsin brain trust; his vigorous defenses of academic freedom, and his leadership in the American Association of University Professors, had also made him an eminent progressive.

That might seem to contradict a common perception (Allen 1975) that the eugenics movement was essentially conservative and racist as opposed to the environmental movement, which has come to be associated more with the left. I would suggest that both are movements of the educated elite, although the social and political character of this elite may have changed with time.

10. I have a certain personal interest in this story. When I finally went public with my objections to the global warming issue, I was initially accused of not having "expertise." When the implausibility of that claim became evident, there was a curious attempt by then-Senator Gore and others to get me to recant my objections. Some of the details of that affair appear in Lindzen (1992).

11. The tendency of advocacy groups to adopt euphemistically misleading names is already apparent.

12. Paul and Spencer (1995) have recently presented a far harsher view of the geneticists of the 1920s.

REFERENCES

Allen, G. "Genetics, Eugenics, and Class Struggle." *Genetics* 79 (1975): 29–45.

Beckwith, J. "A Historical View of Social Responsibility in Genetics." *BioScience* 43 (1993): 327–33.

Boehmer-Christiansen, S. A. "A Scientific Agenda for Climate Policy?" *Nature* 372 (1994): 400–402.

Davenport, Charles B. *The Study of Human Heredity.* Cold Spring Harbor, N.Y.: Cold Spring Harbor Laboratory, 1911.

Jennings, H. S. *Prometheus (or Biology and the Advancement of Man).* New York: E. P. Dutton & Co., 1925.

Kevles, Daniel J. *In the Name of Eugenics.* New York: Knopf, 1985.

Laughlin, Harry H. "Analysis of America's Modern Melting Pot." *Hearings before the House Committee on Immigration and Naturalization.* Washington, D.C.: Government Printing Office, 1922.

————. "Europe as an Emigrant-Exporting Continent." *Hearings before the House Committee on Immigration and Naturalization.* Washington, D.C.: Government Printing Office, 1924.

Lighthill, J., G. Holland, W. Gray, C. Landsea, G. Craig, J. Evans, Y. Kurihara, and C. Guard. "Global Climate Change and Tropical Cyclones." *Bulletin of the American Meteorological Society* 75 (1994): 2147–57.

Lindzen, Richard S. "Climate Dynamics and Global Change." *Annual Review of Fluid Mechanics* 26 (1993): 353–78.

————. "Global Warming: The Origin and Nature of the Alleged Scientific Consensus." *Regulation* 15 (Spring 1992): 87–98.

Ludmerer, K. M. *Genetics and American Society.* Baltimore: Johns Hopkins University Press, 1972.

Paul, D. B., and H. G. Spencer. "The Hidden Science of Eugenics." *Nature* 374 (1995): 302–4.

Pearl, Raymond. Letter to Herbert S. Jennings, November 24, 1923.

Provine, W. B. "Geneticists and the Biology of Race Crossing." *Science* 182 (1973): 790–96.

Ross, Edward A. *The Old World in the New.* New York: Century Co., 1914.

Stevens, William K. "Experts Confirm Human Role in Global Warming." *New York Times* (September 10, 1995), p. 1.

Stone, R. "If the Mercury Soars, So May Health Hazards." *Science* 267 (1995): 957–58.

Chapter 6

BENEFIT-COST ANALYSIS
Do the Benefits Exceed the Costs?

Lester B. Lave

OVERVIEW

Many economists see benefit-cost analysis as a rational, analytic tool
that is neutral in its values. They assert that benefit-cost analysis is
essential for complicated social issues. Our eloquence about the value
of this framework has enabled us to convince Congress to write benefit-
cost analysis into various laws and convinced President Reagan to
embrace it. President Clinton has reaffirmed the Reagan order with
minor changes.

Despite the objections of "unenlightened" environmentalists,
political scientists, ethicists, and others, we economists believe that
social decisions should be subject to benefit-cost analysis and that the
analysis identifies, at least approximately, the social optimum. During
the beginning of the Reagan administration, economists at the Office
of Management and Budget terrorized those who could not produce
analyses with positive net benefits (Clark, Kosters, and Miller 1980).

But from the outset environmental, labor, and other "public interest" groups objected to cost-benefit tests of regulations. Their viewpoint was partly emotional, but they had some valid points, including
the contention that while costs can be measured fairly accurately, benefits are often difficult to quantify, particularly in dollar terms.

The problems go far beyond a focus on costs. Benefit-cost advocates rely, often unwittingly, on a Pandora's box of utilitarian ethical
beliefs as well as assumptions about the quality of current methods. If
they examined those assumptions carefully, economists would reject

many of them. We are perpetrating a fraud on ourselves and decision makers with our unqualified claims about what conclusions can be drawn from our analyses.

Benefit-cost analysis can be an extraordinarily valuable tool for policy analysis. Before it can fulfill its potential, however, economists must strip the tool of the remnants of utilitarian doctrines that we do not believe, recognize the inherent biases, and learn to interpret the outcomes of the analysis. What remains is a much less powerful tool, but one worthy of our confidence.

I begin this chapter with the case for using benefit-cost analysis to help illuminate public policy regarding environmental issues. I then critique formal benefit-cost analysis. The problems are of two sorts—fundamental issues of theory and the many pitfalls in implementation.

The foundation of benefit-cost analysis is flawed; the tool cannot provide what some economists claim. The practical difficulties are even greater. Even if the technique might be valid when implemented by a master with unlimited time and resources for analysis, it is a problematic tool in practice when resources are extremely limited, time is short, and people with little training or experience do the analysis. Finally, I examine how benefit-cost analysis is used in the political arena.

The Case for Benefit-Cost Analysis

Texts (Mishan 1982; Sassone and Schaffer 1978; Stokey and Zeckhauser 1978) praise benefit-cost analysis for a number of reasons. Some textbook authors think of benefit-cost analysis as an "accounting framework" for exploring social decisions. Theorists tend to see it as an optimizing tool that maximizes social welfare. I order the following thirteen descriptions from those needed for an accounting framework to those needed for the tool to optimize social welfare. Benefit-cost analysis encourages a systematic statement of the goals to be accomplished (attribute 1) and encourages analysts to identify and evaluate a wide range of options for accomplishing the stated goals (attribute 2). In addition, it is a systematic, analytic approach that attempts to explore the implications of each option (attribute 3). Benefit-cost analysis requires the analyst to confront the trade-offs among options, both at the detailed level for each individual dimension and at the aggregate level in terms of total expenditures (attribute 4). Moreover, the approach encourages a search for externalities and an evaluation of those that have been identified (attribute 5). Benefit-cost analysis focuses on the allocation of benefits and costs over time and translates them to a single time period (attribute 6). The approach seeks to accomplish the stated goals at least cost (attribute 7). The tool can be used to identify the data and analyses of importance (attribute 8) and to specify a research and development agenda to provide important data not currently available (attribute 9). Benefit-cost analysis seeks to isolate and quantify social interest, not self-interest (attribute 10). The approach recognizes that there are desirable and undesirable aspects of each situation and characterizes them as "benefits" and "costs" (attribute 11). Benefit-cost analysis encourages objective, value-free analysis (attribute 12). Finally, benefit-cost analysis identifies the option with the greatest net benefit, which is described as the one that is best for society (attribute 13).

The first six descriptions characterize an accounting framework that can be extremely helpful in examining social decisions. Attribute 7 sharpens the economic focus by introducing a goal that might not be stated in attribute 1: cost-effectiveness. Attribute 10 adds a further goal, the social interest. With a social goal defined, "benefits" and "costs" can be defined. Attribute 12 is a myth widely believed among benefit-cost analysts; unfortunately, the analysis cannot be value-free, as I shall show below. Attribute 13 is true, as Railton (1990) points out, only under stringent assumptions.

Reagan's Executive Order 12291 assumed that all thirteen attributes are correct. In requiring benefit-cost analysis for every major regulatory decision, the order assumed that the first six attributes are true (and the analysis is not costly). In requiring that the option with the greatest net benefit be chosen (unless precluded by law), the order assumed the validity of all thirteen attributes.

Reagan's advisers praised both the accounting framework and the optimizing roles of benefit-cost analysis. Miller (1989), for example, asserts that the best way to get some discipline and analysis into regulatory agencies that were "out of control" is benefit-cost analysis. Just having to go through the steps of a benefit-cost analysis should prove enlightening for agencies that do not normally use the tool. Miller (1989, 91) also defends the optimizing role:

[Executive Order 12291] . . . is no more than common sense.
. . . Of course, the way an agency has estimated the benefits
and costs can be disputed in particular cases. . . . Without
some check, like that provided by President Reagan's executive order, regulatory decision makers might be tempted to
pander to such moralism [that disdains rational analysis]—or
to other special interests.

Miller sees benefit-cost analysis as the bulwark against moralism and
special interests.

As an accounting framework, benefit-cost analysis satisfies the
government's need for a systematic approach to policy issues. While
an individual might be satisfied with an emotional or ad hoc response,
a governmental agency cannot rely on such reactions. The
Administrative Procedure Act of 1946, which defines the procedures
that must be followed by all regulatory agencies, requires that agencies
hold public hearings and listen and respond to public suggestions and
complaints concerning their proposed regulations. Congress is inun-
dated with emotional or ad hoc responses. Benefit-cost analysis is
designed to stand apart from them because of the framework and systematic analysis. If benefit-cost analysis is not done with care, it does
not deserve greater confidence than ad hoc reactions.

As shown below, except under assumptions that seem indefensi-
ble, benefit-cost analysis does not have a claim to being a tool that
maximizes social welfare. But even being relegated to an accounting
framework can result in misuse. First, some economists assume that
the analysis either is value-free or that they have accounted for differences in values, a claim I shall show to be false. Second, few economists interpret the outcome of the analysis with proper humility.
Instead, they focus on the alternatives with positive net benefits and
tend to dismiss alternatives with negative net benefits. In practice,
economists act as if an estimate that the net benefits are large or even
positive is somehow value-free and reliable, despite their acknowledg-
ment of objections to the methods and estimates.

Laurence Tribe dismisses benefit-cost analysis in hostile terms. He
asserts that analysts have an ideological bias, even though they claim to
be operating in the public interest: "[I]ideology has often sought to masquerade as analysis, deriving a power it could never justly claim from
the garb of neutrality it has at times contrived to wear" (Tribe 1973, 3).

Fundamental Problems with Benefit-Cost Analysis

We begin the discussion of benefit-cost analysis with a theoretical debate in economics that goes back many years. The debate grapples with the question of whether benefit-cost analysis actually maximizes social welfare; the question is not nearly so simple as it may seem on the surface. While, as we shall later see, the huge difficulties in actually *implementing* benefit-cost analysis are even more important than the theoretical problems, the theoretical issue remains significant. Even in theory, benefit-cost analysis has major problems.

Must Compensation Actually Be Paid?

The claim that benefit-cost analysis maximizes social welfare is vitiated by a fundamental problem. In few social decisions is one alternative Pareto superior to others (no one is worse off and at least one person is better off). But, if some people lose, the option with the greatest net benefit may not be socially preferred. Some of the best economic minds have attempted to overcome the difficulty. Kaldor (1939) and Hicks (1939) proposed criteria in 1939: Proposal A is superior to B if the winners could bribe the losers and still be better off and if the losers could not bribe the winners and still be better off. If the compensation is not actually paid, however, the Kaldor-Hicks criteria can lead to outcomes that all reasonable people would reject. Consider a project that would have the king of Saudi Arabia gain $50 billion, but would cost every American whose income is below the subsistence level $100. This project passes the Kaldor-Hicks test, since the king could afford to bribe the poor Americans and still be better off. Assuming it is impractical to compensate the losers, however, few economists would think that the project increases social welfare.

The Kaldor-Hicks criteria implicitly assume that a dollar of benefit is fungible and that a dollar of cost is pretty much independent of who bears it. Those assumptions seem ludicrous to anyone who has studied the operation of political systems, as well as implausible for people with very different income levels.

The Leonard-Zeckhauser defense. Leonard and Zeckhauser (1986) defend the Kaldor-Hicks criteria on different but still mistaken grounds. They concede that "[i]t would of course be preferable to carry out the compensation" (Leonard and Zeckhauser 1986, 33). Since it is not practical to pay compensation, they argue that the Kaldor-Hicks criteria are preferable to "pure politics." But they neglect other options, such as taking no government action.

They propose a Rawlesian contractarian argument concerning the class of all mechanisms that might be used to decide public policy:

> What mechanisms for making decisions would individuals choose if they had to contract before they knew their identities in society or the kinds of problems they would confront? Our answer is that, on an expected-value basis, cost-benefit analysis would serve them best and hence would be chosen. (Leonard and Zeckhauser 1986, 33)

Unfortunately, that argument rests on three assumptions. First, benefit-cost analysis is the (only) efficient decision framework. Second, benefit-cost analysis can be applied to essentially any social decision. Third, the values of the analyst are not important in determining the outcome of the analysis.

Is benefit-cost analysis the most efficient decision framework? Interesting social issues are fraught with ignorance and uncertainty. Rarely can the uncertainty be handled by adding a random error (with mean zero) to the correct answer. Often, important issues are ignored (because they cannot be quantified) or missed, for example, current attempts to do a benefit-cost analysis of controlling emissions of greenhouse gases to arrest global climate change. The uncertainties here are so fundamental that the implications of global warming are largely unknown (National Research Council 1991; Lave 1991). Quantitative and qualitative uncertainties are so pervasive in "interesting" (nontrivial) social issues that the assertion of efficiency is hollow.

Should all issues be decided by benefit-cost analysis? The range of issues to which benefit-cost analysis is applied is a second difficulty. Consider whether to confiscate Zeckhauser's property (to pay tribute to Saddam Hussein) and transform Leonard from professor into a kamikaze pilot (for an attack on Tibetan demonstrators). While they might believe that estimated costs will exceed estimated benefits, Leonard and Zeckhauser are unlikely to agree to submit those proposals to benefit-cost analysis by analysts named by Saddam Hussein or Deng Xiaoping.

Some people object to benefit-cost analysis of mandatory seat belt use, while others object to using benefit-cost analysis to set health and safety standards. If one sees an issue primarily in efficiency terms, benefit-cost analysis might be the best decision framework. If instead the issue is seen in ethical or similar terms, benefit-cost analysis is anathema.

The role of the analyst's values. Subjecting Zeckhauser's property and Leonard's life to benefit-cost analysis may seem absurd. But those proposals are analogous to the way that pacifists see analyses of defense expenditures, environmentalists see analyses of new dams and canals, and urban planners see analyses of new highways. Those with views and values different from the analyst see benefit-cost analysis as an absurd, illogical, inconsistent ritual (Wildavsky 1966), for example, quantifying the dollar value of preventing the extinction of the snail darter. While welfare mothers might find benefit-cost analysis better than autocratic rule, they certainly would not welcome it. The dissident minority would prefer having a constitution that limits the scope of government activities (obviating the need for a benefit-cost analysis). They want to place many questions outside the scope of benefit-cost analysis and the majority values that would victimize them systematically.

> **If one sees an issue primarily in efficiency terms, benefit-cost analysis might be the best decision framework. If instead the issue is seen in ethical or similar terms, benefit-cost analysis is anathema.**

In particular, since benefit-cost analysts need economic training, and since graduate students in economics either self-select based on a belief in the market mechanisms or find it difficult to pass the courses if they do not share that view, there is an inherent bias that we can expect to emerge from benefit-cost analyses. Proponents of regulatory programs are correct in asserting that benefit-cost analysts are biased against their views. That point has a more subtle implication. Suppose that the values of the benefit-cost analyst were quite different from mine. If so, the recommendations are likely to make no sense to me. My benefit-cost analysis would lead to a preferred outcome—the one with the greatest net benefit—quite different from the one the official analyst derived. If benefit-cost analysts have a wide range of values, I might be better off by choosing an alternative framework for analysis or by choosing to have no collective action.[1] In short, the contractarian argument suggested by Leonard and Zeckhauser is an interesting idea, but their assertion is mistaken.

The Trumbull defense. Trumbull (1990) defends benefit-cost analysis and the use of the Kaldor-Hicks criteria on the grounds that they utilize the affected individuals' own valuation of the gains and losses. All economists would agree that individuals' valuation is a legitimate, even important, input to the decision. Does a benefit-cost analysis reflect individuals' preferences if compensation is not paid? People have preferences about the distribution of income, particularly when some individuals are paying and not benefiting. In arguing that the Kaldor-Hicks criteria are a sufficient basis for judging a policy to be superior, Trumbull, Leonard and Zeckhauser, and others are implicitly asserting that the social preferences with respect to income redistribution can be ignored. That is true for projects where the redistribution is small and from rich to poor; it is not likely to be true where there is large redistribution from poor to rich.

Not compensating losers poses subtle difficulties. The magnitude, and even the sign, of benefits and costs depend on the level and distribution of income. If income is concentrated in the hands of those who value boating and swimming, a willingness-to-pay measure will favor damming a river. If income is concentrated in the hands of those who value wildlife and undisturbed nature, a benefit-cost analysis is likely to find negative net benefits for the dam. A project that has a large effect on the income distribution could give rise to contradictory outcomes depending on whether the ex ante or ex post distribution is used.

Zerbe (1991) proposes modified Kaldor-Hicks criteria: Calculate the least expensive way to pay compensation. If benefits still exceed costs, the project has a net social benefit, even if compensation is not paid. Short of actually paying compensation, however, none of those proposals works. Assume, for example, that the cost of compensating individuals for the lost $100 is $120. If so, the king of Saudi Arabia could compensate every individual who lost and still be better off. Nonetheless, unless the compensation is actually paid, Zerbe's criterion only tells us that benefits exceed costs by more than a small amount. That information would not change my judgment that the proposal is objectionable—unless compensation is actually paid.

Although economists have labored long and hard to find a way around having to pay compensation and make everyone better off, we have failed. Many economists have known this for some time, although the profession continues to perform benefit-cost analysis and to place great confidence in the alternative(s) with the greatest net benefit. In doing so, they are implicitly embracing utilitarianism and myths about the neutrality of economic analysis.

What Is Wrong with Being a Utilitarian?

"May we be governed by utilitarians!" Think of living in a society governed by a benevolent despot who works hard to "provide the greatest good for the greatest number." If you hold a Ph.D. in economics from an American university, your heart probably warms to that prospect.

Achieving the "greatest good for the greatest number" defines a relative, in contrast to an absolute, morality. In a relative morality, no constitution or Bible guarantees free speech or praises honesty and self-sacrifice while condemning theft and murder (Kelman 1981, 1982). Zerbe (1991) gives the example of a crowd wishing harm to someone because of his race. The utility of the crowd for seeing the man beaten might be greater than the disutility to the victim. Few people would want to live in a society where one might be beaten or killed because the sum of utilities "for" was greater than the sum of utilities "against."

One way of dealing with that objection is to ask whether the utility of society would be higher if that behavior were forbidden in general, rather than subject to evaluation in each case. Thus, a utilitarian society could arrive at rights, although they would still be relative, not absolute. Those rights would be subject to a continuing benefit-cost analysis; whenever the estimated net benefit of a right became negative, it would no longer be social policy. Unfortunately, those in power frequently find reasons to want to suspend civil liberties, confiscate property, and jail or execute people without due process. To persuade us to give up our constitutional guarantees, a utilitarian leader might promise that those values would ordinarily hold and that he would suspend them only in "unusual" situations. Events such as the internment of Japanese-Americans during World War II, the more recent internment of Iraqis in Great Britain during the Persian Gulf War, and Watergate do not foster trust in the judgment of even democratically elected leaders in the United States and England. Leaders attempt to accomplish their goals. Inevitably, they will regard constraints on the means they may use as unfortunate. They are repeatedly tempted to intrude on the values "slightly" in "compelling" cases. If freedom of speech were subject to a benefit-cost analysis in each case, one would see much less freedom than when it is guaranteed constitutionally.[2]

Other Problems with Benefit-Cost Analysis

Is Everything for Sale?

Kelman (1981) cites other reasons for distrusting utilitarianism.[3] Valuing nonmarket items is difficult and arbitrary and may be repugnant. What price would one put on his daughter's teddy bear? Putting a dollar price on things defines them as being "in commerce" and changes the way we think about them. Saying that one's wedding ring is not for sale means that it is not analogous to a laxative suppository. In theory, there are circumstances under which I would have sold the sexual services of my adolescent daughter and son, but I do not regard thinking through those circumstances as uplifting, calming, or enlightening. Few if any of us will ever face those circumstances; I see no value in torturing myself to sketch the offer curve.[4]

Situation-Specific Values

Another fundamental difficulty is that values and judgments are often situation-specific; they change radically from one setting to another. For example, my willingness to pay to reduce the chance of immediate death by one in 100,000 is different depending on whether the risk comes from a hazardous waste site that I opposed or a ski trip that I welcomed. What is the dollar value associated with not having to shoot someone? Is that value different for shooting a burglar in your home at night from what it is for shooting your child? Our actions have subtle implications that make valuing an item or action dependent on the precise setting. Thus, the dollar values that Viscusi (1983) estimates for lowering the chance of premature death in an occupational setting may have little relationship to the dollar value that people would put on lowering the chance of cancer from tolerating carcinogens in their drinking water. The estimated values did not predict how much the price of a toilet bowl cleaner would have to be reduced to lead consumers to purchase a slightly more dangerous version (Viscusi and Magat 1987).

Fischhoff (1991) points out how sensitive expressions of value are to the precise question, and even the context, including the preceding questions. A respondent's answers often are internally inconsistent. Subjects sometimes give the same value to preventing one lake from being polluted as preventing five, a hundred, or a thousand lakes from being polluted. Clearly, the respondent's answers are not appropriate for detailed analysis.

Valuing Nonmarket Goods and Services

Economists have attempted to quantify and value effects such as unpleasant odors, eye irritation, a greater chance of getting cancer, improved visibility, improved recreation, and the value of preserving a natural setting, including one that will not be visited (Cummings et al. 1986). Clever people have found ingenious ways to value those effects. But we economists rarely ask the question, Can decision makers have confidence in those estimates? Economists have even started challenging the assumption that people have fixed utility functions (Akerlof 1991). The fundamental question is not whether the estimates are clever or the best available, but whether they are reliable. Do we have unbiased estimates with a relatively small error term? I would not want to bet the family jewels on the numbers estimated.[5]

Is Efficiency the Only Important Criterion?

The fundamental basis for benefit-cost analysis is its theoretical efficiency. As shown above, that efficiency is doubtful for social issues. Even if the efficiency were real, benefit-cost analysis neglects other social criteria for evaluation: equity, administrative simplicity, transparency, and improved environmental quality (Lave 1981a). I know of no presumption that maximizing efficiency simultaneously will maximize the other evaluation criteria. Indeed, why would one expect a positive correlation between efficiency and the other evaluation criteria?

Benefit-Cost Analysis for Personal Decisions?

Fischhoff (1977) notes that few people desire to maximize net benefits in their personal decisions. They do not attempt to translate the multiple dimensions into a scalar and certainly do not try to translate everything into dollars. Do people use a formal benefit-cost analysis to decide what career to pursue or which person to ask to be a spouse? Even conceptually, benefit-cost analysis is not likely to be of much help in nonmarginal decisions, such as whether to have children. Before experiencing them, it is hard for someone to know the distribution of pleasure and irritation to be derived from caring for them—it is impossible to gain information without taking a distinctly nonmarginal step.

I can briefly list other difficulties. While the analysis should account for multiple dimensions and interactions among them, that rarely occurs (Lave 1981b, 1984).[6] For many projects we cannot enumerate all the consequences of a decision, which implies that all important consequences may not have been considered.[7] If so, the analysis should be viewed as an exercise in "bounded rationality" (Simon 1955) rather than efficiency or optimizing. Estimating parameters is difficult because available data may represent a different circumstance.[8] People differ in the ways they handle risky situations, and no single method will satisfy all people. For example, Lave and Romer (1984) point out that a safety standard is a public good. Since people have different safety goals, instituting a single standard will make almost everyone unhappy in the sense that the goal will not be as safe as, or will be more expensive than, they desire.

Implementation Difficulties

Whatever the theoretical difficulties, they are dominated by the difficulties of implementing benefit-cost analyses. So many compromises are needed in practice that benefit-cost analysis has been criticized as biased and as serving the incumbent politicians. But, as Leonard and Zeckhauser (1986, 31) point out:

Any technique employed in the political process may be distorted to suit parochial ends and particular interest groups. Cost-benefit analysis can be an advocacy weapon, and it can be used by knaves. But it does not create knaves, and to some extent it may even police their behavior. The critical question is whether it is more or less subject to manipulation than alternative decision processes. Our claim is that its ultimate grounding in analytic disciplines affords some protection.

Selecting a Valuation Concept

Often there are several bases for valuation. Choosing among them can be difficult. If, for example, 100,000 salmon return each year to spawn in a river, and if construction of a dam would prevent spawning, how should the loss of those salmon be estimated? One way is to measure the price of salmon in local fish markets and subtract the cost of catching, transporting, and retailing them. The result is the value of a salmon in the river for consumption. That "producer surplus" probably amounts to less than $1 per pound. That line of reasoning results in such a low value for environmental benefits that society's welfare is likely to be increased by damming the river or making it into a sewer. The price of a salmon carcass on ice has nothing to do with the value of preserving the wilderness habitat. Suspending plastic salmon in a sewer or displaying real salmon in aquariums (where they can be seen more easily and reliably) does not address the environmental values. Some joke that possible extinction of the snail darter was used to try to stop building the Tellico dam, even though the fish is no good to eat (White 1981). Should we value California condors in terms of how good they taste? Would bald eagles be more highly valued if they performed for tourists?[9]

Some fishermen appear to value catching salmon out of all proportion to the value of the salmon on ice at your favorite fishmonger. We see individuals pay more than $1,000 per fish for the sport of catching them. Other individuals—for example, people going to see migrating whales or whooping cranes or going on picture-taking safaris—are willing to pay large amounts of money to see wild animals, without even catching them or shooting them. Indeed, some people are willing to pay to prevent anyone from disturbing wild animals, for example, leaving salmon uncaught and even unseen. I would not be willing to sell the flowers in my front yard for the price of cut flowers in the florist shop. If they were equivalent, it would be less expensive for me to buy flowers than to grow them. Does anyone think the sensible way to value a whooping crane or a spotted owl is in terms of the market price (per pound) of a turkey? Would you feel fairly compensated if someone killed your pet dog and offered as compensation the retail value of that amount of dog meat—less the cost of butchering, transport, and retailing? As a trip to a shopping mall will reveal, many salmon are valued at what the carcass will fetch; many flowers are valued at what they sell for in the florist shop. When should an uncaught salmon be valued at $1 per pound and when at $1,000 per pound? Economists have attempted to estimate existence values and option values and to explore what would be the effect of imbuing the environment with rights, for example, giving trees rights (Baumol and Oates 1988).

Some items have a value in commerce that is quite different from their personal value. If there is no easy way to make marginal substitutions, the value difference can persist. In addition, some people refuse to regard some items as being in commerce, even though they can be purchased, for example, sexual intercourse or old growth forests. If society cannot agree on the valuation of the benefits and costs, social optimization is not possible or at least is not simple. Social decisions are made, but few have even a remote claim to being optimal. Often, wisdom calls for stating the benefits and costs in multidimensional terms, not in dollars.

Neglecting the Primary Objective

The federal government has announced plans to set aside a forest area equal to the combined size of Massachusetts and Vermont to prevent the extinction of the spotted owl. This means that the agency is implicitly valuing a pair of spotted owls at more than $1 million per year. It cannot be that U.S. society values those owls at so great a dollar amount. Furthermore, for a decade the issue of how much forest to set aside has been contentious, calling forth intense opposition from loggers and logging communities. That is not a case where the parties are unaware of what some faceless regulators are doing.

No reasonable benefit analysis could come up with $1 million per year to preserve a nesting pair of spotted owls, or perhaps $1 billion per year to preserve all of those owls in their forest homes. Rather than rush to the media to label that proposal as absurd, economists would do better to assume, for purposes of the discussion, that the decision is a sound one. What social values could justify such a decision? It appears that people want to preserve old growth forest and the species that live there. The spotted owl is no more than an indicator species or "label" for what is desired. Economists incur ridicule by assuming naively that the indicator species is the only issue. Whether the United States should incur a cost of more than $1 billion per year requires examining a large bundle of benefits, including romantic notions about preserving the primeval forest.

In practice, benefit-cost analysis is an unimaginative, bookkeeper's activity. The tool seems to encourage a narrow analysis. All too often, economists miss the primary benefits (or costs) in doing the analysis.

Who Has Standing?

Whose benefits and costs are to be counted? What weights are to be given to each individual? Trumbull (1990) asserts that the benefits of those who violate the law ought not to be counted (the criminal's utility from his act) and that all who are affected by a policy, including future generations, be counted. Zerbe (1991) notes that "standing" is defined by political and legal rights, such as the right to sue. For example, the U.S. Supreme Court decided that the psychological costs of residents around Three Mile Island need not be counted in establishing policy, presumably because the experts agreed that there was no basis for the fear. Thus, a benefit-cost analysis would ignore those costs, even though they were quite real to the individuals. Zerbe (1991) conjectures that the cases where standing is most controversial will be the cases where political and legal decisions masquerade as benefit-cost analyses.

Should a nation be altruistic enough to give full weight to the benefits and costs that occur to those living outside its borders, for example, fishing with monofiliment nets or greenhouse effects? While we might hope that all nations would behave in that way, it seems unlikely that they would do so without some metaauthority to arbitrate conflicts.

Attempting to account for the preferences of future generations runs into the practical difficulty of not knowing what they will want.

Anyone who has bought gifts for other people and has been the recipient of gifts knows how difficult it is to get even a vague idea of the preferences of others. That is all the more true of a generation socialized by different ideas and facing different opportunities and constraints. Imagine an Eskimo's saving a choice piece of blubber for someone or her great grandfather's deliberately not building a privy on the best site so that the site would be available for her use.

The Correct Discount Rates

The difficulties of reducing the disparate benefits and costs to a scalar have their parallel in reducing the time stream of benefits and costs to a single date. A large body of literature has been devoted to determining the proper discount rate for market goods and services that accrue over time (Baumol 1968; Sandmo 1973; Sandmo and Drèze 1973; Jenkins 1973; Parfit 1983). Of particular difficulty is the choice of a rate that will properly account for transfers across generations (Berry 1983; Kneese et al. 1983; Page 1983). Despite general agreement on the proper concept (at least for a time period of less than a generation), there is little agreement on the number that ought to be used in a particular analysis. Discounting nonmarket goods and services may require an entirely different discount rate from that used for market goods and services. What discount rate should be used for future risks of disease, death, and the destruction of environmental amenities? For example, what is the value of a program that prevents the extinction of a species for an additional fifty years?

Valuation in the Presence of Risks

In the 1960s there was growing recognition that benefit-cost analyses of waterway projects had been simplistic (Campen 1986). It was already recognized that social benefits were multidimensional. For example, building a dam could provide not only flood control but also electricity generation, a year-round water supply, and a lake for recreation. Enlarging the dam was also seen to have multidimensional costs. Since land was flooded for the reservoir, some fish and plants would cease to exist here. Other effects were more difficult to classify. Land in the floodplain was now protected from frequent flooding but still subject to large floods. How should we value land where the threat of flooding from frequent small storms has been removed, but there is an increase in the amount of damage that would be done in very rare large storms (National Research Council 1985; Epple and Lave 1988)?

Problems with Benefit-Cost Analysis in Practice

Those conceptual difficulties are the grist for academic theorists. Reality is more bleak. What should EPA Administrator Carol Browner infer from a benefit-cost analysis of a new automobile emissions standard? Suppose she was informed that the analysis was done by a GS-9 with a B.A.—or even an M.B.A.—in six weeks with no supplementary budget? The analyses produced by government agencies often contain major flaws in theory, quantification, and analysis. We economists lose our credibility and risk ridicule by requiring analyses we know will have major flaws and by insisting that the option with the greatest *measured* net benefit is the optimal choice.

Myriad other problems occur in practice. We assume that market prices reflect a purely competitive market, even in concentrated industries. We assume that tastes do not change over time. We assume that many "small" externalities do not need to be included in the analysis because they are unimportant.

A benefit-cost analysis will reveal legions of uncertainties and gaps in knowledge. If they are displayed to the reader, they might create a bias toward concluding that the analysis is unworthy of confidence and would certainly lead to a long, unreadable report. If they are not highlighted, the public might have more confidence in the analysis than is warranted. In practice, what decision makers learn from benefit-cost analysis comes from the executive summary. But no one- or two-page summary can indicate the range of uncertainties and other qualifications that a decision maker must know to use the analysis intelligently. For example, global climate change issues are so awash in uncertainty that definitive actions are not possible (National Research Council 1991). Because the analysis seems to be scientific, it is often presented as if disagreeing with the results is akin to asserting that two plus two do not equal four. I conclude that in neither theory nor practice does benefit-cost analysis have a legitimate claim to be the optimizing framework that many economists believe it is; our current attempts at benefit-cost analysis are probably biased (Lave 1971).

Although we have no conceptual difficulty with how to incorporate nonmarket effects, we do not have accurate ways to incorporate them into current analyses. In short, I conclude that the estimated net benefit of current social issues may be biased and misleading; the deficiencies stem from both theory and practice. Even if we hired the best and brightest economists and gave them essentially unlimited resources, they could not carry out a benefit-cost analysis of complicated issues that would give a confident estimate of the net social benefit.

Consider, for example, an analysis of whether to build a nuclear power plant on Long Island, New York, or whether to open northern Alaska to the production of petroleum. Benefit-cost analysis requires hundreds of value judgments, most of them small and hidden. Which environmental effects are nontrivial will depend on whether the analyst believes that rocks have the same rights as people or whether she believes that nature is nasty and cruel. Does she favor draining swamps or extolling wetlands? Even if both analysts were doing their best to be objective and neutral, their analyses would look very different. Our quest for technocratic neutrality leads to the conclusion that if benefit-cost analyses differ, one must be wrong. In fact, there is a range of uncertainty concerning the extent of physical effects and a range of uncertainty concerning valuation. Benefit-cost analyses could be quite different, and yet each could be equally valid in the sense that disparities are due to value differences in structuring and monetizing, although each structure could be equally valid from a technocratic viewpoint. That recognition leads to a shocking assertion. The same economist might do quite different benefit-cost analyses of the same issue, depending on who the client is. A principled analyst could produce analyses with quite different preferred options (the one with the largest net benefits).

A decision maker cannot interpret a benefit-cost analysis properly without knowing the values of the analyst and sponsoring organization. Although a different analysis could be an indication of technical inadequacy or misconduct, it could also result from value differences. A reviewer has the difficult task of determining whether an analysis is technically accurate and spelling out the values used.

Alternative Frameworks and Criteria

Benefit-cost analysis is one of several decision frameworks that Congress has written into legislation: (1) no-risk, (2) risk-risk,

(3) technology-based standards, (4) risk-benefit analysis, and (5) cost-effectiveness analysis (Lave 1981a). In terms of the breadth of considerations, trade-offs considered, and thus efficiency optimization, the frameworks in rough order lead to benefit-cost analysis. Similarly, they are listed in rough order in terms of the amount of data and analysis required. For example, cost-effectiveness analysis does not require data and theory that would make benefits and cost comparable, but it does not result in optimization unless the goal just happens to be the one with maximum net benefits.

> **Technology-based standards rest on a naive assumption that the technology drives the solution and that other considerations, including health and consumption, either are not important or are handled in an obvious fashion.**

Just as benefit-cost analysis (maximizing net benefits) assumes utilitarian ethics, each of the other decision frameworks implicitly assumes an ethical background. For example, the "no-risk" framework assumes that protecting human health is the only goal; no trade-offs are relevant concerning such other attributes as health versus private or public consumption. The framework is simplistic in not recognizing more complicated implications, such as the risk-risk trade-offs of the second framework. The risk-risk framework continues to focus only on health. Technology-based standards rest on a naive assumption that the technology drives the solution and that other considerations, including health and consumption, either are not important or are handled in an obvious fashion. Risk-benefit analysis examines the health risks and general benefits of a technology. It assumes that other types of risk are not relevant. Finally, cost-effectiveness is based on the premise that efficiency is the most important attribute, that choosing the desired goal is simple or not possible analytically. Although Congress could be forthright in declaring its goals, more often it expresses its values more subtly by choosing one of those decision frameworks. Economists value efficiency and tend to downplay the importance of value judgments—we joke that one does not want to know the details of how sausage, legislation, or regulations are made.

Does Benefit-Cost Analysis Change Political Decisions?

Like our utilitarian predecessors, economists seek to optimize social decisions. In distinction from special interest groups, we economists see ourselves as providing neutral advice that is essential to making social decisions that serve the public interest (Miller and Yandle 1979; Clark et al. 1980; White 1981). At the opposite extreme, political economists see government decisions as resulting from interest groups that are able to put together winning coalitions. Decisions are not "good" or "bad." Rather they are successful (adopted) or unsuccessful (not adopted). In this view benefit-cost analysis is simply an attempt by one special interest group (economists, who think of themselves as virtuous and helpful) to influence the agenda and voting.

Indeed, in practice, benefit-cost analysis is a means by which an interest group can secure the support of uncommitted voters or legislators. If one side thinks that a benefit-cost analysis will be favorable—that is, their proposal can be shown to be efficient—they should commission an analysis. The other side might counter by focusing on the advantages of their proposal, such as helping a deserving group or improving the environment; they might also attack the benefit-cost analysis as mean-spirited or inconclusive and show the tenuous nature of some parameter estimates or the arbitrariness of some valuations. For example, in the 1980s business groups attacked environmental proposals by commissioning benefit-cost analyses that showed the high costs of the improvement; environmental groups defended the proposals by saying that no price could be put on environmental improvements; they also showed flaws in the benefit-cost analysis (Gruenspecht and Lave 1991). Such a view leads to the question, Which group will play the benefit-cost card, and under what circumstances?

In the usual political interpretation, a small interest group with a great deal to gain (representing a small proportion of the voters) battles a small interest group that has a great deal to lose; most congressmen have no direct interest in the matter. The proponents try to put together a winning coalition while the opponents try to block it. In their efforts to gain supporters, each side will claim that it is acting in the public interest and will want data and analyses to support its claim. One way of convincing people is a benefit-cost analysis. The analysis could convince those with no direct interest that the proposal is in the public interest; more likely, it could convince others that they have a fair amount to gain or lose if the legislation is passed. For example, a benefit-cost analysis of the 1977 Clean Air Act Amendments showed western coal producers that they had much to gain if regulation were simply on the basis of emissions, while the eastern coal producers had much to lose. The benefit-cost analysis clarified who would win and lose and by how much and showed that there would be a large net efficiency loss (Ackerman and Hassler 1980).

The Presidency versus Congress

Our system of government checks and balances means that no individual or institution has the power to make policy. Melnick (1990, 26) asserts:

> Dispersion of power has three important consequences for environmental policy making. First and foremost is the dispersion of responsibility. In the United States, it is easy to shift the blame for nearly everything to someone else. Second, because no one controls the entire policy making process, each participant tries to squeeze as much as possible out of the limited portion he or she controls. Third, given the complexity of the entire process, it is difficult to see the connection between the decisions of each participant and eventual outcomes.

In an attempt to impose some discipline on the system, Gerald Ford and his successors have issued executive orders to executive branch agencies. The orders require agencies to investigate a wider range of considerations than Congress wrote into legislation, or at least a wider range of considerations than the relevant oversight committee wants to stress. The executive orders also rule out considerations that Congress thought were paramount, namely equity.

American presidents have been "political," just like Congress. In general, presidents have not been more courageous than Congress in revealing their values in major controversies concerning food additives, occupational safety and health, waterway projects, or toxic substances in the environment. Nonetheless, the institution of the presidency is different from the institution of Congress. Compared with the president, Congress gives more weight to seniority—getting along by going along and forming coalitions for public works—and is better able to hide behind rules committees and not scheduling issues for debate and votes.

Benefit-cost analysis has drawn fire because it is used to circumvent the value judgments Congress wrote into legislation. What sense is there in doing a benefit-cost analysis of the snail darter if Congress passed legislation that attempts to prevent species extinction? If Congress specified that no carcinogens should be added to food, why perform a benefit-cost analysis? Since Congress has instructed the administrator of the EPA to set ambient air quality standards for the criteria pollutants that protect public health with an ample margin of safety (1970 Clean Air Act Amendments), what is the point of finding the standard that maximizes net benefit? The Office of Management and Budget might answer that it is valuable to know how great the difference in net social benefit is between the best option and the one mandated by Congress. If that difference is large, Congress and the public ought to rethink the congressional mandate.

Unfortunately, that answer neglects the inadequacies of benefit-cost analysis. When the analysis does not deal with equity issues, and at best brushes past the criteria of transparency, administrative simplicity, and goal achievement, the results must be interpreted with care.

That point is more general: Benefit-cost analysis, in practice, is static. It does not account for new discoveries, advances in technologies, or many other adjustments. In principle, the adjustments could be included, even though they are highly uncertain. The analyses must be defended against hostile critics, however. An agency speculating that technology forcing will be successful would find it difficult to defend its numerical estimates. I remarked more than two decades ago that a carefully done benefit-cost analysis will tend to be biased toward understating benefits and overstating costs (Lave 1971).

Inherent Problems with Environmental Regulation

Environmental regulation is in trouble for many reasons (Portney 1990; Swartzman 1982). First, the EPA and the other agencies do not have a clear idea of what they should accomplish. Legislation is contradictory or full of pious hopes rather than working goals, for example, "no discharge in waterways by 1985" (1972 Clean Water Act).

Without goals, efficiency is not defined; benefit-cost analysis and other economic tools are irrelevant or at least less relevant (Gruenspecht and Lave 1991). For example, cost-effectiveness analysis can be used to attain some goal (or small number of goals) efficiently, even though no precise goal is specified; such a framework is severely limited, however. The lack of goals results in small part from the reluctance of congressmen to take stands that will earn them enemies. More important is the rapidly changing nature of public opinion regarding environmental issues. If, as time passes, incomes rise, more people become educated, people with less enlightened views die, and environmental abatement occurs without catastrophic consequences to the economy, environmental issues will become more important to the public. If incomes fall and defense or other issues grow in importance, environmental issues likely will become less important. Thus, the secular trend is toward greater concern, with business cycles and regional wars reversing the trend temporarily. Federal judges are subject to the same pressures and trends, and the nature and aggressiveness of court intervention change over time and across regions of the country.

Second, the environmental sciences and ecology are inherently complicated. The ability to predict the effects of a discharge on human health or ecology is primitive. Thus, there is sharp disagreement among experts, for example, about the effects of the *Valdez* oil spill. Eventually those issues get settled, but the public rarely hears about the resolution, although the problem initially was front-page news.

Third, as environmental expenditures have become significant, they have become more important to the political process. A new regulation can affect the president's public image. The effects are too important to escape White House review and reformulation.

Fourth, in the debate, the sides become more polarized until the issue ceases to be examined and is transformed into a test of strength. For example, public opinions about the environmental effects of acid rain were shaped by preliminary scientific data from the late 1970s; government studies of the 1980s seemed to be regarded as irrelevant, even when they contradicted the earlier conclusions that acid rain was acidifying many lakes and killing trees. Under some circumstances, scientific data become irrelevant, even if the vote is still years away (Oversight Review Board of the National Acid Precipitation Assessment Program 1991).

Fifth, there is no agreement about how the issues ought to be framed. Is the fundamental concern environmental preservation or a healthy local economy? Is the focus now, the next century, or all of future time?

Beyond Benefit-Cost Analysis

Benefit-cost analysis is inherently a time- and resource-consuming analysis. For formal benefit-cost analysis to convey a net social benefit, it must be applied only to issues of sufficient importance that the resource expenditures are worthwhile. Many issues can be handled with simpler frameworks, such as "no-risk," "technology-based standards," or "cost-effectiveness." Using one of the other frameworks would, at least in theory, result in lower efficiency. Only in economic models are information gathering and analysis free, however. Accounting for those costs and the inherent limitations of benefit-cost analysis, a formal analysis will be socially beneficial only for a limited number of cases. More limited analyses, from one of the other decision frameworks, or a quick and dirty benefit-cost analysis, should be preferred for most social issues.

A decision analysis is likely to be more enlightening if it emphasizes nine steps. First, it should define the problem—the issues to be considered, the possible remedies, and the goals. The analysis should also state the goals. Otherwise, a complicated social problem degenerates into peoples' talking past each other as they address different goals. The analysis should identify all reasonable means to accomplish the stated objectives. An overly limited set of options will lead to suboptimization, while an excessively broad set will waste resources and time. There are an infinite number of unreasonable alternatives. The analysis should quantify the benefits and costs of each alternative, and if reasonably possible, they should be translated into dollars. Where the translation is controversial, the analysis must be careful to summarize the effects in terms of a multidimensional array—although one of minimum size. In cases of deep controversy, the analysis should emphasize a systematic, analytic approach that uses all relevant data and helps to structure a research agenda for gathering the crucial missing data. The analysis should specify the perspective and values used and should consider other important perspectives and values, although the possible list is endless. For example, is the perspective current U.S. society, U.S. society in two decades, current advanced countries, current third world countries, or the world? Are the values of those who believe that industrialization is the only hope or of those who believe that industry inherently creates more problems than it solves? Equity issues associated with who pays and who benefits are of primary importance. Eastern and Western religions display quite different values. The analysis should spell out the implications of using different discount rates. Furthermore, it should analyze uncertainties. Each of the previous steps is filled with uncertainties, from quantification to choosing a discount rate. Finally, the analysis should interpret the results, because neither the facts nor the analysis will "speak for themselves." The analyst must interpret them for the reader. Those nine steps, adapted from the Office of Technology Assessment (1982), define a systematic analysis—a framework for pulling together diverse data and analyzing them. The framework emphasizes uncertainty and values; it does not claim that it will find a social optimum. As Railton (1990, 62) asserts, "Once benefit-cost analysis is understood as a process meant to yield information rather than to make decisions, practitioners of benefit-cost analysis need not take sides in controversies over the nature of justice."

What Should Be Analyzed?

I hinted above that benefit-cost analysis is helpful for only a fraction of social issues. How can decision makers know when a benefit-cost analysis is warranted and when a less resource-intensive method is superior? For example, when should an issue be resolved by negotiation among the most knowledgeable parties without any explicit attempt to determine a social optimum? One answer comes from the nine steps specified above. If those nine steps cannot be accomplished with confidence, a benefit-cost analysis will not result in a confident answer.

Another answer is that benefit-cost analysis is the best way of deciding which issues should be subject to benefit-cost analysis and which components are to be the focus. In other words, benefit-cost analysis can function as a metanalysis to define what tools to use. I do not know of any systematic attempt to investigate this metanalysis role for benefit-cost analysis.

Conclusion

I join dozens of people who have scrutinized benefit-cost analysis in concluding that the tool is a useful way of structuring a complicated problem. With the exception of economists who are utilitarians or unwitting utilitarians, there is general agreement that the option identified as having the largest net benefit does not have a strong claim to being the best social choice. The time has come to purge the utilitarian foundation from benefit-cost analysis. This means identifying the tool as a decision analysis rather than as a means for prescribing optimal decisions. We want to praise the virtues of systematic analysis and straight thinking, not the utilitarian properties of maximizing net benefits in complicated social decisions.

We need to admit that many benefit-cost analyses are biased; some are simply worthless. We should stop defending this tool with religious fervor and give more attention to the cases where it leads to results quite different from what Congress and the public appear to desire. Efficiency is not the most important attribute of a public program. We need to admit that benefit-cost analysis is costly to perform; it ought not to be applied to every problem or applied lightly. Few issues are worthy of a formal benefit-cost analysis. A one- or two-semester course in benefit-cost analysis, even at the Ph.D. level, does not transform a neophyte into a master or even a journeyman practitioner. The economic aspects of the analysis are sufficiently difficult and subtle that an apprenticeship system is needed, with few apprentices being promoted to journeymen, and few journeyman becoming masters.

Economists who are regarded as masters are sometimes

> **Economists need to admit that even the best available estimates of benefits and costs can be so uncertain that they are unlikely to enlighten.**

alarmingly ignorant about the limitations of their methods. We need to spend more time identifying attributes and must be more careful not to eliminate important attributes. We need to take a much more critical view about elicited values. Insisting on translating all benefits and costs into dollars is folly. In many cases the translation cannot be done with confidence. When the analyst does so despite the problems, the result is estimates almost certain to mislead or to generate controversy. At the least, the benefits and costs should be summarized in multidimensional arrays before the square pegs are pounded into round holes. More generally, we need to give more attention to tossing out inadequate parameter estimates, even if they are the best available. We need to admit that even the best available estimates can be so uncertain that they are unlikely to enlighten. We need to admit in many cases that a confident benefit-cost analysis is not possible. The basic approach can be used to structure the problem and to give values to parts of the problem, but it simply may not be possible to derive a meaningful estimate of net social benefits. Finally, we need to be more conscious of how we, and the analysis, are used. This is policy analysis, not fundamental research. Partial information can mislead, and analysts can, even inadvertently, become advocates. It is not enough to provide a caveat that such analysis may be underestimating costs and overestimating benefits. We must investigate the extent of the possible bias.

Along with other proponents of benefit-cost analysis, I praise it for forcing analysts to think systematically about social issues, collect data, and do analyses to clarify the implications of decisions. Unfortunately, the median application of the tool not only does not point to the best policy, but tends to mislead. We economists have a great deal of work to do before we can make benefit-cost analysis into the helpful tool that we know it can be.

NOTES

I thank Robert Axtell, Hadi Dowlatabadi, Carol Goldburg, Robert Hahn, Ben Harrison, Mark Kamlet, Daniel Nagin, Tom Romer, Kenneth Small, and Richard Zeckhauser for comments.

1. Still another approach to rescuing benefit-cost analysis has been the attempt to find special conditions under which superiority can be asserted without having to pay compensation (Small 1987).
2. The counterargument is that the utilitarian leader would have a more credible basis for asserting that the values would not be sacrificed except for stated circumstances, since the circumstances would have been thought through. Does detailing the circumstances under which the freedoms would be sacrificed add or subtract credibility? Would one vote for a candidate who detailed the exceptional circumstances under which he would lie, cheat, and steal or for a candidate who said he would not lie, cheat, and steal under any circumstances?
3. Van Doren (1989) defends benefit-cost analysis against the usual political science argument that it does not attend to symbols. He argues that preserving symbols has a cost and that the public does not have uniform values that praise the same symbols; the costs of preserving symbols should be taken more seriously. The political process is filled with rent-seeking, with an interest group seeking wealth and favoritism. Benefit-cost analysis alerts people to the implications of proposed legislation or regulation and causes them to protect their own interests. Van

Doren does insist that compensation actually be paid to those who are injured.
4.   MacLean (1990, 103) asserts:

> To argue that the sacred value of human life in those situations must be respected is not to deny in any way the value of efficiency in life-saving and the importance of saving more lives rather than fewer whenever possible. That point is rather a more subtle one. It is to suggest that there may be irresolvable tensions between our rationalistic, revisionist sentiments, on the one hand, and our conservative, ritualistic sentiments on the other. A rationalistic decision procedure may unavoidably threaten some of those sentiments, which may suggest that it is better not to make that procedure too absolute, too open, or too openly identified with public agencies like the Environmental Protection Agency that were created to pursue moral as well as other goals. It may perhaps be necessary to live with some controversies rather than to resolve them technocratically, and to tolerate "pockets" or modest levels of inefficiency for that purpose.

Compare Van Doren (1989).
5.   Miller has no patience with questions about whether government officials should be able to interpret estimates, even if they are not very reliable:

> If we have given government officials the power to impose costs on the activities of private citizens or otherwise control them, we cannot say they cannot be trusted to weigh benefits and costs in determining what they do. If regulatory statutes allow discretion, the enforcing agency would be irresponsible—and in my view unfair—not to weight the benefits and costs of its policies (Miller 1989, 92).

6.   For example, when Congress (or the National Highway Transportation Safety Administration) sets standards for safety, fuel economy, and pollution emissions, it must recognize that adding safety features increases weight and thus decreases fuel efficiency, just as does tightening emissions standards (Lave 1981b). A benefit-cost analysis must account for those interactions (Lave 1984).
7.   For example, the evaluation of the safety of nuclear power reactors got too large for the computers available (Rasmussen 1981).
8.   For example, there has been an evolution in the design of cooling pumps for nuclear reactors. Modern pumps are made of different materials with different quality control (Atomic Energy Commission 1974, 1975; Primack 1975).
9.   Should a trained seal be the national symbol?

REFERENCES

Ackerman, Bruce A., and William T. Hassler. *Beyond the New Deal: Coal and the Clean Air Act*. New Haven: Yale University Press, 1980.

Akerlof, George A. "Procrastination and Obedience." *American Economic Review* 81 (1991): 1–19.

Atomic Energy Commission. "Reactor Safety Study: An Assessment of Accident Risks in U.S. Commercial Power Plants." Washington, D.C.: Government Printing Office, 1974, 1975.

Baumol, William J. "On the Social Rate of Discount." *American Economic Review* 58 (1968): 788–802.

————, and Wallace E. Oates. *The Theory of Environmental Pollution*. New York: Cambridge University Press, 1988.

Berry, Brian. "Intergenerational Justice in Energy Policy," in D. MacLean and P. G. Brown, eds., *Energy and the Future*. Totowa, N.J.: Rowman and Littlefield, 1983.

Campen, James T. *Benefit, Cost, and Beyond: The Political Economy of Benefit-Cost Analysis*. Cambridge, Mass.: Ballinger, 1986.

Clark, Timothy B., Marvin H. Kosters, and James C. Miller III. "Introduction," in T. B. Clark, M. H. Kosters, and J. C. Miller III, eds., *Reforming Regulation*. Washington, D.C.: American Enterprise Institute for Public Policy Research, 1980.

Cummings, Robert G., David S. Brookshire, and William Schultze. *Valuing Public Goods: The Contingent Valuation Method*. Totowa, N.J.: Rowman and Allanheld, 1986.

Epple, Dennis, and Lester Lave. "The Role of Insurance in Managing Natural Hazard Risks: Private versus Social Decisions." *Risk Analysis* 8 (1988): 421–33.

Fischhoff, Baruch. "Cost-Benefit Analysis and the Art of Motorcycle Maintenance." *Policy Sciences* 8 (1977): 177–202.

————. "Value Elicitation: Is There Anything in There?" *American Psychologist* 46 (1991): 835–47.

Gruenspecht, Howard, and Lester Lave. "Increasing the Efficiency and Effectiveness of Environmental Decisions: Benefit-Cost Analysis and Effluent Fees." *Journal of the Air and Waste Management Association* 41 (1991): 680–93.

Hicks, John R. "The Foundations of Welfare Economics." *Economic Journal* 49 (1939): 696–712.

Jenkins, Glenn P. "The Measurement of Rate of Return and Taxation from Private Capital in Canada," in W. A. Niskanen, A. C. Harberger, R. H. Haveman, R. Turvey, and R. Zeckhauser, eds., *Benefit-Cost Analysis, 1972: An Aldine Annual on Forecasting, Decision-Making, and Evaluation*. Chicago, Ill.: Aldine, 1973.

Kaldor, Nicholas. "Welfare Propositions in Economics." *Economic Journal* 49 (1939): 549–52.

Kelman, Steven. "Cost-Benefit Analysis: An Ethical Critique." *Regulation* 5 (1981): 33–40.

————. "Cost-Benefit Analysis and Environmental, Safety, and Health Regulation: Ethical and Philosophical Considerations," in D. Swartzman, R. A. Liroff, and F. G. Croke, eds., *Cost-Benefit Analysis and Environmental Regulations: Politics, Ethics, and Methods*. Washington, D.C.: Conservation Foundation, 1982.

Kneese, Allen V., Shaul Ben-David, and William D. Schulze. "The Ethical Foundation of Benefit-Cost Analysis," in D. MacLean and P. G. Brown, eds., *Energy and the Future*. Totowa, N.J.: Rowman and Littlefield, 1983.

Krupnick, Alan J., and Paul R. Portney. "Controlling Urban Air Pollution: A Benefit-Cost Assessment." *Science* 252 (1991): 522–28.

Lave, Lester B. "Air Pollution Damage," in A. Kneese and B. Bower, eds., *Environmental Quality Analysis*. Baltimore: Johns Hopkins University Press, 1971.

———. "Conflicting Federal Regulations Concerning the Automobile." *Science* 11 (1981b): 893–99.

———. "Controlling Contradictions among Regulations." *American Economic Review* 74 (1984): 471–75.

———. "Formulating Greenhouse Policies in a Sea of Uncertainty." *Energy Journal* 12 (1991): 9–21.

———. *The Strategy of Social Regulation*. Washington, D.C.: Brookings Institution, 1981a.

———, and Thomas Romer. "Specifying Risk Goals: Inherent Problems with Democratic Institutions." *Risk Analysis* 3 (1984): 217–27.

Leonard, Herman B., and Richard J. Zeckhauser. "Cost-Benefit Analysis Applied to Risks: Its Philosophy and Legitimacy," in D. MacLean, ed., *Values at Risk*. Totowa, N.J.: Rowman and Allanheld, 1986.

MacLean, Douglas E. "Comparing Values in Environmental Policies: Moral Issues and Moral Arguments," in R. B. Hammond and R. Coppock, eds., *Decision Making: Report of a Conference*. Washington, D.C.: National Academy Press, 1990.

Melnick, R. Shep. "The Politics of Benefit-Cost Analysis," in R. B. Hammond and R. Coppock, eds., *Decision Making: Report of a Conference*. Washington, D.C.: National Academy Press, 1990.

Miller, James C., III. *The Economist as Reformer: Revamping the FTC, 1981–1985*. Washington, D.C.: American Enterprise Institute for Public Policy Research, 1989.

———, and Bruce Yandle, eds. *Benefit-Cost Analyses of Social Regulation*. Washington, D.C.: American Enterprise Institute for Public Policy Research, 1979.

Mishan, Edward J. *Cost-Benefit Analysis: An Informal Introduction*, 3rd ed. London: George Allen and Unwin, 1982.

National Research Council. *Policy Implications of Greenhouse Warming*. Washington, D.C.: National Academy Press, 1991.

———. *Safety of Dams: Flood and Earthquake Criteria*. Washington, D.C.: National Research Council, 1985.

Office of Technology Assessment. *Evaluation of Medical Technologies*. Washington, D.C.: Government Printing Office, 1982.

Oversight Review Board of the National Acid Precipitation Assessment Program. "The Experience and Legacy of NAPAP." Washington, D.C.: National Acid Precipitation Assessment Program, 1991.

Page, Talbot. "Intergenerational Justice as Opportunity," in D. MacLean and P. G. Brown, eds., *Energy and the Future*. Totowa, N.J.: Rowman and Littlefield, 1983.

Parfit, Derek. "Energy Policy and the Further Future: The Social Discount Rate," in D. MacLean and P. G. Brown, eds., *Energy and the Future*. Totowa, N.J.: Rowman and Littlefield, 1983.

Portney, Paul R., ed. *Public Policies for Environmental Protection*. Washington, D.C.: Resources for the Future, 1990.

Primack, J. "An Introduction to the Issues." *Bulletin of the Atomic Scientists* 31 (1975): 15–19.

Railton, Peter. "Benefit-Cost Analysis as a Source of Information about Welfare," in R. B. Hammond and R. Coppock, eds., *Decision Making: Report of a Conference*. Washington, D.C.: National Academy Press, 1990.

Rasmussen, Norman C. "The Application of Probabilistic Risk Assessment Techniques to Energy Technologies," in J. Hollander, M. Simmons, and D. Wood, eds., *Annual Review of Energy*. Palo Alto, Calif.: Annual Reviews, 1981.

Sandmo, Agnar. "Discount Rates for Public Investments under Uncertainty," in W. A. Niskanen, A. C. Harberger, R. H. Haveman, R. Turvey, and R. Zeckhauser, eds., *Benefit-Cost Analysis, 1972: An Aldine Annual on Forecasting, Decision-Making, and Evaluation*. Chicago, Ill.: Aldine, 1973.

———, and Jacques H. Dreze. "Discount Rates for Public Investments in Closed and Open Economies," in W. A. Niskanen, A. C. Harberger, R. H. Haveman, R. Turvey, and R. Zeckhauser, eds., *Benefit-Cost Analysis, 1972: An Aldine Annual on Forecasting, Decision-Making, and Evaluation*. Chicago, Ill.: Aldine, 1973.

Sassone, Peter G., and William A. Schaffer. *Cost-Benefit Analysis: A Handbook*. New York: Academic Press, 1978.

Simon, Herbert A. "A Behavioral Model of Rational Choice." *Quarterly Journal of Economics* 59 (1955): 99–118.

Small, Kenneth A. "A Constitutional Rationale for Welfare Measurement." Working paper, Department of Economics, University of California at Irvine, 1987.

Stokey, Edith, and Richard Zeckhauser. *A Primer for Policy Analysis*. New York: W. W. Norton, 1978.

Swartzman, Daniel. "Cost-Benefit Analysis in Environmental Regulation: Sources of the Controversy" in D. Swartzman, R. A. Liroff, and K. G. Croke, eds., *Cost-Benefit Analysis and Environmental Regulations: Politics, Ethics, and Methods*. Washington, D.C.: Conservation Foundation, 1982.

Tribe, Laurence H. "Policy Science: Analysis or Ideology," in W. A. Niskanen, A. C. Harberger, R. H. Haveman, R. Turvey, and R. Zeckhauser, eds., *Benefit-Cost Analysis, 1972: An Aldine Annual on Forecasting, Decision-Making, and Evaluation*. Chicago, Ill.: Aldine, 1973.

Trumbull, William N. "Who Has Standing in Cost-Benefit Analysis?" *Journal of Policy Analysis and Management* 9 (1990): 201–18.

Van Doren, Peter. "Should Congress Listen to Economists?" *Journal of Politics* 51 (1989): 319–26.

Viscusi, W. Kip. *Risk By Choice: Regulating Health and Safety in the Workplace*. Cambridge: Harvard University Press, 1983.

———, and Wesley A. Magat. *Learning about Risk: Consumer and Worker Responses to Hazard Information*. Cambridge: Harvard University Press, 1987.

White, Lawrence J. *Reforming Regulation: Process and Problems*. Englewood Cliffs, N.J.: Prentice-Hall, 1981.

Wildavsky, Aaron. "The Political Economy of Efficiency: Cost-Benefit Analysis, Systems Analysis, and Program Budgeting." *Public Administration Review* 26 (1966): 292–310.

Zerbe, Richard O., Jr. "Comment: Does Benefit-Cost Analysis Stand Alone? Rights and Standing." *Journal of Policy Analysis and Management* 10 (1991): 96–105.

Chapter 7

THE DANGERS OF UNBOUNDED COMMITMENTS TO REGULATE RISK

W. Kip Viscusi

OVERVIEW

For economists, determining the appropriate degree of risk regulation should not differ much from any other policy choice we make. We should consider the policy options, assess their benefits and costs, and select the policy that is in society's best interests. Ultimately, some trade-offs must be made as society decides how vigilant to be in promoting safety.

If it were relatively inexpensive to make life risk-free, those concerns would not be an issue. Unfortunately, life is inherently risky. All forms of transit pose risks, as do meat, alcohol, and many widely consumed and very healthful foods, such as celery and broccoli.[1] The limited nature of our resources is apparent when we realize that if the entire U.S. gross domestic product were devoted to avoiding fatal accidents, we would have only $55 million to spend per life at risk. That expenditure would leave us no available resources to combat cancer and AIDS or to provide for other health-related needs, such as food and housing.

Although the notion that some balance must be struck in our quest for safety differs from the normal popular intuition that when lives are at risk we should spare no expense to save them, that commitment is largely with respect to identified lives in which there is the certainty of life or death rather than statistical lives involving cases with typically small probabilities. To take but one common example, the chlorination of our drinking water poses a potential risk of cancer, albeit quite small and much less than the other risks posed by unchlorinated water. It is quite feasible for us to eliminate those risks by providing all people with distilled water for drinking and food preparation. Policy makers have not mandated distilled drinking water not because they have been remiss or because the underlying scientific base is false. Rather, the resource expenditures involved are so large relative to the magnitude of the risks that it makes little sense to embark on such a strategy.

Our willingness to accept many known hazards is more general. Few of us consider mining or construction work an attractive means of earning a living. The risks are substantial, and the jobs often involve unpleasant environmental exposures. The fact that those jobs do not accord with our own preferences does not, however, imply that we should ban those pursuits or alter their fundamental character. Doing so would not advance the well-being of those who have chosen to work on such jobs.

This chapter assesses how we should distinguish which risks to regulate and, in particular, where we should set the expenditure limits in our efforts to reduce risk. In establishing those thresholds, we shall not attempt to impose some external judgment. Thus, our task is not to impose our value of safety or that of policy makers. Instead, in a democratic society, policy should reflect the values of those affected by the policy. In particular, what are the individual values that members of society attach to risk reductions, and how can those values be translated into policy guidelines? This exercise is based on an underlying recognition that life is inherently risky. Inevitably, we shall choose risks both individually and collectively. Our task is to choose those risks wisely to reduce the serious risks that we can eliminate with an appropriate expenditure of funds.

As I shall demonstrate, making sensible choices in the balancing of costs and risk entails more than limiting expenditures because they do not generate substantial risk reductions. If we are extremely profligate in our expenditures, the net effect may make our lives even riskier. Single-minded efforts to eliminate particular identified hazards such as asbestos, for which both Environmental Protection Agency and Occupational Safety and Health Administration regulations impose a cost in excess of $100 million per life saved, may adversely affect the health of society, not simply our financial well-being.

I begin by examining the principles for valuing life and reviewing the empirical evidence that will provide guidelines for government valuation of risk. How government agencies will regulate risk will be defined in large part by their legislative mandates, and that is the subject of the second section of this chapter. Then I examine the risk regulation outcomes in terms of the level of expenditures actually devoted to life-saving activities. The risk-risk considerations that arise from excessive regulation are the focus of the following section. I then offer conclusions.

How Should We Value Risks to Life and Health?

The man in the street—and the ordinary member of Congress—has an instinctive aversion to placing a dollar value on a life. But economists do not calculate such values because they are unfeeling technicians. They do so because sensible regulation—the making of sound choices—in many cases requires it. There is no escape from this aspect of regulatory policy.

Two decades ago government agencies did not attach a value to lives saved by policies. Indeed, even raising those issues was too controversial, at least within the context of publicly disseminated documents and public ex-penditures. That silence did not mean that our life-saving efforts were unbounded. For example, we did not install

> **If we are extremely profligate in our expenditures to reduce risk, the net effect may make our lives even riskier.**

guardrails on every highway where a guardrail might diminish the probability of an accident.[2] Expenditures were undertaken without the kind of explicit policy analysis one would expect today.

When government agencies did begin assessing the benefits associated with reducing risks to life and health, they did not attempt to value life but rather to calculate the monetary costs of death. Those costs, which consisted of income losses and medical expenses, would be incorporated into a benefits analysis. To make that assessment, agencies calculated the present value of the individual's earnings stream. How much income would be lost after death? Even combined with the medical expenses en route to death, that procedure yields a very low estimate of the value of life, on the order of several hundred thousand dollars.

Those who resisted such approaches to assess the "economic value" of life as being incomplete and possibly even immoral were correct in their uneasiness with the concept. Our lives are certainly worth much more than what we make. Indeed, if faced with the prospect of certain death, there are few of us who would not work overtime or perhaps even resort to illegal activities in an effort to fend off that outcome. Moreover, those who do not work or who are retired and who have a zero present value of earnings might well find returning to the labor force desirable if doing so were necessary for the government to view their lives as worthwhile.

Much more is wrong with the human capital approach to valuing life than its failure to capture such nuances. We are not dealing with situations in which we can alter the probability of death from one to zero. Rather, we are dealing with contexts in which the shift in the probabilities is quite small. For example, the average probability of death to a blue-collar worker from a job accident is on the order of one in ten thousand. No existing government regulations eliminate all of that risk, only individual components that are linked to specific hazards that regulation targets. Thus, the range of manipulation of the probabilities is often quite narrow. Many federal agencies, for example, have a restrictive threshold value such as a one in a hundred thousand lifetime risk that will trigger regulatory action. Infinitesimal risks such as those differ significantly in character from situations in which one faces death with certainty and has the opportunity to purchase reductions in that risk.

A second distinctive feature is that the lives are not identified. Unlike in the case of a child trapped in a well—an identified individual with a stark shift in the probabilities of life and death depending on our action—the child who may die because of his parents' failure to require that he use automobile seat belts cannot be identified *ex ante* but is instead subject to a random risk of death. The importance of identifying the life at risk is clearly influential. Even beached whales evoke from society such substantial concern that we spend thousands of dollars in an effort to save them.

I contend that we should adopt the same principle for valuing risks to life and health that governs any other benefit assessment process. When valuing a public park, the building of a new bridge, or a homeless shelter, the appropriate valuation is society's willingness to pay for those public goods. In much the same manner, the appropriate value of a risk regulation policy is society's willingness to pay to reduce the risk. What is being valued is a lottery, where the value is the amount that we would place on reducing the risk if we understood the probability and could react rationally to it.

The requirement that we base risk regulation on rational respons- es that would take place if those affected by the policies accurately understood their implications is a nontrivial restriction. In many instances the public substantially misperceives the risk. The press often exaggerates hazards such as the risks associated with Superfund sites and creates unwarranted public alarm. If that concern is based on a misperception of the risk, then the government agency should perform an educational function. Just as the government has an obligation to convey information about products and activities whose risk the public cannot accurately perceive, government also has an obligation to fos- ter responsible behavior with respect to exaggerated risks. Moreover, in the presence of alarmist responses to risk, the government should not institutionalize those behavioral errors. For much the same reason that we should regulate risks that are underestimated and not well under- stood, we should also not rush to regulate inconsequential risks that the public incorrectly believes are important. Somewhat surprisingly, the response to exaggerated public concerns regarding risks is still regarded in many quarters as a legitimate basis for policy intervention.

Another recurring issue is that government programs deal with statistical lives rather than identified lives. The following example illustrates the problems that arise when we use the identified life approach. Suppose that each of us in a town of 100,000 is willing to spend $10 to reduce the risk of death to any particular individual in that town, possibly ourselves. Together, we can raise $1 million in an effort to prevent the loss of one statistical life, which will become our implicit value of life. Suppose, however, that after the victim has been identified, our willingness to pay is $2 million. Moreover, assume that no matter who the victim is, after the fact we would be willing to spend $2 million to save the life. Does this inconsistency in our *ex ante* and *ex post* values imply that we have been inconsistent in our valuations? Have we overreacted because the life has been identified or are our assessments of the value of risk lotteries excessively low because they are an abstraction? Most of our concern with the value of life will reflect the private value to the individual at risk. Once altruistic concerns begin to enter as a factor, however, the range of difficulties such as this increases.

Assessing the benefit derived from expenditures to reduce risk is complicated by the need to consider the altruistic gains that society would have derived from alternative uses of the funds. The pertinent altruistic benefit measure is the net altruistic gain. If the costs of regulating risk had been spent on some other utility-raising activity, such as lower taxes, then welfare would have been enhanced as well. If our altruism stems from concerns about utility levels as well as mortality, then the only altruistic component will be the value derived from the net increase in the individual's expected utility from the life-saving effort as compared with other possible private expenditures that would have been made. Thus, one must net out altruistic concerns from alternative uses of the funds.

To ascertain risk-money trade-offs, economists in the United States have used the implicit rates of trade-off reflected in risk-taking decisions in the marketplace, primarily the labor market. In contrast, the foreign literature focuses primarily on survey valuations of risk (Jones-Lee 1989). That difference in approach may stem in part from the greater competitiveness of U.S. labor markets, where labor unions play a less influential role than in many European countries.

The advantage of using market-based estimates of money-risk trade-offs is that those exposed to risk have a greater incentive to think carefully about the implications of the risks for their lives than do respondents who are quickly briefed on potential risk trade-offs. The advantages of revealed preference data are underscored by the fact that economists usually rely on market data to estimate demand curves, supply curves, and other economic relationships of interest instead of using survey data for hypothetical choices.

Carefully constructed surveys can, however, yield reliable trade-off values. Moreover, survey techniques have proven very useful in establishing the implicit value of avoiding cancer and other outcomes not readily estimated with market data. But the valuations of life from available surveys tend to be fairly similar to those obtained from market evidence, and market evidence is much more extensive. Therefore, I shall focus my review on the market-based studies of the value of life.

In particular, I shall ask how much individual workers require to face greater risks of death. Such a procedure respects the integrity of individual preferences and inquires how valuable the avoidance of risks are to those affected by them. Such valuations will not be confined to human capital concerns and, if workers are informed of the risk, will reflect preferences in a reliable manner. For the types of acute accident risks considered in those analyses, I have shown that workers' beliefs about risk accord quite closely with objective measures of the risk so that there is a sound basis for placing confidence in the market evidence (Viscusi 1979, 1983; Viscusi and O'Connor 1984).

Table 7-1 summarizes the estimates of the value of life obtained from labor market studies of the wage premiums commanded by job risks. The value-of-life estimates obtained in those different studies vary for several reasons. First, the value of life is not a natural constant. Different samples with different mixes of workers will have different implicit values of life. In the case of nonfatal job injuries, for example, I have shown (Hersch and Viscusi, 1990) that workers who smoke have an implicit value of avoiding job injuries of $30,781, whereas workers who wear seat belts have an implicit value of $92,245. A similar heterogeneity in preferences will affect the job risk studies of fatalities as well. The differences arise particularly because workers who are more willing to bear risk self-select themselves into the higher risk occupations. The substantial differences in risk being examined in the studies account for the discrepancy in valuations. The Thaler and Rosen (1976) study, for example, focuses on workers in very high risk jobs with an annual fatality rate on the order of one in a thousand. In contrast, my estimates (Viscusi 1978, 1979) deal with workers in more typical jobs with risks on the order of one in ten thousand and yield an implicit value of life of $4.1 million—five times as great as the value Thaler and Rosen found. That discrepancy is to be expected because of the self-selection of workers who place a low value on risk to relatively high risk jobs. Other sources of heterogeneity among the studies include differences in income level across the sample and differences in labor market conditions that will influence the amounts firms are willing to pay and the amounts workers are willing to accept for risky jobs.

Most of the labor market estimates of the value of life are clustered in the range from $3 million to $7 million, with a midpoint of $5 million. The studies such as those I undertook with Michael Moore (Viscusi and Moore 1989) that yielded very high values of life tend to be unreliable for inferring a value of life because their intent was to estimate very complicated econometric models focusing on many aspects of job-related behavior, such as individuals' implicit rates of interest with respect to years of life at risk, rather than to attempt to isolate more directly the wage-risk trade-off.

TABLE 7-1 Summary of Labor Market Studies of the Value of Life

Study	Sample	Risk Variable	Mean Risk	Nonfatal Risk Included?	Workers' Comp. Included?	Average Income Level (1990 U.S.$)	Implicit Value of Life ($ million)
Smith (1974)	Industry data: Census of Manufactures, U.S. Census, Employment and Earnings	Bureau of Labor Statistics (BLS)	NA	Yes	No	22,640	7.2
Thaler and Rosen (1976)	Survey of Economic Opportunity	Society of Actuaries	0.001	No	No	27,034	0.8
Smith (1976)	Current Population Survey (CPS), 1967, 1973	BLS	0.0001	Yes, not signif.	No	NA	4.6
Viscusi (1978, 1979)	Survey of Working Conditions, 1969–1970 (SWC)	BLS, subjective risk of job (SWC)	0.0001	Yes, signif.	No	24,834	4.1
Brown (1980)	National Longitudinal Survey of Young Men 1966–1971, 1973	Society of Actuaries	0.002	No	No	NA	1.5
Viscusi (1981)	Panel Study of Income Dynamics, 1976	BLS	0.0001	Yes, signif.	No	17,640	6.5

Olson (1981)	CPS	BLS	0.0001	Yes, signif.	No	NA	5.2
Marin and Psacharcpoulos (1982)	U.K. Office of Population Censuses and Surveys, 1977	Occupational Mortality, U.K.	0.0001	No	No	11,287	2.8
Arnould and Nichols (1983)	U.S. Census	Society of Actuaries	0.001	No	Yes	NA	0.9
Butler (1983)	S.C. Workers' Compensation Data, 1940–1969	S.C. Workers' Compensation Claims Data	0.00005	No	Yes	NA	1.1
Leigh and Folsom (1984)	Panel study of Income Dynamics, 1974; Quality of Employment Survey, 1977	BLS	0.0001	Yes	No	27,693; 28,734	9.7; 10.3
Smith and Gilbert (1984)	Current Population Survey, 1978	BLS	NA	No	No	NA	0.7
Dillingham (1985)	Quality of Employment Survey, 1977	BLS; constructed by author	0.00008; 0.00014	No	No	20,848	2.5–5.3; 0.9
Leigh (1987)	Quality of Employment Survey, 1977; Current Population Survey, 1977	BLS	NA	No	No	NA	10.4

(Table continues)

TABLE 7-1 (continued)

Study	Sample	Risk Variable	Mean Risk	Nonfatal Risk Included?	Workers' Comp. Included?	Average Income Level (1990 U.S.$)	Implicit Value of Life ($ million)
Herog and Schlottman (1987)	U.S. Census, 1970	BLS	NA	No	No	NA	9.1
Moore and Viscusi (1988a)	Panel Study of Income Dynamics, 1982	BLS, NIOSH National Traumatic Occup. Fatality Survey	0.00005, 0.00008	No	Yes	19,444	2.5, 7.3
Moore and Viscusi (1988b)	Quality of Employment Survey, 1977	BLS, discounted expected life years lost; subjective risk of job (QES)	0.00006	No	Yes	24,249	7.3
Garen (1988)	Panel Study of Income Dynamics, 1981-82	BLS	NA	Yes	No	NA	13.5
Cousineau, Lacroix, and Girard (1988)	Labor Canada Survey, 1979	Quebec Compensation Board	0.00001	No	No	NA	3.6

Study	Sample	Risk variable	Risk			Value
Viscusi and Moore (1989)	Panel Study of Income Dynamics, 1982	NIOSH National Traumatic Occupational Fatality Survey, Structural Markov Model	0.0001	No	No	19,194	7.8
Moore and Viscusi (1990a)	Panel Study of Income Dynamics, 1982	NIOSH National Traumatic Occupational Fatality Survey, Structural Life Cycle Model	0.0001	No	No	19,194	16.2
Moore and Viscusi (1990b)	Panel Study of Income Dynamics, 1982	NIOSH National Traumatic Occupational Fatality Survey, Structural Integrated Life Cycle Model	0.0001	Yes	Yes	19,194	16.2
Kniesner and Leeth (1991)	Two-digit mfg. data, Japan, 1986	Yearbook of Labor Statistics, Japan	0.00003	Yes	No	34,989	7.6
	Two-digit mfg. data, Australia, by state, 1984–1985	Industrial accident data, Australia	0.0001	Yes	Yes	18,177	3.3
	Current Population Survey, U.S., 1978	NIOSH National Traumatic Occupational Fatality Survey	0.0004	Yes	Yes	26,226	0.6

Notes: All values are in December 1990 dollars. NA = not available.

In other cases the studies' procedures to infer a value of life were quite elaborate and involved very strong assumptions regarding missing parameters needed to construct the value of life. To estimate the implicit value of life based on seat belt use, one must, for example, establish some monetary value for the discomfort and time required to use the seat belt. Table 7-2 summarizes value-of-life studies based on trade-offs outside the labor market. The most direct counterparts to the labor market studies are the automobile accident risk studies of Atkinson and Halvorsen (1990), who find an implicit value of life of $4 million, and of Dreyfus and Viscusi (1995), who find an implicit value of life of from $2.9 million to $4.2 million.

In general, the estimates of the value of life from labor market evidence indicate an amount in the range of $5 million. The variation in risks and preferences across different samples and the choice of different econometric methodologies make the range of estimates less precise than one might like. Nevertheless, that figure serves as an approximate measure of the value of life for a prime-age individual exposed to a fatal risk. One would, for example, believe that there was a serious misallocation of resources if the value of life cutoff was $500,000 or $10 million.

Those estimates of the value of life represent a population average, since the risk-money preferences among individuals will differ, as do other tastes. One particularly important correlate with the value of life is the income level of the person at risk. Individual willingness to pay to avert risks is positively and approximately proportionally related to income.[3] Although we can make refinements in an effort to set different value-of-life estimates based on income differences and age differences in those whose lives are at risk, doing so is more controversial than simply using a uniform value of life. Nevertheless, suppressing those differences is clearly not a reasonable economic approach. Quantity adjustments, such as establishing a value per discounted life year, would recognize the differences in the amount of life at risk. An individual would clearly prefer to be protected from a fatal risk of a particular magnitude when young rather than old since he would have a greater amount of life to save. Estimates of individual rates of time preference with respect to the years of their life at risk suggests that this quality concern may be substantial (Viscusi and Moore 1989). Recognizing those differences is problematic only if one views lives as being of infinite duration rather than of a finite magni-

TABLE 7-2 Summary of Value-of-Life Studies Based on Trade-offs Outside the Labor Market

Study	Nature of Risk	Implicit Value of Life ($ millions)
Ghosh, Lees, and Seal (1975)	Highway speed/value of time trade-off, 1973	0.07
Blomquist (1979)	Automobile death risks/seat belt use, 1972	1.2
Dardis (1980)	Smoke detector risk reduction, 1974–1979	0.6
Portney (1981)	Property value response to air pollution risk, 1978	0.8
Ippolito and Ippolito (1984)	Cigarette smoking cessation, 1980	0.7
Garbacz (1989)	Smoke detector risk reduction, 1968–1985	2.0
Atkinson and Halvorsen (1990)	Automobile accident risks/price trade-off, 1986	4.0
Dreyfus and Viscusi (1995)	Prices of used automobiles	2.9–4.2

Note: All values in December 1990 dollars.

tude whose length is consequential. Acknowledging those concerns in the abstract is, however, more straightforward than making the somewhat difficult policy judgment that the lives of the elderly who die from air pollution should receive a lower value than the lives of children killed in school bus crashes.

The influence of income differences on the value of life is, quite legitimately, more controversial. In those policy instances in which the beneficiary of the risk regulation will bear the cost, however, recognition of income differences is compelling. Consider the case of air travel. Whereas the average worker in Viscusi (1978a, 1979a) had an implicit value of life of $4.1 million, for the income level of a typical airline passenger that value would be $5.7 million if we assume an income elasticity of the value of life of one. Since airplane passengers in effect pay for more stringent safety standards through higher ticket prices, the government is not conferring a windfall gain on that group. The current U.S. Department of Transportation practice of requiring that the same value of life be used for highway safety as for airline safety effectively provides suboptimal protection to air travelers at risk. Not only is the value-of-life estimate (under $3 million) excessively low, even for the average American at risk, but it fails to reflect the greater concern airplane passengers have with safety. If a market for safety existed in which the customers could buy airplane safety explicitly, they would demand higher levels of safety than they are currently receiving through the policies that they pay for in the current regulatory regime. An interesting example of the price-safety trade-off is USAir's 1994 program to reduce fares to lure passengers back after two major crashes of its Boeing 737s.

Throughout the federal government, agencies use value-of-life estimates such as those presented in tables 7-1 and 7-2 to value the benefits associated with policies to reduce risk. But using those numbers to value benefits is quite different from making policy decisions based on such assessments of benefits. As I shall demonstrate in the next section, there is little evidence that the estimates of the value of life constrain those decisions.

Indeed, a particularly ominous trend has emerged in the Clinton administration. OSHA has begun to abandon explicitly assessing the beneficial effects of regulations on mortality. For both the proposed environmental tobacco smoke regulations and the asbestos regulations, the agency estimates no explicit value of life. Instead, OSHA simply asserts that the risks are "significant" and consequently must be regulated, given its legislative mandate.

Although restrictive legislative mandates ultimately limit the potential role of executive oversight, without a comprehensive assessment of benefits, the oversight process may be short-circuited altogether. Moreover, policy makers can use the significant risk threshold, to the extent that it exists, to justify highly intrusive government regulations. In its environmental tobacco smoke proposal, for example, OSHA cited the Supreme Court's benzene decision, which noted that the risks posed by drinking water were not significant but did not set higher cutoff risk levels.[4] Indeed, OSHA cites that particular passage in the Court's decision in its analysis of environmental tobacco smoke (OSHA 1994). If OSHA is free to regulate all risks greater than are posed by drinking water without comprehensively assessing benefits, then the agency in effect will be completely unconstrained. Following the drinking water logic, one should eliminate most blue-collar jobs as well. The current regulatory impact approach represents a retrogression to the pre-Ford era of policy analysis. The Carter administration, which was Clinton's Democratic predecessor, required comprehensive assessments of benefits, costs, and cost-effectiveness. That practice should not be abandoned. Legislation passed by the House of Representatives in 1995 and pending in the Senate would require benefit-cost tests and honest risk assessment.

We should note that the perfunctory risk analyses now undertaken are being coupled with fanciful cost assessments as well. Increasingly, OSHA has begun claiming that firms adopting government regulations will earn profits in the billions of dollars. If such economic gains were potentially available, however, enterprises would exploit those opportunities without the compulsion of government regulation.

The trend toward abandoning realistic cost assessment and comprehensive valuation of risks will surely worsen attempts to strike a reasonable balance between cost and risk. Both Democratic and Republican administrations over the past two decades have recognized the importance of assessing the consequences of policies, even in a world of restrictive legislative mandates. Without such information, we cannot know what we are paying for poorly conceived legislation. As I shall show, that price is often in terms of our health, not simply wasted expenditures.

Legislative Mandates of Risk Regulation Agencies

When evaluating the risk policies agencies adopt, it is instructive to assess what their enabling legislation permits them to do. From an economic standpoint, we might view the ideal policy as one that maximizes the net gains to society or provides the greatest difference between the benefits and costs. Although there is not unanimous endorsement of that criterion, the notion that the benefits of a policy should exceed the costs before it is undertaken has been adopted as a guideline for governmental regulatory oversight. That procedure recognizes that not all benefits can be monetized, and the Clinton administration has correctly emphasized the role of nonmonetary concerns.

Even if the enabling legislation did not require benefit-cost trade-offs, if it were framed in a manner that permitted agency officials to make such judgments in setting policy, then it would be possible to use such an approach. Benefit-cost orientation presumably would be in conjunction with the urging of the executive branch's regulatory oversight by the Office of Management and Budget.

Unfortunately, circumstances do not favor permitting agency officials to use the benefit-cost approach. OSHA's enabling legislation, the Occupational Safety and Health Act of 1970, for example, requires that the agency "assure so far as possible every man and woman in this Nation safe and healthful working conditions."[5] Although that mandate may seem to be quite broad, the U.S. Supreme Court has interpreted it more narrowly in its benzene decision.[6] In particular, the Court has ruled that the agency cannot use benefit-cost analysis in setting its standards. That restriction is not so narrow as it might appear; it does not necessarily imply that benefits and costs cannot be considered or that some balance cannot be struck in the setting of regulations to reflect what is "possible."

On the practical level, such trade-offs have been made since the founding of the agency. If our objective were truly to eliminate all risks, then a natural starting point would be to abolish the construction industry. Construction activity is inherently risky, and as long as we engage in it, fatalities will result. Presumably, agency officials have made some judgment that the economic gains to society from continuing construction activity outweigh the risks that are present within the industry.

OSHA has continued to tinker with various construction industry risks, but those efforts are far less pervasive than would be warranted if OSHA were truly to commit itself to eliminating all such significant risks.

The enabling legislation for various programs administered by the EPA is also quite narrow. The Clean Air Act completely prohibits the agency from considering costs when it sets ambient air quality standards. Similarly, in the case of the cleanup of hazardous waste at Superfund sites, the focus of the initial legislation was on eliminating those risks rather than on having a more balanced approach. As a result, the "how clean is clean?" issue surfaced as a salient policy controversy in the 1994 reauthorization debate over Superfund. We have increasingly come to realize that the cleanup costs are quite high and, in some cases, that society should ensure that the risk reductions are commensurate with the resources expended. To address that problem, the 1995 legislation passed by the U.S. House of Representatives (H.R. 1022) would require a benefit-cost test for the cleanup of each Superfund site.

The failure of those agencies to adopt balanced policies is by no means the exception. In its approval process for new drugs, the Food and Drug Administration focuses on two criteria—the safety and efficacy of the drugs. Consumers'

The public has a well-documented tendency to overestimate risks with low probabilities and risks that have received substantial media attention.

willingness to pay for the drugs or corporate profits that may result from the drugs do not enter the calculations. The risk-reduction benefits of new drugs relative to the risks generated by possibly dangerous drugs are also not weighted appropriately.

Although the formal legislative criteria are generally quite narrow, in practice agencies find various ways to strike informal balances. In the case of its safety standards, OSHA regulations often focus on how affordable the regulations will be. How many firms will be forced to cease operations if the regulations are adopted? The OSHA cotton dust standard, for example, did not reduce cotton dust exposures to the lowest level possible or to the lowest level that was feasible with available technologies. Rather, the stringency of the controls stopped at the point where there was a substantial increase in the degree to which costs would accelerate as the standard was tightened.

The feasibility and the availability of the technology also enter the EPA's decisions. The agency has begun to exploit the potential for trade-offs indirectly by soliciting community support for less stringent regulations. The 1994 draft of proposed Superfund legislation, for example, included explicit provisions fostering community involvement. That phenomenon represents an example of the increasing emphasis in the 1990s on eliciting local viewpoints on the desirability of reducing pollution or cleaning up hazardous waste sites. Ascertaining local support for a less stringent standard, possibly because it will bolster local employment, may in effect serve as a politically acceptable way to deal with the legislative restrictions.

Unfortunately, the less formalized ways of introducing trade-offs do not always make a sensible basis for policy. The costs of risks or regulations should not be so great that they force the closure of businesses or produce a local public uproar before policy makers recognize that they are consequential. Citizen group meetings may also not always constitute a suitable springboard for a national dialogue about risk. The technical issues are often quite complex and unfamiliar. For example, the public has a well-documented tendency to overestimate risks with low probabilities and risks that have received substantial media attention. A preferable alternative would permit the agency to make more balanced choices and to solicit explicit public involvement only when the agency had a legitimate interest in learning about the public's attitude toward conflicting policy effects.

Similarly, we should not need a public lobbying effort by identified victims suffering from AIDS before the government realizes that expeditious drug approval is warranted for all high-risk groups, not simply AIDS victims. Expediting the approval of potentially beneficial drugs involves conflicting risk gains and losses, not simply the errors that result when bad drugs are approved.

Risk Policy Outcomes

It is useful to compare any reasonable threshold for the value of life with the amount government agencies actually expend per statistical life saved. Table 7-3 summarizes estimates of the costs per life saved that were prepared primarily by OMB regulatory oversight economist, Dr. John F. Morrall III, from the regulatory impact analysis and other information prepared for the rulemaking record.

Some regulations would clearly pass a test of economic desirability. Regulatory policies of the National Highway Traffic Safety Administration and the Federal Aviation Administration clearly are relatively efficient in terms of promoting life-saving activities. Indeed, those agencies' efforts may not be vigilant enough, as they may have forgone pursuing measures that would have passed a benefit-cost test. The U.S. Department of Transportation traditionally used as its value of life the present value of the lost earnings of those whose lives were at risk. Since a narrowly based legislative mandate to reduce risks did not constrain the DOT, as was the case for the EPA and OSHA, the department has taken less aggressive life-saving efforts than the willingness-to-pay criterion might justify. Although the DOT has since adopted the willingness-to-pay approach, its historical method of valuing lives by their present value has served as the starting point from which the agency has steadily increased the implicit value of life. At the present time, that value is under $3 million per life, which is below the figure used by other agencies, such as the EPA.

Compared with the performance of the DOT, the EPA and OSHA are clearly out of sync. Very few of the regulations issued by those agencies have a cost per life saved of $5 million or less. For example, OSHA's 1986 asbestos standard imposed a cost per life saved of $90 million, and in 1994 OSHA established an additional tightening of its asbestos exposure limits. Although asbestos is clearly a hazardous substance meriting regulation, the major health damages from asbestos arose from the massive exposures of shipyard workers during World War II. They and most other asbestos disease victims contracted illnesses when asbestos was unregulated. Instead of playing a neutral role, the government actually contributed to the risk. Government shipbuilding specifications mandated asbestos use. Although asbestos is clearly a "bad actor" meriting regulation, there is a need for balance even in the case of substances that should be regulated. The Consumer Product Safety Commission's ban on asbestos in products consumed by the general public may have led to the *Challenger* disaster.[7]

Until the advent of the Reagan administration in 1981, the Council on Wage and Price Stability, in a regulatory oversight role, required agencies to assess the merits of regulatory policies to ensure that those efforts were desirable. In the Ford administration the council focused on assessing the costs and broader economic impacts. In the Carter administration the council required agencies to assess ben-

TABLE 7-3 The Cost of Various Risk-Reducing Regulations per Life Saved

Regulation	Year and Status[a]	Agency	Initial Annual Risk[b]	Annual Lives Saved	Cost per Life Saved (millions of 11/90 $)
Pass Benefit-Cost Test:					
Unvented space heaters	1980 F	CPSC	2.7 in 10^5	63.000	.13
Oil and gas well service	1983 P	OSHA-S	1.1 in 10^3	50.000	.13
Cabin fire protection	1985 F	FAA	6.5 in 10^8	15.000	.26
Passive restraints/belts	1984 F	NHTSA	9.1 in 10^5	1,850.000	.39
Underground construction	1989 F	OSHA-S	1.6 in 10^3	8.100	.39
Alcohol and drug control	1985 F	FRA	1.8 in 10^6	4.200	.64
Servicing wheel rims	1984 F	OSHA-S	1.4 in 10^5	2.300	.64
Seat cushion flammability	1984 F	FAA	1.6 in 10^7	37.000	.77
Floor emergency lighting	1984 F	FAA	2.2 in 10^8	5.000	.90
Crane-suspended personnel platform	1988 F	OSHA-S	1.8 in 10^3	5.000	1.55
Concrete and masonry construction	1988 F	OSHA-S	1.4 in 10^5	6.500	1.80
Hazard communication	1983 F	OSHA-S	4.0 in 10^5	200.000	2.32
Benzene/fugitive emissions	1984 F	EPA	2.1 in 10^5	0.310	3.61
Fail Benefit-Cost Test:					
Grain dust	1987 F	OSHA-S	2.1 in 10^4	4.000	6.83
Radionuclides/uranium mines	1984 F	EPA	1.4 in 10^4	1.100	8.89
Benzene	1987 F	OSHA-H	8.8 in 10^4	3.800	22.03

Arsenic/glass plant	1986 F	EPA	8.0 in 10^4	0.110	24.73
Ethylene oxide	1984 F	OSHA-H	4.4 in 10^5	2.800	32.97
Arsenic/copper smelter	1986 F	EPA	9.0 in 10^4	0.060	34.13
Uranium mill tailings inactive	1983 F	EPA	4.3 in 10^4	2.100	35.55
Uranium mill tailings active	1983 F	EPA	4.3 in 10^4	2.100	68.27
Asbestos	1986 F	OSHA-H	6.7 in 10^5	74.700	115.03
Asbestos	1989 F	EPA	2.9 in 10^5	10.000	134.22
Arsenic/glass manufacturing	1986 R	EPA	3.8 in 10^5	0.250	182.91
Benzene/storage	1984 R	EPA	6.0 in 10^7	0.043	260.19
Radionuclides/DOE facilities	1984 R	EPA	4.3 in 10^6	0.001	270.50
Radionuclides/elem. phosphorous	1984 R	EPA	1.4 in 10^5	0.046	347.73
Benzene/ethylbenzenol styrene	1984 R	EPA	2.0 in 10^6	0.006	622.14
Arsenic/low-arsenic copper	1986 R	EPA	2.6 in 10^4	0.090	984.09
Benzene/maleic anhydride	1984 R	EPA	1.1 in 10^6	0.029	1,056.23
Land disposal	1988 F	EPA	2.3 in 10^8	2.520	4,508.29
EDB	1989 R	OSHA-H	2.5 in 10^4	0.002	20,094.08
Formaldehyde	1987 F	OSHA-H	6.8 in 10^7	0.010	92,741.89

a. Status classified as proposed (P), rejected (R), or final (F) rule.
b. Annual deaths per exposed population. An exposed population of 10^3 is 1,000.
Source: Viscusi (1992), based on Morrall (1986, 30). These statistics were updated by John F. Morrall III via unpublished communication with the author, July 10, 1990.

efits and costs and to select the most cost-effective policy alternative. That process was, however, advisory, as the council relied on written submissions to the public record and subsequent lobbying by White House officials. The Reagan administration strengthened the oversight process by moving it to the OMB and requiring that regulations pass a benefit-cost test. Agencies also began explicitly valuing risks to life, but overriding legislative mandates impeded those favorable developments. The Bush and Clinton administrations have continued that general approach, but agencies seem to be increasingly exploiting the risk orientation of the legislative mandates and have become less vigilant in undertaking sound regulatory analysis.

Because risk regulation has faced at least a nominal benefit-cost test since the Reagan administration, it is instructive to examine the performance of those regulatory efforts. Have agencies attempted to foster balance in setting the stringency of regulations, and has the OMB succeeded in blocking the most undesirable regulatory measures?

The record of the OMB's regulatory battles is shown by the second column in table 7-3, which indicates which regulations were rejected and which were adopted. Clearly, the OMB totally eliminated some of the least cost-effective regulations. Doing so prevented the agencies from promulgating regulations that were very expensive relative to what they would have achieved. The thresholds that must be reached before the OMB takes regulatory action are also quite high, however. In particular, table 7-3 lists no regulation for the cost per life saved at $150 million or less that has not been issued. The OMB nevertheless may have had some beneficial effect on the other regulations by altering their structure and making them less onerous than they would otherwise have been. The OMB was, for example, influential in leading OSHA to include performance-oriented alternatives in its grain dust regulations. But the regulatory oversight process alone is not sufficient to strike an appropriate regulatory balance. That inadequacy has held true in Democratic and Republican administrations, including administrations with a strong public commitment to regulatory reform. The imbalance will continue as long as legislative mandates take on an absolutist approach to risk reduction instead of recognizing society's legitimate competing concerns.

At the most superficial level, society is squandering resources and getting little in return. In addition, when we compare policies across agencies, we see that we are not saving as many lives as we could if resources were allocated more effectively. If we were to place greater emphasis on stringent transportation safety regulations and less emphasis on environmental regulations or job safety regulations, then we would be able to save more lives than we do now at a more modest allocation of resources. Doing so would be in all of our interests, but it is not possible without some central coordinating mechanism that could ensure that we are obtaining the same amount of safety benefit per dollar expended across agencies. That coordinating function lies within the OMB's jurisdiction, but the restrictive legislative mandates give the agency very little discretion in that regard.

One additional role that the OMB could serve would be to urge the DOT to adopt a higher value of life for its policies. Such an effort would be in contrast to the agency's usual disciplinary role in discouraging excessive regulations. But the OMB also has a constructive function to serve in promoting sound regulations when they are desirable. Transportation safety regulations appear to be the greatest outlier meriting increased regulatory effort. Advocates of responsible regulation may resist such an effort to bolster the attractiveness of any regulatory policies, with the belief that the agency will ultimately err in the direction of excessive regulation. For example, many of the DOT's fuel economy standards are of questionable validity, and many other transportation regulatory analyses have had questionable elements. Ideally, however, one should not suppress the value of life to a suboptimal level in an effort to create regulatory discipline. Distortions such as that violate the integrity of policy analysis and ultimately will impede its value for making policy judgments.

The Dangers of Excessive Regulation

By definition, any regulation that has costs in excess of its benefits does more harm than good. In the case of extremely wasteful regulations, however, that observation may be even more striking than is apparent at first glance.

One kind of damage a regulation can do is to create risks other than those that the regulation itself addresses. In the case of an automobile recall in which individuals are required to bring their cars back to the dealership to have a defect repaired, there is some chance that the driver will be killed en route. All motor vehicle transportation is risky, killing 50,000 Americans annually, so that there is some expected life cost arising from a recall. It is of course true that had the individual not driven the car to the dealership, he would have driven somewhere else, such as to work. But when making the private driving choice in the absence of the recall, the driver would have determined that the benefits of driving the car to that destination exceeded the costs of doing so. It is not appropriate simply to neglect the risk costs of returning the vehicle to the dealer because other driving would have taken place. As a result, it is appropriate to recall a vehicle only when the risk reduction and other benefits of repairing the vehicle exceed the risk and time costs of the consumer's having the vehicle repaired.

The risks entailed in responding to a motor vehicle recall represent in many respects simply a special case of the more general phenomenon that regulations generate risky activities. Almost all regulations entail some kind of industrial activity, whether it is construction efforts associated with removing waste from a Superfund site or manufacturing activity to produce pollution control equipment. In each case regulation directly stimulates economic activity and indirectly stimulates the inputs to the industries. For example, the construction equipment used at the Superfund site is produced at firms where workers suffer injuries or death in the manufacturing process. Moreover, the steel used to make the bulldozer is produced in a risky manner, as is the coal used to provide the electric power to the steel plant. This example generalizes to all regulatory contexts in which a regulation stimulates economic activity that is in no way specific to the environmental intent of the regulatory effort.

To assess the risk linkages associated with economic activities, Richard Zeckhauser and I (Viscusi and Zeckhauser 1994) have calculated the mortality costs and injury costs of expenditures associated with different industries. Table 7-4 summarizes those mortality cost estimates for different broad industry groups. The figures pertain to the total monetary cost of the statistical lives lost that is associated with each dollar of production from the industries. The typical industries that are associated with government regulatory efforts are manufacturing processes and construction, for which fatality costs are about 1 percent of expenditures. We have also developed estimates of the injury costs associated with expenditures, which are much greater than the mortality costs and are available on a more refined industry basis. In construction, for example, fatality and injury risk costs are 4 percent of expenditures.

TABLE 7-4   Fatality Costs of Output Valued at $5 Million per Fatality

Industry	Allocated Fatalities	Valuation of Losses ($ million)	Ratio: Valuation to Output
Agriculture, forestry, and fisheries	396	1,978	0.0107
Mining	103	516	0.0042
Construction	866	4,329	0.0073
Manufacturing	1,416	7,082	0.0029
Transportation and utilities	602	3,011	0.0046
Wholesale and retail trade	424	2,120	0.0020
Finance, insurance, and real estate	194	971	0.0008
Services	672	3,358	0.0025

In general, we find that we may be embarking on a losing effort with respect to the health costs of expenditures if the cost per life saved amounts are excessive. For each dollar of construction expenditures, total injury and fatality costs average four cents per dollar. In effect we create four cents of risk costs for each dollar of expenditures. If the value of the lives saved by a policy constitutes less than 4 percent of the costs, then we shall be doing more harm than good from the standpoint of those direct risk effects.

There is a second type of risk-risk trade-off as well. It is less indirect in character but potentially of greater consequence. In addition to the direct risk costs noted above, risk regulations and other government expenditures in effect make society poorer since they deprive us of resources that could have been spent elsewhere. In some cases workers incur the opportunity costs. In other cases taxpayers or consumers must pay more for more expensive products. Stockholders may also suffer loss in income to pay for the regulatory expenditures. The analysis that I shall present will not distinguish which of those groups incurs the loss but instead will show average estimates for the U.S. economy.

The most direct way to ascertain the effect of decreasing income on mortality is to estimate directly the relationship between mortality in different groups and individual income levels. Keeney (1990) and Lutter and Morrall (1993) have used that approach. At the close of the Bush administration, the OMB raised those risk offsets as a poten-

tial concern with respect to OSHA regulations. Although the underlying methodology was sound, OSHA had not precisely established
the empirical basis for implementing the policy.

　The evidence available at that time consisted of studies of the
relationship between income levels and mortality. In table 7-5 I set
out the results of those studies. The statistics show that the expenditure level that will lead to the loss of a statistical life because of the
negative relationship between income levels and mortality varies con-
siderably from one study to another. Keeney (1990) and Lutter and
Morrall (1993) both have placed greatest emphasis on studies that
indicate the loss of a statistical life in the general range of $10 mil-
lion.

Unfortunately, isolating the income-mortality trade-off based on
such studies will remain problematic. Multiple causes of mortality are
highly correlated with income, such as educational levels. Moreover,
the two-directional causality between health and income confounds
any attempts to reliably isolate the relationships. Perhaps because of
those difficulties, many estimates of the statistical expenditures that
will lead to the loss of a statistical life appear implausible, as they are
inconsistent with other evidence regarding risk trade-offs. At the
same time that society appears to be willing to spend $5 million to
prevent the loss of a statistical life, the studies suggest that with an
expenditure of a bit more or perhaps double that amount, there will
be the loss of a statistical life. In effect, saving lives becomes a break-
even proposition where every time we are willing to spend money to
save a life, we lose a life because we become poorer in doing so. Such
a relationship is clearly implausible, as any life-saving expenditures
would become quite unattractive in such an instance.

In an effort to resolve that inconsistency, I have developed estimates of the value of expenditures that will lead to the loss of a statistical life that are based on estimates of the implicit value of life. The
procedure I have developed links the estimate of the expenditure
level that leads to the loss of a statistical life to the value people are
willing to spend to save a statistical life. Those magnitudes are closely
linked theoretically, and by exploiting that linkage we can avoid relying on the controversial direct estimates of the income-mortality relationship. Moreover, we can use that approach to formulate a policy in
which there is internal consistency between the value of life and the
income loss level that leads to the loss of a statistical life. My proce-

TABLE 7-5 Summary of Income-Mortality Studies

Study	Nature of Relationship	Income Loss per Statistical Death ($ million, 11/1992)
Hadley and Osei (1982)	One percent increase in total family income for white males age 45–64 leads to .07 percent decline in mortality.	33.2
U.S. Joint Economic Committee (1984)	Three percent drop in real per capita income in 1973 recession generated 2.3 percent increase in mortality.	3.0
Anderson and Burkhauser (1985)	Longitudinal survey, Social Security Administration Retirement History Survey, 1969–1979. $1 difference in hourly wage levels in 1969 generates 4.2 percent difference in mortality rates over next 10 years.	1.9
Duleep (1986)	Social Security mortality data 1973–1978 for men age 36–65 imply a higher mortality rate of .023 for income group $3,000–$6,000 compared with income group $6,000–$9,000.	2.7
Keeney (1990), based on Kitagawa and Hauser (1973)	Mortality rate-income level data fit exponential curve relating mortality rates to income; 1959 data on mortality of whites, age 25–64, death certificate information.	12.5
Lutter and Morrall (1993)	International data on mortality-income relationship from the World Bank, 1965 and 1986.	9.3
Chapman and Hariharan (1994)	Social Security Administration Retirement Study, 1969–1979, controlling for initial health status; trade-off of $12.2 million per life in 1969 dollars.	13.3

dure, which is described in Viscusi (1994), indicates that the expenditure that will lead to the loss of a statistical life is on the order of ten times the value of life, or $50 million. What that figure indicates is that every time we spend $50 million on a life-saving effort, the income loss that will result will generate a statistical death because of the income-mortality linkage.

That estimate and the direct evidence on the expenditure-risk linkage demonstrate that there are dangers to agencies' unbounded commitments to regulate risk. Imposing regulatory costs generates risks directly by stimulating economic activity and indirectly through the mortality-income relationship. Even if our sole concern is risk reduction, irrespective of costs, current policies are often ill-conceived. Applying those various risk-risk concerns would lead to rejection of regulatory proposals at a lower level of the costs per life saved than has ever been pertinent for a regulation rejected by the OMB.

> **Every time we spend $50 million on a life-saving effort, the income loss that will result will generate a statistical death because of the income-mortality linkage.**

Since legislative mandates make benefit-cost concerns largely inapplicable, the OMB should focus its efforts on whether policies achieve risk reductions. Policies that endanger our lives more than they protect them should be rejected. Such an approach ideally would enable agencies to abandon their institutional myopia and recognize the broader implications that excessive regulations have for our well-being.

Conclusion

Several results are quite striking. First, the cost-effectiveness of risk-regulation policies differs greatly across government agencies. We could clearly save more lives for less money through a reallocation of regulatory resources. Second, the trade-offs that are made are out of line with reasonable efforts to reduce risk. The cost per life saved amounts are inconsistent with measures of society's willingness to pay to save the lives.

Since the nature of the agencies' legislative mandates is a principal contributor to those inadequacies, Congress should rethink the legislation to permit more explicit balancing. Proposed amendments to various risk regulation agencies' legislation that require benefit-cost analysis represent sensitivity to that issue. Broader legislation requiring benefit-cost analysis and overriding legislative mandates could address those inadequacies for all agencies. Why should society not pursue only regulations that are in our best interests? That is all a benefit-cost test would require.

Finally, focusing only on risk reduction achieved by a policy makes little sense. The "conservative" approach to risk reduction has, in effect, generated more increases than decreases in risk. The extremely high costs per life saved often endanger more lives and impose much greater mortality costs than if we are not to undertake those efforts at all. The unbounded commitment to saving statistical lives not only is fiscally irresponsible but also endangers the health of the citizens whom the government is intending to protect.

NOTES

1. See Ames, Magaw, and Gold (1987) for a review of a variety of natural and synthetic carcinogens to which we are exposed.
2. Indeed, that is still not the case, as those who drive south on the Pacific Coast Highway (Route 1) in California—along the edge of the cliff overlooking the Pacific Ocean—can attest.
3. In particular, the elasticity of the implicit value of job injuries with respect to income is one. See Viscusi and Evans (1990).
4. *Industrial Union Department, AFL-CIO v. American Petroleum Institute*, 448 U.S. 607 (1980).
5. Section 26 of the Occupational Safety and Health Act of 1970, 29 U.S.C. §651(1976).
6. See the decision of the Supreme Court in *Industrial Union Department, AFL-CIO v. American Petroleum Institute*, 448 U.S. 607 (1980).
7. Although the ban did not apply to the asbestos-containing putty that the Fuller-O'Brien Company supplied to Morton Thiokol, the manufacturer chose to discontinue producing the putty, which represented only 1 percent of sales, to limit legal liability. Morton Thiokol bought the patent rights to the putty but could find no manufacturer willing to produce it. Finally, Morton Thiokol contracted with Randolph Products Company, which made putty for jet engines, to produce a substitute putty that also contained asbestos but had a different composition. Before the *Challenger* fire, engineers noticed that the substitute putty charred, and referred to Fuller-O'Brien's putty as "lucky putty" (Bennett 1991).

REFERENCES

Ames, Bruce N., R. Magaw, and Lois S. Gold. "Ranking Possible Carcinogenic Hazards." *Science* 236 (1987): 271.

Anderson, Katherine H., and Richard Burkhauser. "The Retirement-Health Nexus: A New Measurement of an Old Puzzle." *Journal of Human Resources* 20 (1985): 315–30.

Arnould, R., and Nichols, L. M. "Wage-Risk Premiums and Worker's Compensation: A Refinement of Estimates of Compensating Wage Differentials." *Journal of Political Economy* 91 (1983): 332–40.

Atkinson, S. E., and R. Halvorsen. "The Valuation of Risks to Life: Evidence from the Market for Automobiles." *Review of Economics and Statistics* 72 (1990): 133–36.

Bennett, Michael J. *The Asbestos Racket: An Environmental Parable.* Bellevue, Wash.: Free Enterprise Press, 1991.

Blomquist, G. "Value of Life Saving: Implications of Consumption Activity." *Journal of Political Economy* 96 (1979): 675–700.

Brown, C. "Equalizing Differences in the Labor Market." *Quarterly Journal of Economics* 94 (1980): 113–34.

Butler, R. J. "Wage and Injury Rate Responses to Shifting Levels of Workers' Compensation," in John D. Worrall, ed., *Safety and the Work Force.* Ithaca, N.Y.: ILR Press, 1983.

Chapman, Kenneth S., and Govind Hariharan. "Controlling for Causality in the Link from Income to Mortality." *Journal of Risk and Uncertainty* 8 (1994): 85–94.

Cousineau, J., R. Lacroix, and A. Girard. "Occupational Hazard and Wage Compensating Differentials." University of Montreal Working Paper, 1988.

Dardis, R. "The Value of Life: New Evidence from the Marketplace." *American Economic Review* 70 (1980): 1077–82.

Dillingham, A. "The Influence of Risk Variable Definition of Value on Life Estimates." *Economic Inquiry* 24 (1985): 277–94.

Dreyfus, Mark, and W. Kip Viscusi. "Rates of Time Preference and Consumer Valuations of Automobile Safety and Fuel Efficiency." *Journal of Law and Economics* 38 (1995).

Duleep, Harriet Orcutt. "Measuring the Effect of Income on Adult Mortality Using Longitudinal Administrative Record Data." *Journal of Human Resources* 20 (1986): 238–51.

Garbacz, C. "Smoke Detector Effectiveness and the Value of Saving a Life." *Economics Letters* 31 (1989): 281–86.

Garen, J. "Compensating Wage Differentials and the Endogeneity of Job Riskiness." *Review of Economics and Statistics* 70 (1988): 9–16.

Ghosh, D., D. Lees, and W. Seal. "Optimal Motorway Speed and Some Valuations of Time and Life." *Manchester School of Economic and Social Studies* 43 (1975): 134–43.

Hadley, J., and A. Osei. "Does Income Affect Mortality? An Analysis of the Effects of Different Types of Income on Age/Sex/Race-Specific Mortality Rates in the United States." *Medical Care* 20 (1982): 901–14.

Hersch, Joni, and W. Kip Viscusi. "Cigarette Smoking, Seatbelt Use, and Differences in Wage-Risk Trade-Offs." *Journal of Human Resources* 25 (1990): 202–27.

Herzog, H. W., Jr., and A. M. Schlottmann. "Valuing Risk in the Workplace: Market Price, Willingness to Pay, and the Optimal Provision of Safety." University of Tennessee Working Paper, 1987.

Ippolito, Pauline M., and R. A. Ippolito "Measuring the Value of Life Saving from Consumer Reactions to New Information." *Journal of Public Economics* 25 (1984): 53–81.

Jones-Lee, M. W. *The Economics of Safety and Physical Risk.* Oxford: Basil Blackwell, 1976.

Keeney, Ralph L. "Mortality Risks Induced by Economic Expenditures." *Risk Analysis* 10 (1990): 147–59.

Kitagawa, Evelyn M., and Philip M. Hauser. *Differential Mortality in the United States: A Study in Socioeconomic Epidemiology.* Cambridge: Harvard University Press, 1973.

Kniesner, Thomas J., and John D. Leeth. "Compensating Wage Differentials for Fatal Injury Risk in Australia, Japan, and the United States." *Journal of Risk and Uncertainty* 4 (1991): 75–90.

Lave, Lester B. "Health and Safety Risks Analyses: Information for Better Decisions." *Science* 236 (1987): 291–95.

Leigh, J. P. "Gender, Firm Size, Industry and Estimates of the Value-of-Life." *Journal of Health Economics* 6 (1987): 255–73.

———, and R. N. Folsom. "Estimates of the Value of Accident Avoidance at the Job Depend on Concavity of the Equalizing Differences Curve." *Quarterly Review of Economics and Business* 24 (1984): 56–66.

Lutter, Randall, and John F. Morrall III. "Health-Health Analysis: A New Way to Evaluate Health and Safety Regulation." *Journal of Risk and Uncertainty* 8 (1993): 43–66.

Marin, A., and G. Psacharopoulos. "The Reward for Risk in the Labor Market: Evidence from the United Kingdom and a Reconciliation with Other Studies." *Journal of Political Economy* 90 (1982): 827–53.

Moore, M. J., and W. K. Viscusi. *Compensating Mechanisms for Job Risks: Wages, Workers' Compensation, and Product Liability.* Princeton: Princeton University Press, 1990a.

———. "Discounting Environmental Health Risks: New Evidence and Policy Implications." *Journal of Environmental Economics and Management* 18 (1990b): S51–S62.

———. "Doubling the Estimated Value of Life: Results Using New Occupational Fatality Data." *Journal of Policy Analysis and Management* 7 (1988a): 476–90.

———. "The Quantity-Adjusted Value of Life." *Economic Inquiry* 26 (1988b): 369–88.

Morrall, John F., III. "A Review of the Record." *Regulation* (November/December 1986): 25–34.

Occupational Safety and Health Administration. "Indoor Air Quality." *Federal Register* 59 (April 5, 1994): 15968–6039.

Olson, C. A. "An Analysis of Wage Differentials Received by Workers on Dangerous Jobs." *Journal of Human Resources* 16 (1981): 167–85.

Portney, Paul R. "Housing Prices, Health Effects, and Valuing Reductions in Risk of Death." *Journal of Environmental Economics and Management* 8 (1981): 72–78.

Smith, R. S. "The Feasibility of an 'Injury Tax' Approach to Occupational Safety." *Law and Contemporary Problems* 38 (1974): 730–44.

———. *The Occupational Safety and Health Act: Its Goals and Achievements.* Washington, D.C.: American Enterprise Institute, 1976.

Smith, V. Kerry, and C. Gilbert. "The Implicit Risks to Life: A Comparative Analysis." *Economics Letters* 16 (1984): 393–99.

Thaler, R., and Sherwin Rosen. "The Value of Saving a Life: Evidence from the Labor Market," in Nestor Terleckyz, ed., *Household Production and Consumption.* New York: Columbia University Press, 1976.

U.S. Joint Economic Committee. *Estimating the Effects of Economic Change on National Health and Social Well-Being.* Study prepared by M. Harvey Brenner, Congress of the United States. Washington, D.C.: Government Printing Office, 1984.

Viscusi, W. Kip. *Employment Hazards: An Investigation of Market Performance.* Harvard Economic Studies No. 148. Cambridge: Harvard University Press, 1979.

———. *Fatal Tradeoffs: Public and Private Responsibilities for Risk.* New York: Oxford University Press, 1992.

———. "Labor Market Valuations of Life and Limb: Empirical Estimates and Policy Implications." *Public Policy* 26 (1978): 359–86.

———. "Mortality Effects of Regulatory Costs and Policy Evaluation Criteria." *RAND Journal of Economics* 25 (1994): 94–109.

———. "Occupational Safety and Health Regulation: Its Impact and Policy Alternatives," in J. Crecine, ed., *Research in Public Policy Analysis and Management* 2. Greenwich, Conn.: JAI Press, 1981.

———. *Risk by Choice: Regulating Health and Safety in the Workplace.* Cambridge: Harvard University Press, 1983.

———. "The Value of Risks to Life and Health." *Journal of Economic Literature* 31 (1993): 1912–46.

———, and William Evans. "Utility Functions That Depend on Health Status: Estimates and Economic Implications." *American Economic Review* 80 (1990): 353–74.

Viscusi, W. Kip, and Michael J. Moore. "Rates of Time Preference and Valuations of the Duration of Life." *Journal of Public Economics* 38 (1989): 297–317.

Viscusi, W. Kip, and Charles O'Connor. "Adaptive Responses to Chemical Labeling: Are Workers Bayesian Decision Makers?" *American Economic Review* 74 (1984): 942–56.

Viscusi, W. Kip, and Richard J. Zeckhauser. "The Fatality and Injury Costs of Expenditure." *Journal of Risk and Uncertainty* 8 (1994): 271–93.

Chapter 8

THE OPPORTUNITY COSTS OF HAPHAZARD SOCIAL INVESTMENTS IN LIFE-SAVING

Tammy O. Tengs and John D. Graham

OVERVIEW

Numerous authors and studies have concluded that our current "portfolio" of social investments in life-saving appears haphazard (Graham and Vaupel 1981; Morrall 1986; Zeckhauser and Viscusi 1990). To regulate the flammability of children's clothing, for example, we spend $1.5 million per year of life saved, while some 30 percent of those children live in homes without smoke alarms, an investment that costs about $200,000 per year of life saved.

Physicians don gloves and masks and follow "universal precautions" to protect themselves against HIV and other diseases at a cost of $2.4 million per year of life saved, but those same physicians often fail to take the time to advise their patients to stop smoking, an intervention that, even taking into account poor compliance, costs only $6,000 per year of life saved. We regulate potentially carcinogenic benzene emissions during waste operations at a cost of $19 million per year of life saved, while 70 percent of women over age fifty do not receive regular mammograms, an intervention that costs roughly $17,000 per year of life saved.

That pattern of resource allocation is important because all investments, including investments in survival, carry some opportunity cost. That is, when we spend resources on interventions that save lives at high cost, we forgo the opportunity to spend those same resources on interventions that save lives at low cost. This means that we save fewer lives than we might, at greater expense than necessary.

But how can all those losses be quantified? In this chapter we develop a new methodology for doing so and reach some striking conclusions. The primary purpose of this chapter is to assess the opportunity costs of our present pattern of social investments in life-saving. Opportunity costs are expressed as the financial loss as well as the loss of human life resulting from apparent inefficiencies.

We begin by describing our efforts to collect data on the costs and effectiveness of hundreds of interventions designed to avert premature death. Next, we estimate the annual resources currently consumed by those interventions, as well as the annual survival benefits they produce. Then, we determine the "optimal" portfolio of life-saving investments and calculate the additional survival benefits or cost savings that such a portfolio would provide. The results are impressive: the investments could be at least twice as effective as they are.

Finally, we conclude with some suggestions on how to improve the allocation of scarce life-saving resources. Even though the methodology is not perfect—none could be—the conclusion is inescapable that our regulatory and other investments in life-saving could and should be far better directed.

Data Collection and Refinement

To identify information on the cost and effectiveness of life-saving interventions, we performed a comprehensive search for publicly available economic analyses. We defined a "life-saving intervention" as any behavioral or technological strategy that reduces the probability of premature death among a specified target population.

Two trained reviewers (from a total of eleven) read each document. Each reviewer recorded fifty-two items, including the nature of the life-saving intervention, the base-case intervention with which it was compared, the target population, the resources consumed by the intervention, total lives saved, total life-years saved, cost per life saved, and cost per life-year saved. The two reviewers worked independently, then met and came to a consensus on the content of the document.

To increase the comparability of cost-effectiveness estimates drawn from different economic analyses, we established nine definitional goals. When an estimate failed to comply with a goal, reviewers attempted to revise the estimate to improve compliance. The first definitional goal is that cost-effectiveness estimates should be in the form of "cost per year of life saved." Estimates of the cost per life saved should be transformed to cost per life-year by considering the average number of years of life saved when a premature death is averted.

Second, costs and effectiveness should be evaluated from the social perspective. Third, costs should be "direct." Indirect costs, such as forgone earnings, should be excluded. Fourth, costs and effectiveness should be "net." Any resource savings or mortality risks induced by the intervention should be subtracted out.

The fifth goal is that costs, lives, and life-years saved should all be discounted to their present value at a rate of 5 percent. Sixth, cost-effectiveness ratios should be marginal or "incremental." Both costs and effectiveness should be evaluated with respect to a well-defined baseline alternative. Seventh, costs should be expressed in 1993 dollars using the general consumer price index.

Our eighth goal is that total costs, total lives saved, and total life-years saved should be annual, annualized over a meaningful time horizon suggested by the author of the economic analysis or annualized over a ten-year time horizon if no time horizon was suggested. Costs, lives, and life-years should reflect the total consequences of implementing the intervention nationwide.

Finally, total costs, total lives saved, and total life-years saved should be measured with respect to the "do nothing" alternative that involves no additional expenditure and results in no additional survival benefits relative to the status quo.

Although the full data set contains cost-effectiveness estimates for 587 interventions (Tengs et al. 1995), *national* cost and effectiveness estimates were available for only 185 of those interventions. For the others, the original authors reported estimates for single individuals, fixed cohorts, or specific geographical areas. Even the national estimates were often not immediately comparable. They were typically reported as some combination of the following: one-time, cumulative, annualized, or annual. To ensure that the published estimates were scaled in the same way, they were reexpressed in constant annual units using standard methods.

For each intervention, we supplemented cost-effectiveness data with two measures of the degree to which that intervention was implemented. For the subset of interventions where a "go/no-go" decision was made (for example, laws, regulations, or uniform building codes), we collected binary data on the implementation decision (B_{ijk}). Because some degree of implementation can exist even in the presence of a "no-go" decision or can be absent even with a "go" decision, however, we also collected data on "percent implementation" (P_{ijk}). We defined that measure as "the percent of people in the target population who received the life-saving intervention as of 1992."

To gather data on percent implementation, we elicited independent estimates from two experts. For example, we contacted two experts in cervical cancer to estimate the percentage of women over age twenty who receive annual cervical cancer screening, two experts in school bus safety to estimate the percentage of school buses that have passenger seat belts, and two experts in radiology to estimate the percentage of radiologists who wear protective leaded gloves. Where appropriate, experts also provided binary information on implementation decisions. When experts' estimates of percent implementation differed by ten percentage points or less, we averaged them. When their estimates differed by more than ten percentage points, the estimate that appeared to be the most valid was used.

Model of Life-Saving Investments

To estimate the total annual resource consumption associated with current life-saving investments, we multiplied the annual cost (C_{ijk}) of intervention ijk by its percent implementation (P_{ijk}) and summed the products over all interventions:

$$\sum_{i=1}^{I} \sum_{j=1}^{J} \sum_{k=1}^{K} C_{ijk} P_{ijk}. \tag{1}$$

To estimate the lives that are currently being saved, we multiplied the annual lives saved for each intervention (L_{ijk}) by percent implementation (P_{ijk}) and summed those products as well:

$$\sum_{i=1}^{I} \sum_{j=1}^{J} \sum_{k=1}^{K} L_{ijk} P_{ijk}. \tag{2}$$

This method of estimating the resources that are currently being consumed and the lives that are currently being saved assumes that costs and benefits are proportional to implementation. That is, if 50 percent of the target population receives the intervention, then we assume that 50 percent of the total resources are consumed and that 50 percent of the survival benefits are achieved. In reality, the relationships might be nonlinear (for example, the first 50 percent of implementation might result in 70 percent of the resource consumption and 30 percent of the life-saving). Thus, this method of estimation should be thought of as yielding approximate results.

We can estimate the *average* cost per life saved associated with our current portfolio of investments as the annual expenditures calculated with equation (1), divided by annual lives saved calculated with equation (2). The *marginal* cost-effectiveness of our current investments is impossible to estimate because we do not adhere to a single threshold. Some cost-*in*effective interventions are fully implemented while other more cost-effective interventions are not.

To assess opportunity costs, we performed two hypothetical reallocations. In the first reallocation we constrained costs to remain less than or equal to the amount determined with equation (1) in the descriptive model and maximized the number of lives saved. In appendix 8-A we define the variables. The linear programming model for this constrained optimization appears in appendix 8-B. We recorded the shadow price of the budgetary constraint and took the reciprocal of that shadow price as the marginal cost per life saved of the last

> **Some cost-*in*effective interventions are fully implemented while other more cost-effective interventions are not.**

intervention funded. To calculate the average cost per life saved associated with that "optimal" portfolio, we divided annual costs by the maximum number of lives saved.

In the second reallocation we constrained lives saved to be greater than or equal to the value assessed with equation (2) in the descriptive model and performed a cost minimization. We took the shadow price of the lives saved constraint to be equivalent to the marginal cost per life saved for the last intervention funded. To calculate the average cost per life saved associated with that portfolio, we divided the minimum annual costs by the descriptive value for lives saved.

We then performed the same two experiments substituting life-years saved for lives saved as the measure of effectiveness. In addition to the single-constraint models described above, we performed several more hypothetical reallocations with multiple constraints to ensure that resources remained within a specified sector. We describe those models in more detail later.

We can express the opportunity costs of our present pattern of investments in terms of additional expenditures, the loss of lives, or the loss of years of life. We define the monetary opportunity cost of our present pattern of investments as the difference between the resources consumed under the descriptive model and the smaller amount of resources that would be consumed under a model where costs are minimized while life-saving benefits remain constant. We define the human opportunity cost of our present pattern of investments as the difference between the lives (or life-years) saved under the descriptive model, and the larger number of lives (life-years) that could be saved under a model that maximizes survival while expenditures remain constant.

Results

In figure 8-1 we find no apparent relationship between the cost-effectiveness of the 185 life-saving interventions and their implementation. The annual resources consumed by those interventions total approximately $21.4 billion. For such a sum, we avert approximately 56,700[1] premature deaths and save 592,000 years of life annually. On average, we spend about $376,000 per life or $36,100 per year of life saved. Below we describe the opportunity costs of that pattern of investment.

First, we consider the question, How many lives could we save if we were to spend the same amount of money but invest it in those interventions that, taken together, would save the greatest number of lives possible? Results indicate that if we hold investments constant at $21.4 billion and make funding decisions so as to maximize lives saved, we could save a total of 117,000 lives annually. That represents an additional 60,200 lives saved, or about twice as many lives saved relative to the status quo. To accomplish those gains, we could simply invest in all interventions costing less than the marginal cost per life value of $7.57 million and in none of the interventions costing more than $7.57 million. On average, we would spend $183,000 per life saved.

By maximizing "lives saved," we are treating all premature deaths as equally undesirable, regardless of when they occur. Suppose that we instead took into account the age of death and considered the years of

Figure 8-1   Implementation of Life-Saving Interventions as a Function of Cost-Effectiveness

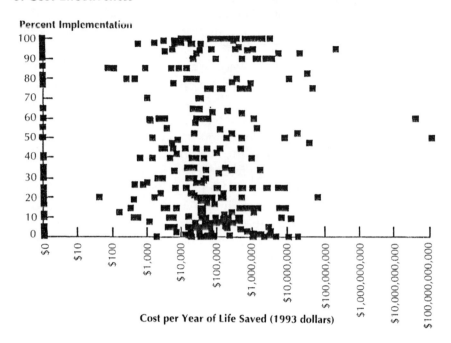

Percent Implementation

Cost per Year of Life Saved (1993 dollars)

life that are saved when a premature death is averted. To do this, we substitute "years of life saved" as our measure of survival gains, so that when we avert the death of a forty-year-old who would have lived to age seventy-seven, we save approximately thirty-seven years of life. Here, results indicate that for $21.4 billion we could save 1,230,000 years of life annually. That represents an additional 636,000 life-years over the status quo, and we could achieve that result by investing in all interventions costing less than $607,000 per year of life saved. On average, we would spend $17,400 per year of life saved.

Next, we consider the question, How little could we spend while still maintaining our present level of survival benefits? Results indicate that if we hold life-years saved constant at 592,000 or lives saved constant at 56,700 and make funding decisions so as to minimize expenditures, we could save about $31.1 billion over the status quo. In fact, because there are many untapped investment opportunities that save both lives and money, the result would be a net monetary savings. That is, not only would we save the $21.4 billion that we are currently spending, but another $10 billion—all while maintaining our present level of survival benefits. We could achieve that result by simply investing in all interventions costing less than $16,500 per life or $565 per life-year saved.

Figure 8-2 shows the number of years of life that could be gained for varying levels of annual investment. Notice that the first few interventions that we might fund actually save more resources than they cost, so that the curve begins in the quadrant where negative costs and positive survival benefits occur. The slope of that piece-wise linear function at any point is the marginal cost per life-year saved.

Figure 8-2 also plots our present level of investment in life-saving. That point is at approximately $21.4 billion for 592,000 life-years. The length of the line-segment stretching vertically from that point to the curve represents the human opportunity costs of such a pattern of investments, or 636,000 life-years. The length of the line-segment stretching horizontally from that point to the curve represents the monetary opportunity costs of that pattern of investments, or $31.1 billion.

In the thought experiment described above, we implicitly assumed that resources could simply be reallocated from one intervention to another. For example, we assumed that if a current Occupational Safety and Health Administration rule were lifted, we could somehow reinvest the social resources consumed by that rule to immunize children or to improve safety features in automobiles. Since we can challenge that assumption as being somewhat unrealistic, we now consider the question, What survival and resource gains are possible if resources *cannot* be transferred across sectors?

To consider that question, we first classified all life-saving interventions into three sectors—injury reduction, medicine, and toxin control—and assumed that resources that are currently being consumed within each sector must continue to be consumed within that same sector. Thus, resources currently consumed by heart transplants could be reinvested in prenatal care, but not in air bags in cars or pollution control equipment for industry. To perform that hypothetical reallocation, we added constraints to the original linear programming models.

When we hold resources in each sector constant and make funding decisions to maximize life-years saved, results indicate that we can save a total of 1,190,000 life-years each year. That represents an additional 595,000 life-years saved over the status quo and is nearly equiv-

Figure 8-2   Total Annual Life-Years Saved as a Function of Total Annual Resources Expended (n=185)

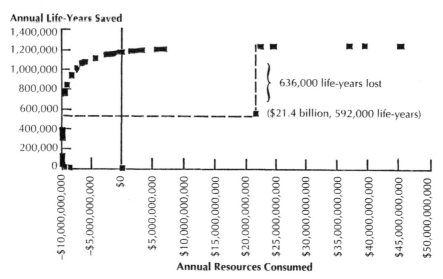

Annual Resources Consumed

alent to the years of life that might be saved if resources could flow across sectors. To accomplish that we would fund only those injury-reduction interventions costing less than $2,610,000 per life-year, medical interventions costing less than $7,550 per life-year, and toxin control interventions costing less than $607,000 per life-year.

If we instead held constant life-years saved in each sector and made funding decisions so as to minimize expenditures, we could save about $29.2 billion over the status quo—nearly the same amount saved in the original model. The marginal cost per life-year would be $5,400 within the injury reduction sector, $869 for medical interventions, and $55,000 for toxin control. Again, on average, we would save rather than spend resources.

Next we consider only the 134 interventions that one of five government agencies—the Consumer Product Safety Commission, the Environmental Protection Agency, the Federal Aviation Administration, the National Highway Traffic Safety Administration, and the Occupational Safety and Health Administration—proposed. To analyze those interventions, we substituted binary implementation (B_{ijk}) for percent implementation (P_{ijk}) so as to model regulatory decision making. Those

134 agency rules consume about $4.11 billion annually and save 94,000 life-years. On average, interventions resulting from those regulations cost $44,000 per life-year saved.

If we hold investments constant at $4.11 billion and make funding decisions so as to maximize life-years saved, we could save a total of 211,000 life-years each year. That represents an additional 117,000 life-years saved over the status quo, and at the margin we would be spending $110,000 per life-year saved. On average, we would spend $19,500 per life-year saved.

If we instead held life-years saved constant at 94,000 and made funding decisions so as to minimize expenditures, we could save about $4.76 billion over the status quo. On average, we would save rather than spend money.

As before, the above analysis assumes that the savings associated with forgoing an EPA regulation would somehow be available to ensure the safety of a product regulated by the CPSC. Because that is a questionable assumption, we now constrain the resource consumption resulting from regulations associated with each agency so that, for example, the resources currently consumed owing to EPA regulation remain constant, as do the resources currently consumed owing to CPSC regulation.

> **Retaining our present pattern of investments in the 185 life-saving interventions considered here results in the loss of $31.1 billion, 636,000 life-years, or 60,200 lives every year. That is, we could more than double the life-saving potential of our current investments.**

With those added constraints, we find that we could save a total of 180,000 life-years each year. That represents an additional 86,300 life-years saved over the status quo and about as many years of life that might be saved if resources could in fact flow without regard to agency boundaries. The marginal cost per life-year saved would be $1,510,000 for CPSC regulations, $35,200 for EPA regulations, $45,700 for FAA regulations, $11,300 for NHTSA regulations, and $497,000 for OSHA regulations. On average, we would spend $23,800 per life-year saved. Thus, even if each agency had consistently used those differing decision thresholds, the result would be $4.11 billion in resource consumption and 180,000 life-years saved.

If we instead held constant life-years saved for each agency and made funding decisions so as to minimize expenditures, we would spend about $926 million. That represents a savings of about $3.19 billion over the status quo. The marginal cost per life-year saved would be $30,000 for the CPSC, $35,200 for the EPA, $45,700 for the FAA, less than $0 for NHTSA, and $347,000 for OSHA. On average, we would spend $9,850 per life-year saved.

Discussion

This analysis demonstrates that retaining our present pattern of investments in the 185 life-saving interventions considered here results in the loss of $31.1 billion, 636,000 life-years, or 60,200 lives every year. That is, we could more than double the life-saving potential of our current investments. Alternatively, we could maintain our present level of risk reduction and, in addition, save money.

It is important to realize, however, that our analysis has certain limitations. For example, the life-saving interventions comprising our data set do not represent a random sample of all life-saving interventions. We included interventions because information on total costs and total survival benefits was readily available in the economics literature. In addition, our analysis ignores the important controversies and uncertainties about the cost consequences and survival benefits of some interventions. Further, our mathematical methods assume that noncompeting life-saving interventions are independent of one another, so that implementing one intervention has no effect on the costs and survival benefits of the other interventions. In addition, as discussed previously, our method of estimating current annual expenditures and current annual survival benefits assumes linearity.

Further, we calculate opportunity costs for only two scenarios: the scenario in which current resource consumption is held constant and the scenario in which current survival benefits are held constant. In reality, any point on the efficient frontier pictured in figure 8-2 would represent an efficient portfolio of investments that simultaneously maximized survival benefits for a given level of resources expended and minimized resource expenditures for a given level of survival benefits.

So where should we be on the efficient frontier? That decision must be constrained by the resources available and should reflect the value we place on small improvements in survival. Viscusi (1993) notes that even if we expended our entire gross national product on minimizing risk, we could only spend an average of $55 million per fatality averted and would have nothing left over for roads, or schools, or any of the other things that we value. He further notes that most studies imputing the value of a life from wage-risk trade-offs arrive at estimates in the range of $3 million to $7 million dollars. Reexpressed in terms of years of life saved, that translates into a few hundred thousand dollars per life-year. In figure 8-2 the slope of the efficient frontier where the vertical segment touches the curve is $7.57 million per life saved, or $607,000 per year of life saved. Thus, the optimal point reflecting our willingness to pay for survival benefits is probably slightly to the left of that point. This suggests that, rather than investing $21.4 billion in the 185 interventions considered here, we should invest somewhat less. If we invested some smaller amount but did so wisely, the outcome would be cost savings, survival benefits, and improvements in the trade-off between investments in survival and investments in all other goods, relative to the status quo.

How can policy makers make decisions so that we might save more lives at less expense? The good news is that fancy mathematical programming techniques are not needed to achieve the optimal portfolio. The following rule of thumb, elegant in its simplicity, will achieve the same results: Invest in all interventions costing less than some threshold (for example, $5 million per life saved) and in none of the interventions costing more.

Putting that rule into practice is the hard part, requiring knowledge, bravery, and restraint. First, note that employing such a decision rule means that public health decision makers must abandon old ways of thinking. For example, the common inclination to invest resources in the most worrisome health problems, the problems affecting the most people, or the most effective solutions will not maximize health gains, given limited resources. Public health decision makers must be retrained to consider the "bang for the buck," not just the "bang." Graduate schools of public health and public policy must teach students that to maximize health gains they cannot consider only health gains. They must also consider cost. Further, they must be taught that by bravely saying "no" to public health interventions that represent poor investments, society will likely be rewarded by even bigger health gains elsewhere in the economy.

Managed care organizations and insurers are already implementing this rule of thumb. Some hospitals, for example, substitute drugs with more attractive cost-effectiveness ratios into their pharmaceutical formulary. More could be done, however. Physicians could be encouraged and trained to counsel all patients to stop smoking—an intervention with very favorable cost-effectiveness characteristics for all types of smokers.

Another way to implement that rule of thumb would be to require regulatory agencies to adhere to the same cost-effectiveness threshold. If we passed all the regulations with cost-effectiveness ratios less than some threshold and none of the regulations with cost-effectiveness ratios exceeding that threshold, our results demonstrate that we could double the life-saving potential of our regulations. The current regulatory reform effort requiring that cost-benefit analysis be performed for rules costing more than $50 million and that the benefits of

> **Our analysis suggests that we pay a large price for our current haphazard pattern of social investments in life-saving.**

regulations justify their costs is an important positive step in that direction. Note that in those cases where the benefits of regulations are limited to improvements in survival, the language "benefits must justify the costs" is consistent with the decision rule of using a single cost-effectiveness decision threshold for all agencies.

The previous discussion assumes that the interventions described here save lives and cost money—but nothing more. In reality, most interventions that reduce fatal injuries also reduce nonfatal injuries. Environmental regulations save lives, but they also protect the ecosystem. Public health and medical interventions improve survival, but they also reduce the morbidity associated with illness. Further, some interventions such as speed limits or helmet laws have disadvantages, such as reducing personal freedom. In addition, we may wish to value lives differently by assigning a higher value to identifiable lives than to unidentifiable statistical lives, for example, or by preferring to reduce risks imposed on us without our knowledge or consent over risks we assume voluntarily. To the extent that we value those other concerns, we should be willing to give up some survival or economic resources in return for those values. Thus, we may not even want to be on the efficient frontier pictured in figure 8-2, in which we make investment decisions based only on cost and survival outcomes.

On the other hand, our present pattern of investment also clearly fails to make optimal trade-offs among those variables. Even taking those other factors into account, it is hard to defend the regulation of some toxins at a cost of billions of dollars per life saved while children go without immunizations and women cannot afford good prenatal care. Our analysis suggests that we pay a large price for our current haphazard pattern of social investments in life-saving. Policy makers would be well advised to examine whether the benefits obtained from our current life-saving investment portfolio are worth the cost and loss of human life.

Appendix 8-A: Definition of Variables

The variables in our model of life-saving investments are as follows:

L_{ijk} represents total lives saved annually if intervention ijk is fully implemented.

C_{ijk} is total cost (resources consumed) if intervention ijk is fully implemented.

B_{ijk} represents the binary implementation of intervention ijk. For those interventions where there was a "go/no-go" decision, this variable takes on the value zero if the decision was "no-go" and the value one if the decision was "go."

P_{ijk} is the percent implementation of intervention ijk. It is defined as the percentage of the target population members who received life-saving intervention ijk and is scaled between zero and one in the model.

D_{ijk} is the decision variable. It is set to zero if the optimal decision is to not implement program ijk or to one if the optimal decision is to implement program ijk. We assume infinite divisibility, so the decision variable could take on values between zero and one.

i is the group. This is any collection of life-saving interventions that form a natural category. Category definitions change depending on the research question that is being posed. For example, a group might be the type of intervention (1 = injury reduction, 2 = medicine, 3 = toxin control) or a group might be the governmental agency responsible for the intervention (1 = CPSC, 2 = EPA, 3 = FAA).

j is the competing cluster. Programs belonging to the same competing cluster "compete" with one another in the sense that they all reduce risks to members of the same target population, and a particular target population member would receive only one intervention in a cluster.

k is the program, the specific life-saving intervention.

I denotes the total number of groups.

J represents the total number of competing clusters in a particular group.

K is the total number of interventions in a particular competing cluster.

Appendix 8-B: Linear Programming Model to Maximize Annual Lives Saved Subject to a Constraint on Annual Resource Consumption

Maximize

$$\sum_{i=1}^{I} \sum_{j=1}^{J} \sum_{k=1}^{K} L_{ijk} \, D_{ijk} = Z$$

subject to

$$\sum_{i=1}^{I} \sum_{j=1}^{J} \sum_{k=1}^{K} C_{ijk} \, D_{ijk} \leq \sum_{i=1}^{I} \sum_{j=1}^{J} \sum_{k=1}^{K} C_{ijk} \, P_{ijk}$$

$$\sum_{k=1}^{K} D_{ijk} \leq 1 \; \forall i,j$$

$$D_{ijk} \geq 0 \; \forall i,j,k.$$

NOTES

This work was conducted at the Harvard Center for Risk Analysis and supported by research grant SES-9110225 from the National Science Foundation (Drs. Tengs and Graham), Medical Informatics Training Grant number 1T15LM07092 from the National Library of Medicine (Dr. Tengs), a predoctoral fellowship from the Merck Foundation (Dr. Tengs), and unrestricted funds from the Harvard Center for Risk Analysis (Drs. Tengs and Graham).

We wish to thank our colleagues on the Lifesaving Team including Miriam Adams, Amy Bensen, Paul Eisenstadt, Dana Gelb Safran, David Paltiel, Joseph Pliskin, Laura Rose, Joanna Siegel, Milton Weinstein, and Alex Zaleski. For their efforts in searching the literature we thank Michael Kamat, Kayla Laserson, Lori Leonard, Adil Najam, Francine Wiest, and Karen Worthington. For gathering data on the level of implementation, we thank Brian Ash, Nancy Beaulieu, Sherri-Ann Burnett, Heidi Hoffman, and Cynthia Lopez. In addition, Deborah Servi provided able management of the project database. Richard Zeckhauser made helpful suggestions.

1.   All estimates are rounded to three significant figures to stress their approximate
nature.

REFERENCES

Graham, John D., and J. Vaupel. "Value of a Life: What Difference Does It Make?"
Risk Analysis 1 (1981): 692–704.
Morrall, John F., III. "A Review of the Record." *Regulation* (November/December
1986): 25–34.
Tengs, Tammy O., Miriam E. Adams, Joseph S. Pliskin, Dana Gelb-Safran, Joanna E.
Siegel, Michael C. Weinstein, and John D. Graham. "Five-Hundred Life-Saving
Interventions and Their Cost-Effectiveness." *Risk Analysis* 15 (1995): 369–90.
Viscusi, W. Kip. "The Value of Risks to Life and Health." *Journal of Economic Litera-
ture* 31 (1993): 1912–46.
Zeckhauser, Richard, and D. Shepard. "Where Now for Saving Lives?" *Law and Con-
temporary Problems* 40 (1976): 5–45.

Chapter 9

MAKING SENSE OF RISK
An Agenda for Congress
John D. Graham

OVERVIEW

The American people are suffering from what can be called "a syn-drome of paranoia and neglect" about potential dangers to their health, safety, and the environment. This leads to a paradox that is becoming increasingly recognized. Large amounts of resources are devoted to slight or speculative dangers while substantial and well-documented dangers remain unaddressed.

Congress can take a modest step toward curing that syndrome by embracing a risk-analysis approach to public decision making. Omnibus legislation covering federal agencies should include

- requirements for responsible quantitative risk assessment before making protective decisions
- periodic risk rankings for setting priorities on the basis of science and citizen preferences
- public reporting of estimated risks, costs, and benefits of new rulemakings
- external peer review of analyses to enhance quality and credibility
- a presumptive burden that costs are reasonably related to benefits (without insisting on full-scale quantification, monetization, and positive net benefits)
- the opportunity for affected citizens to seek judicial review in the event that agencies do not use the risk-analysis framework.

Such omnibus legislation, applying to the entire regulatory process, would greatly improve outcomes, but it must be crafted carefully. This chapter outlines components of such legislation.

To avoid "paralysis of analysis," Congress should authorize agencies to tailor the intensity of analysis to the importance and complexity of the specific problems. Congress should provide adequate budgetary and technical resources for agencies to discharge their analytical functions.

Statement of the Problem

Each day Americans are confronted with new information about potential dangers to their health and safety: childhood cancer from exposure to electric and magnetic fields, male infertility from exposure to chlorinated chemicals, brain cancer from using cellular telephones, subtle neurologic effects in children from ingesting small amounts of lead in house dust, premature death from inhaling fine particles in urban air, heart disease from ingesting margarine and other sources of transfatty acid, and non-Hodgkin's lymphoma from exposure to phenoxy herbicides on the farm.

Although most objective indicators suggest that America's burden of mortality and morbidity risk is steadily declining (Department of Health and Human Services annual), citizens are confused about the growing number of hazards in daily life reported in the media that appear to have some degree of scientific support (Singer and Endreny 1993). Misperception of risk may be widespread. For example, a majority of Americans perceive that "things in the environment" are *at least as important* as "personal habits" in causing sickness and poor health (Dunlap 1991). Yet the best available scientific data indicate that personal habits are a much more important cause of poor health than environmental agents (McGinnis and Foege 1993).

The public's general reaction to health, safety, and environmental dangers may best be described as a syndrome of paranoia and neglect. We are paranoid in the sense that we devote large amounts of resources and attention to alleged dangers that are speculative (at best) and probably small (or even nonexistent). Examples of "overblown" hazards include soil and groundwater contamination at many abandoned hazardous waste sites (Environmental Protection Agency 1990; National Research Council 1991a), the pesticide residues on fruits and vegetables purchased in grocery stores (Ames 1992; Archibald and Winter 1990), the benzene in the ambient air of urban and rural communities (Graham 1993), and the residual chloroform found in drinking water after disinfection of water supplies through chlorination (Larson, Wolf, and Butterworth 1994). None of those hazards constitutes a major public health problem, but the media and government agencies treat them as if they are.

Accompanying that paranoia is a disturbing degree of tolerance of well-documented and substantial dangers to public health and environmental quality. Examples of "neglected" hazards include violence in families and communities (National Committee for Injury Prevention and Control 1989), deteriorating lead paint in older homes (Florini and Silbergeld 1993), inadequate use of basic preventive health services such as childhood immunizations, influenza vaccinations, and breast cancer screening, and hazardous lifestyles characterized by smoking, abuse of alcohol, high-fat diets, lack of physical exercise, and failure to use basic safety devices such as smoke detectors and lap/shoulder belts in cars (U.S. Department of Health and Human Services 1990). These are all major public health problems that receive less than their fair share of attention in media stories and public policy.

Even within a single domain of public policy, such as environmental health, the syndrome of paranoia and neglect is evident. In 1990 Congress passed 1,200 pages of amendments to the Clean Air Act Amendments of 1970 that are estimated to cost the nation an additional $30 billion per year (Portney 1990). The beneficial consequences of that intensified effort to reduce outdoor air pollution are considerable and include a variety of ecological, aesthetic, and human health benefits. Nonetheless, there is a growing scientific consensus that exposure to indoor air pollution is a more serious human health problem than exposure to outdoor air pollution (Samet and Spengler 1991; National Research Council 1991b). Yet no powerful political demand or sustained advocacy effort has aimed at new legislation to assess and improve indoor air quality.

The syndrome is also revealed by simple comparisons of the policy debates about health care reform and environmental policy. Consider, for example, the relative cost-effectiveness of reducing cancer through pollution prevention versus early detection and treatment of tumors.

Mrs. Clinton and her task force proposed to Congress a basic health security package that included coverage of preventive screening every two to three years for breast and cervical cancer. The estimated cost of those measures is as low as $1,000 to $10,000 per year of life saved. More frequent screening intervals, say once a year, would have offered slightly more protection, but at an incremental cost in excess of $100,000 per life-year saved (Eddy 1990). Mrs. Clinton's proposal was therefore a form of "implicit rationing" of insurance coverage.

At the U.S. Environmental Protection Agency, the "shadow prices" for an extra life-year are far more extravagant than what Mrs. Clinton proposed. For example, the EPA recently justified a series of new regulations aimed at reducing benzene emissions from various industrial sources on the grounds of cancer prevention (with no stated expectation of accompanying benefits from diminished noncancer health effects or ecological protection). The cost of those benzene rules, using EPA's figures, ranges from $200,000 to $50,000,000 per year of life saved (EPA 1989).

In defense of pollution prevention, citizens would certainly prefer to prevent a tumor from forming rather than simply treat it early, since a family experiences considerable emotional trauma when a tumor is detected. If we knew that particular pollutant exposures were increasing the risk of breast cancer, the case for primary prevention would certainly merit priority attention. Yet one wonders whether citizens would support up to fiftyfold differences in the fiscal priorities that the government is now placing on life-years saved by different cancer prevention policies (Mendeloff and Kaplan 1989).

Winds of Change

The syndrome about risk will not be easy to change because to do so will require us to reexamine our current mental models of risk. Change may also require challenges to various power structures in Washington, D.C., and elsewhere that have capitalized and prospered from the syndrome. Fortunately, a small but growing coalition of reformers is calling attention to the syndrome about risk.

Scientists are questioning the logic behind traditional policies of risk assessment and management. For example, biochemist Bruce Ames of the University of California at Berkeley has raised serious questions about whether findings of carcinogenicity in high-dose animal tests are valid indicators of dangers to people from low-level exposures to chemicals in the environment (Ames, Profet, and Gold 1990). Less vocal yet influential concerns have also been expressed by committees of the National Academy of Sciences and selected leaders of the American Association for the Advancement of Science (National Research Council 1992, 1994; Abelson 1993).

In the all-important mass media, Keith Schneider of the *New York Times*, Boyce Rensberger of the *Washington Post*, David Shaw of the *Los Angeles Times*, and John Stoussel of ABC News have begun to expose the syndrome in highly visible stories and documentaries. Those efforts are stimulating reporters and the public to ask harder questions about which dangers receive media coverage and which ones are overblown and neglected.

Governors and mayors, citing the "unfunded mandates" emanating from Washington, D.C., are frustrated about their lack of freedom to allocate resources to the dangers that are most evident and prevalent in their states and communities. In Columbus, Ohio, for example, environmental mandates from the EPA are forcing cuts in basic public health services typically provided by the state's health department (Environmental Law Review Committee 1991). The mayor of Anchorage, Alaska, has engaged in a concerted effort to expose the distorted view of health problems that emerges from the federal government's view of risk (Municipality of Anchorage 1992). Since the probability of major tax increases to expand governmental services is low, the sobering reality is that resources for protection against dangers are being rationed—even during good economic times!

Business firms, both large and small, are questioning whether the speculative risks of industrial activities should be regulated to vanishingly small levels without regard to the economic costs of such regulations. The growing costs of the tort liability system, which also reflect public perceptions of risk as much as science, are also a significant cost to important segments of industry (Foster, Bernstein, and Huber 1994). Since American firms operate increasingly in a competitive global economy, each addition to the cost structure of American firms— including those generated by a "better safe than sorry" approach to risk regulation and liability—is coming under increasing scrutiny by government as well as industry (Business Roundtable 1994).

In the deliberations of the 102d Congress, one can see the first clear indications that governmental mismanagement of risk has emerged as a national political issue. The indications began with a straightforward effort by Senator Bennett Johnston (D-Louisiana) to require risk assessment, risk comparison, and benefit-cost analysis as an amendment to a bill calling for the elevation of the EPA to cabinet status in the executive branch. That amendment passed on the floor of the Senate by a vote of 95 to 3.

In the House of Representatives, the Clinton administration and the Democratic leadership made a sustained effort to avoid a Johnston-style risk amendment on the theory that a "clean bill" would be less likely to offend certain advocacy groups or legitimize a string of more controversial amendments. When the House Democratic leadership, at the urging of Vice President Al Gore and EPA Administrator Carol Browner, sought to impose a procedural rule blocking such amendments, they were stunned to lose the floor vote by a considerable margin. A loose yet potent bipartisan coalition of representatives led by Gary Condit (D-California), Karen Thurman (D-Florida), Pete Geren (D-Texas), John Mica (R-Florida), and Richard Zimmer (R-New Jersey) expressed their determination to pass significant risk-related legislation.

Since those two floor votes occurred, proper treatment of "risk" has become a major legislative issue. Numerous bills calling for more or better risk analysis were introduced in both the House and Senate. Risk-related amendments were prominent in debates over reauthorization of Superfund, the Safe Drinking Water Act, the Clean Water Act, the U.S. Department of Agriculture, and even an environmental technologies bill. Republicans and Democrats are beginning to compete to take credit for championing the emerging "risk issue," and new risk-protection legislation is unlikely to pass until Congress has the opportunity to consider a new risk-based approach to managing public health and environmental dangers.

What Kind of Change?

While there is a growing political consensus that something needs to be done, the hard thinking has only begun about what Congress can do to help cure the country's syndrome of paranoia and neglect. An implicit assumption of the reform movement is that the federal government has failed to conduct risk analyses or make proper use of risk analysis in public policies aimed at protecting human health, safety, and environmental quality.

The phrase *risk analysis*, following the interdisciplinary interests of the Society for Risk Analysis, refers broadly to the related analytical tools of risk assessment, risk characterization, risk comparison, risk ranking, risk-based priorities, risk management, risk-benefit analysis, benefit-cost analysis, cost-effectiveness analysis, decision analysis, and risk communication.

Although there are important and subtle differences in these tools (Merkhofer 1987), the term *risk analysis* often refers to the collection of them.

But risk analyses of various sorts are already used widely (if not uniformly and consistently) by agencies such as the Consumer Product Safety Commission, the Department of Energy, the Department of Transportation, the Environmental Protection Agency, the Nuclear Regulatory Commission, and the Occupational Safety and Health Administration. In fact, the Clinton administration's 1993 executive order on regulatory planning requires risk analyses to be submitted in support of all significant rulemaking initiatives. It is important therefore to be clear about what specific legislative steps are needed to attack the syndrome of paranoia and neglect.

Responsible Risk Assessments

When potential dangers are brought to the attention of federal agencies, agencies need to assess those dangers in a responsible manner. Congress can work to inculcate a strong sense of responsibility by requiring agencies to follow several basic principles of sound risk assessment practice.

First, Congress should compel agencies to make use of the *best available scientific information*. While that expectation may seem like nothing more than a plea for "apple pie and motherhood," agencies occasionally neglect or reject high-quality scientific information. They do so because they may prefer the apparent consistency provided by use of "default" assumptions and models and because bureaucracies have difficulty innovating without a clear statutory mandate. The EPA, for example, is only beginning to use innovative biological studies that suggest that low doses of unleaded gasoline vapors, chloroform, and formaldehyde pose less risk to people than previously thought (Graham 1991a). When new scientific studies suggest that a hazard is more dangerous than previously thought (for example, dioxin and fine particles), agencies also tend to be slow to respond to new information. Some degree of skepticism about new discoveries is appropriate, but the government's current risk-assessment process can hardly be accused of being overly responsive to scientific developments.

Second, when scientific knowledge about risk is imperfect or deficient, Congress should require agencies to employ *probabilistic methods of uncertainty analysis*. Agencies should report a range of risk estimates, accompanied by each estimate's likelihood of being correct, to decision makers in publicly available documents (Morgan and Henrion 1991). Single-point estimates, such as plausible upper bounds or worst-case scenarios, should generally be accompanied by lower-bound (optimistic) and realistic (or likely) estimates of risk (Graham 1991b), unless a worst-case figure is being used strictly for "screening purposes" (where the objective is to rule out exposures or hazards that are too tiny to worry about). Agencies should follow an iterative procedure that calls for more detailed uncertainty analysis as the importance of the decision increases (National Research Council 1994). Qualified experts in formal uncertainty analysis should be recruited and trained to participate in the preparation of risk assessment reports (Cooke 1991). Some agency scientists and advocates may perceive that only worst-case estimates of risk will induce regulators to provide the maximum degree of public health protection, but Congress needs to insist that value judgments about the proper margins of safety be made by accountable regulators and not be buried in the choice of particular assumptions or models used to compute risk (Federal Focus Inc. 1991; Zeckhauser and Viscusi 1990).

Third, when the same hazard poses more danger to some citizens than others, Congress should insist that agencies report that information through *distributional methods of variability analysis*. For example, some citizens are more sensitive to environmental agents than others for genetic or lifestyle reasons (Brain, Beck, Warren, and Shaikh 1988). Some citizens are also exposed more to hazards than others (for example, those who live directly downwind from a factory). Agencies should present to decision makers a public document with information about the number of citizens exposed to various levels of risk. Since low-income and minority citizens often incur a disproportionate share of public health and environmental risks, agencies should make a special effort to investigate those citizens' degree of exposure and susceptibility to hazards (Zimmerman 1993). Without that kind of information, risk managers are in a poor position to incorporate equity and justice considerations into their decisions.[1]

Fourth, to nurture the public's sense of perspective about risk, Congress should require agencies to make thoughtful use of *risk comparisons* (Wilson 1979). Analogies are a powerful communication and learning tool if they are crafted with forethought. For example, when agencies report that the extra cancer risk from eating pesticide residues on food is one in a million lifetimes, they should state how large this risk is compared with other risks in daily life. A baby born today, at current mortality rates, incurs a risk of four in a million of being struck and killed on the ground by a crashing air-

Congress needs to insist that value judgments about the proper margins of safety be made by accountable regulators and not be buried in the choice of particular assumptions or models used to compute risk.

plane (Goldstein, Demak, Northridge, and Wartenberg 1992). Although the airplane hazard is far better documented than the estimated risk of ingesting pesticide residues, such a comparison can help citizens and journalists develop an intuition about relative magnitudes. Since the purpose of those risk comparisons is educational and is *not* an explicit part of a formal priority-setting process, it is neither necessary nor appropriate for an agency to restrict the comparisons to hazards that happen to fall within its jurisdiction. As long as the comparison does not force or constrain any value judgment about acceptability, it is not crucial for the agency to ensure that the risks are comparable in terms of other dimensions such as controllability or preventability (Roth, Morgan, Fischhoff, Lave, and Bostrom 1990). If an agency is making a value judgment about acceptability, then it should also consider dimensions of risk other than numerical magnitude (Fischhoff, Lichtenstein, Slovic, Derby, and Keeney 1981).

Finally, Congress should require agencies to assess a *broad range of potential human health and environmental effects*. Historically, agencies have tended to focus on mortality effects (especially from cancer). While premature death is obviously important, citizens are concerned about a much broader range of effects on functional status and quality of life. As the EPA's proposed reassessment of dioxin has indicated, the levels of exposure associated with negligible cancer risk are not necessarily low enough to eliminate concern about potential threats to the immune and reproductive systems (EPA 1994a). Providing protection for human health also does not always ensure protection of nonhuman life forms and ecosystems (Hegner 1994). In the field of traumatic risks, federal agencies are also beginning to recognize the long-term functional consequences of nonfatal head and brain injuries (National Highway Traffic Safety Administration 1994).

As Congress becomes more serious about promoting sound risk assessment practice, agencies will need adequate budgetary and technical resources to get the job done. Under some conditions, it may make sense to move the assessment function outside the mission-oriented regulatory agencies to achieve a greater degree of objectivity and credibility. Again, such organizations will have extra start-up costs, will require adequate budgetary and technical resources, and will complicate the challenge of coordinating risk assessment and management (National Research Council 1993). For assessment units to provide attractive career paths for young scientists, they must also have access to exciting intramural and extramural research and training opportunities—an aspect of risk analysis that currently exists nowhere in the federal government. Hence, the emerging coalition for reform of risk regulation needs to be sensitive to the analyst's need for various kinds of resources. Without such commitments, we cannot expect significant and sustained improvements in analytical practice.

In the 102d Congress, improved risk assessment was the subject of important bills introduced by Representatives Carlos Moorehead (R-California) and Herbert Klein (D-New Jersey). Then, after the 1994 election, the momentum for reform increased in the 103d Congress, and by late summer of 1995 very significant legislation had passed the House and was under consideration in the Senate. The House-passed bill (H.R. 1022), with a few revisions, will provide the public with more protection against genuine risks at less total cost than under present law. That is the case despite often-emotional attacks on the bill by journalists, environmentalists, and others.

Although the House bill has flaws—for example, its obtrusive standard of court review—it is based on sound scientific principles and provides regulators with the necessary flexibility to make tough calls about specific hazards.

Risk-Based Priority Setting

Although the federal government undertakes numerous risk analyses each year, few of them address the "big picture" questions about how resources are allocated among various dangers. For example, why are we spending billions of dollars cleaning up lead in soil at industrial sites, where the probability of childhood exposure is low, when we spend few resources to protect urban children against the neurotoxic effects of ingesting deteriorating lead paint in old homes? In the absence of risk rankings, it is difficult for Congress, regulatory agencies, and the public to gain a sense of perspective about the relative importance of each new danger reported in the mass media.

To counteract the "risk-of-the-month" syndrome, Congress should require the executive branch to periodically rank hazards according to their seriousness and the available opportunities for cost-effective reduction. If such rankings were publicly available, reporters could frame questions and write stories about how newly alleged hazards might rank in seriousness relative to hazards that have already been ranked. For example, which is a more serious threat: contracting cancer from inhaling environmental tobacco smoke or contracting cancer from exposure to radon in the basements of homes? Each agency should be responsible for ranking hazards that fall within their jurisdiction, while the Office of Science and Technology Policy should work with an interagency committee to produce a general ranking of hazards (Carnegie Commission on Science, Technology, and Government 1993).

Since risk-ranking exercises are technically demanding and require delicate value judgments, agencies should undertake them with care and in accordance with well-considered guidelines. Congress should authorize the OSTP and the Office of Management and Budget to develop jointly guidelines governing the proper conduct of risk-ranking exercises. Agencies should also issue an "annual report on risk" indicating how their allocation of resources reflects their ranking of hazards, including what they accomplished in the previous year.

The OMB should also use the agency rankings as a contribution to continuing discussions about agency budgets—a modest form of "risk-based budgeting"—including potential limitations on the "off-budget" or unfunded expenditures made by states and localities and the private sector. Trends in staffing and budgets for risk-protection agencies have never been compared with scientific information on agency performance in problem solving. The years from 1984 to 1994 were good for the EPA but fairly lean for most other risk-protection agencies (Warren 1994). Yet there is certainly no hard evidence that the EPA's performance in cost-effective risk reduction has been superior to the performance of other risk-protection agencies.

In recent years the EPA and many state environmental agencies have acquired significant experience in risk-ranking exercises (EPA 1993b). On the basis of that experience, Congress should insist that agencies develop guidelines on several critical issues.

First, there is at least some degree of scientific uncertainty about the seriousness of every hazard. In some cases, such as the catastrophic consequences of rapid global warming from greenhouse gases, the uncertainties are so large that analysts wield enormous discretion in the assessment and ranking process. If "worst-case" estimates of risk are used to characterize hazard A while realistic estimates of risk are used to characterize hazard B, the ranking of risks will be biased toward placing hazard A at the top of the ranking. While there are many valid approaches to resolving that issue (for example, reporting ranges or probability distributions that reflect uncertainty, or on occasion simply refusing to rank poorly understood hazards), Congress should compel the OSTP and the OMB to develop guidelines about treating uncertainty consistently.

Second, informed lay persons as well as experts must explicitly acknowledge and consider the value judgments in risk ranking. Cognitive psychologists have demonstrated that lay people often harbor genuine concerns about risks that are not captured by standard technical estimates of risks (Fischhoff et al. 1978). For example, if one hazard creates 100 "involuntary" cancers, while another hazard creates 1,000 "voluntary" cancers, which hazard should be assigned the higher ranking? Public participation by interest groups is not always the best approach, since there may be a clear incentive to "game" the value-judgment process in a way that favors industry, environmentalists, or consumers. A better approach may be to elicit critical information on value judgments (for example, the relative importance of an equal number of cancer, trauma, and neurologic effects) from a representative citizen panel objectively selected by a panel of social and physical scientists (Fischhoff 1994).

Considerable scientific progress has been made in formally eliciting thoughtful value judgments. Those techniques are already beginning to influence the practice of medicine through the physician-patient rela tionship (Drummond, Stoddart, and Torrance 1987). When post-menopausal women decide whether to undergo long-term estrogen thera-py, they are making a value judgment about the relative importance of cancer risks, which therapy increases, versus hip fracture and heart dis-ease risks, which therapy reduces. Congress should require the OSTP and the OMB to develop guidelines on the development and application of those forms of science-based "public participation" in risk ranking.

Finally, since optimal risk reduction is the ultimate goal of risk policy, the risk-ranking process should include a component that entails considering the relative cost-effectiveness of alternative mea-sures to reduce risk. The most serious dangers should not always be ranked the highest since the available risk-reduction strategies may be fairly ineffective or costly, although research into new interventions may merit high priority. Risks of only a moderate degree of seriousness may be ranked high if it is feasible to eliminate them at a low cost to society. Congress should require the OMB and the OSTP to develop guidelines on how to incorporate considerations of policy effective-ness and cost into the process of setting risk-based priorities (Graham and Hammitt forthcoming).

Report Risks, Benefits, and Costs

When policy makers work to reduce risks, they should routinely quan-tify the target risks and consider what benefits and costs are anticipat-ed to result from their favored policies. Legislators in particular need to recognize the need to assess risks, benefits, and costs before passing new laws. Many states have ignored that principle in laudable efforts to promote "pollution prevention" and "toxics use reduction" (Laden and Gray 1993). Unfortunately, those approaches offer no analytic framework for deciding whether it makes sense to spend scarce resources substituting chemical A for chemical B. The Clinton administration's proposed study and phase-out of chlorine suffers from a similar problem: there is no requirement for a comparative *economic* evaluation of chlorine and its likely substitutes in various uses!

The administration's chlorine initiative does call for a compari-son of the relative *safety* of chlorine and its substitutes. Congress must embrace the principle of considering the competing risks of regulation as well as the target risks in broad-based legislative language (Graham and Wiener 1995). Congress should do so either by clarifying that the risks induced by regulation are "costs" or by clarifying that the risk assessment report should include substitution risks as well as target risks.

Congress needs to mandate consideration of risk trade-offs because agencies sometimes have incentives to downplay risks that are being induced by their policies. In the 1980s, for example, the National Highway Traffic Safety Administration refused to acknowledge that automobile fuel economy rules were decreasing occupant safety by encouraging vehicle manufacturers to build smaller and lighter cars (Graham 1992). NHTSA is beginning to acknowledge that competing risk but only reluctantly, following a federal court order (*Competitive Enterprise Institute* v. *National Highway Traffic Safety Institute*, 956 F.2d 321 (D.C. Cir. 1992)).

President Clinton's 1993 executive order on regulatory planning does require federal agencies to analyze competing risks, costs, and benefits, but only if the proposed rule is a "significant one"—for example, incurring national costs in excess of $100 million. When the statutory criteria governing an agency's decision do not permit the agency to weigh the benefits and costs of alternatives, the agency may be inclined not to invest the time and resources in a risk analysis—a decision that the Clinton administration has been inclined to tolerate.

> **Congress needs to mandate consideration of risk trade-offs because agencies sometimes have incentives to downplay risks that are being induced by their policies.**

It is useful to examine in some detail an example of the problems and flaws in current practice that the suggested omnibus legislation should correct. A good example—it is by no means the only one, but it illustrates the point—is the EPA's implementation of Title III of the Clean Air Act Amendments of 1990. I briefly contrast that with the more reasonable procedures of the National Highway Traffic Safety Administration.

In Title III Congress required the EPA to promulgate technology-based standards for numerous industrial source categories that emit so-called hazardous air pollutants. On the basis of a survey of the rules proposed and finalized to date under Title III, it appears that the EPA is reporting costs but making less effort to report benefits.

In one of the first rules finalized under Title III, the EPA required technological controls of 110 different hazardous organic pollutants in the chemical manufacturing industry. The EPA reported that the rule would induce up-front capital expenditures of $450 million and net annualized costs of $230 million per year. The official rulemaking notice includes no estimate of the rule's benefits, except that the mandated controls would reduce the quantity of hazardous air pollutants by 510,000 tons per year and the quantity of other volatile organic compounds by 490,000 tons per year. The EPA provides no information about the target risks or the number of adverse health effects prevented. The EPA does refer to a regulatory analysis in the public docket prepared at the OMB's request, but the cover page of that document indicates that insufficient time and data were available to produce "scientifically supportable" estimates of benefit (EPA 1994c).

In the case of a similar proposed rule under Title III covering 190 petroleum refineries in the United States, the EPA reported initial capital costs of $207 million and net annualized costs of $110 million per year. The estimated reduction in the quantity of pollutants was 54,000 megagrams per year of hazardous air pollutants and 300,000 megagrams per year of other volatile organic compounds. An accompanying regulatory analysis in the public docket projects that the rule will avert less than one case of cancer per year.[2] The EPA does project $148.3 million per year in health benefits from the reductions in emissions of volatile organic compounds, assuming that each megagram of volatile organic compound is assigned a dollar value. The agency acknowledges that the uncertainty in this critical "shadow price" ranges from $25 to $1,574 per megagram. That wide range was based on a secondary source (the Office of Technology Assessment), with no independent peer review by health scientists or health economists on the agency's Science Advisory Board.

Even when an agency develops a rule through a "regulatory negotiation" involving affected interests, the agency does not necessarily consider the rule from the perspective of social risks, costs, and benefits. In 1993 the EPA finalized a negotiated rule aimed at reducing hazardous air pollutants at thirty coke production plants through two phases of technological controls: the maximum achievable control technology and the lowest achievable emission rate. The EPA reports that the up-front capital cost of the maximum achievable control technology for existing plants will be $66 million, with net annual costs of $25 million. The standards for the lowest achievable emission rate may require $510 million in capital costs and net annualized costs of $84 million. The final rule reports no estimate of risks from hazardous air pollutants or benefits from their reduction, although a 1992 study commissioned by the EPA's Office of Policy Analysis estimated that the maximum achievable control technology and the lowest achievable emission rate rules together would avert less than one case of cancer per year (Considine, Davis, and Marakovits 1992). The EPA concluded that this rule does not require OMB review, in part because it does not cost more than $100 million per year (EPA 1993a).

Most recently, the EPA issued a proposed rule under Title III covering the aerospace industry that would impose $503 million to $714 million in up-front capital costs and net annualized costs of $16.7 million. The agency reported no risk estimates or health benefits except an estimate that the proposed rule would prevent 208,000 tons per year of hazardous air pollutants. The EPA stated that since annual costs were less than $100 million and since Congress did not require benefit-cost analysis, the agency would not report a regulatory analysis for OMB review (EPA 1994b).

Other risk-protection agencies do not share the EPA's proclivity to impose expensive regulations on the economy without conducting any serious analysis of their benefits. NHTSA, for example, reports a rough estimate of costs and benefits for every rulemaking, regardless of whether its cost exceeds $100 million.[3] That practice reflects more the agency's analytical tradition than any specific statutory requirement to perform benefit-cost analysis of all rules. To prevent analytical burdens from creating excessive delays in rulemaking, NHTSA tailors the intensity and precision of the regulatory analysis to the importance of the rule. Thus, less important rules receive less detailed analyses.

The decision not to invest in benefits analysis will ultimately make it difficult for the EPA to present a persuasive case to Congress and the public that their rulemakings on hazardous air pollutants have been worthwhile. Interestingly, an explicit provision in the 1990 Amendments to the Clean Air Act calls for a comprehensive benefit-cost assessment of the 1990 amendments. The EPA has made little progress toward building a database for that assessment and is now making decisions under Title III that will make such an assessment very difficult to perform in the future.

The missteps of the EPA under Title III demonstrate why it is important for Congress to pass an across-the-board statutory requirement that all risk-protection rules be accompanied by risk estimates and estimates of benefits and costs. Even if an agency's statutory mandate does not require or permit consideration of risk or benefit-cost comparisons, Congress and the public need to be informed of what risk regulation accomplishes and sacrifices. Otherwise, a future public debate about whether an agency's authority and resources should be contracted, retained, or expanded will have no factual basis.

It is desirable to prevent excessive analytical burdens, but Congress should not accomplish that by simply exempting regulations that cost less than $100 million per year. Such a move creates perverse incentives for rules to be subdivided into smaller components and for cost estimates to be trimmed to come in under the $100 million threshold. Thus, Congress should simply authorize agencies to tailor the complexity of the analysis to the importance of the rule.

Reasonable Relationship between Cost and Risk Reduction

In the 1960s and 1970s Congress was understandably hesitant to require agencies to show that every risk regulation has marginal monetary benefits in excess of marginal monetary costs. Even today, despite twenty-five years of progress in the science of quantifying and monetizing risks, it would not be wise to impose a strict net-benefit test on rulemaking.

Many human health and environmental benefits remain difficult to quantify (for example, the monetary value of slightly improved visibility on summer days). Progress has been made in methods of "contingent valuation" of health and environmental benefits, but substantial obstacles remain in the confident application of those tools to risk regulation (Freeman 1993). At the same time, many of the more subtle economic effects of rules are difficult to quantify (such as the indirect impacts on industrial productivity and innovation). In addition, fairness and justice considerations may persuade us to adopt some rules that would "flunk" a strict net-benefit test. For instance, a proposed rule that does not satisfy a net-benefit test but promises a significant reduction in the risks and costs incurred by low-income and minority populations may be worth adopting on equity grounds.

While a strict net-benefit test is ill-advised, Congress should require agencies to make a plausible case that the benefits of a rule (quantitative and qualitative) bear a reasonable relationship to costs (quantitative and qualitative). *Reasonable relationship* is intended here as an intuitive narrative standard rather than a specific mathematical balance (Portney 1990). Of course, what one person perceives to be intuitively reasonable may seem nutty to someone else. Various federal agencies are clearly operating under different norms about what kinds of investments in risk reduction are reasonable.

Consider, for example, a little-noticed discrepancy between FDA and EPA decision making. Soon after the onset of the AIDS epidemic, the FDA ordered routine testing of the blood supply to protect recipients of donated blood from contracting the virus. Recently, the FDA considered and rejected the option of adding a special test for the immunodeficiency virus antigen (HIV-Ag) to prevailing procedures for testing donated blood for HIV. The estimated cost of applying that special test to all donated blood in the United States is $48 million per year. The estimated health benefit would be two to four fewer cases of AIDS per year, or a cost-effectiveness ratio of $12 million to $24 million per case of AIDS averted (Gelles 1993).[4]

If the EPA had proposed the same investment, it would very likely have been considered reasonable. Consider, for example, the EPA's final rule requiring the reformulation of gasoline in an effort to reduce human exposures to carcinogens such as benzene, a known human leukemogen, and volatile organic compounds, which are precursors to smog. The estimated annual costs of that rule are $700 million per year in Phase I plus an additional $250 million in Phase II. The estimated benefits of Phase I are twenty fewer cases of cancer plus 115,000 fewer tons of volatile organic compounds emitted into the atmosphere. Phase II benefits are estimated to be four fewer cancer cases, 42,000 fewer tons of volatile organic compounds, and 22,000 fewer tons of nitrogen oxides. Those benefit estimates are based on assumptions that are far more likely to exaggerate benefits than underestimate them.

If we make the further assumption that each ton less of volatile organic compound or nitrogen oxide produces $5,000 in general health and ecological benefits (which the EPA regards as generous), then the net benefits of Phases I and II (excluding the cancers avoided) are –$125 million and –$140 million, respectively. The resulting incremental cost-effectiveness ratios are $6.25 million and $35 million per case of cancer avoided (EPA 1994d).

This comparison of FDA and EPA decisions suggests that either the government values the lives of patients receiving donated blood less than the lives of potential cancer patients or that the FDA and the EPA are not behaving consistently. I tend to favor the latter conclusion, since in a recent study covering hundreds of medical and environmental health policies, we found that federal regulators frequently make investments in toxin control that would not be considered reasonable by the norms of preventive medicine (Tengs, Adams, Pliskin, Gelb-Safran, Siegel, Weinstein, and Graham 1995). Congress should address that discrepancy by requiring agencies to achieve a reasonable and consistent balance between benefits and costs. The OMB should be required to develop formal guidance on what magnitudes of investments in health protection are likely to be supportable by reference to the burgeoning literature on the public's willingness to pay for health protection (Viscusi 1992). By applying the same guidance to all agencies, the OMB would take a step toward effecting consistency in norms.

External Mechanisms of Scientific Peer Review

Since analysts wield a subtle yet important power when conducting various types of risk analysis, Congress should insist that their analytical products be scrutinized and improved through the *external mechanism of peer review* (Burack 1987; Graham 1991a). A useful model for review, one the EPA and FDA often use, is a public advisory committee of nongovernmental scientists from academia and nonprofit research organizations. Members are selected on the basis of their technical expertise rather than on the basis of their affiliation with particular stakeholder groups. Advisory committees may consider comments from stakeholders in a public forum, scrutinize a draft agency report, and provide written technical advice to an agency (Lippman 1987). Studies have shown that a public process of external peer review improves both the quality of the technical analysis and the degree of public confidence in decisions that are ultimately made based on the analysis (Jasanoff 1990).

When writing peer review requirements into risk legislation, Congress should insist that such review be applied to economic and engineering analyses as well as to public health and ecological analyses. The extent of peer review should match the importance and complexity of the issue.

Some agencies, such OSHA, NHTSA, and the CPSC, do not yet make widespread use of external advisory groups. The EPA has an improving track record in that area (EPA annual), but serious problems remain. The EPA's Integrated Risk Information System, which supplies sensitive information on cancer and noncancer effects in computerized form to the public, has not yet been subjected to a rigorous yet flexible mechanism of peer review. Problems also occur when agencies such as the EPA or OSHA accept a "science-policy" determination made by an international organization without independent peer review. For example, the World Health Organization's International Agency for Research on Cancer categorizes chemicals and processes as "carcinogenic" without considering information on biological mechanisms of action and extent of human exposure. Congress should insist that federal agencies consider the recommendations of international organizations such as IARC, but only in conjunction with independent review by a public advisory committee of scientists in the United States.

> If Congress believes in risk analysis, it should not be bashful about authorizing judicial review of an agency's use of risk analysis in rulemaking decisions.

Judicial Review under the Principle of Deference

Were agencies already making optimal use of risk analysis, legislation would not be urgent. The country needs legislation precisely because the rate of progress in the analytic practices of agencies is uneven and often slow (Stone 1994; Landy, Roberts, and Thomas 1990). Legislation can spur agency activities, but only if parties outside the agency have the opportunity to bring the agency to court for failure to do so.

If Congress believes in risk analysis, it should not be bashful about authorizing judicial review of an agency's use of risk analysis in rulemaking decisions under a deferential standard of review such as the "arbitrary and capricious" test in the Administrative Procedures Act and subsequent case law (Breyer 1982) Congress should not authorize judges to substitute their scientific or policy judgments for those of the agency (Graham, Green, and Roberts 1988). Risk analysis is unlikely to influence administrative decision making if decision makers are not compelled to consider seriously the findings of analysis when making decisions (Melnick 1983). Legislative reform can be influential in addressing the misallocation of resources resulting from the public's current syndrome of paranoia and neglect about risk (Cross 1994).

Analytical Resources

The congressional commitment to risk analysis should include more budgetary and technical resources as well as more analytical requirements. A recent report by the OTA (1994) documented the minimal resource commitments in the federal government that have been made to advancing the field. Supreme Court Justice Stephen Breyer (1993) has also highlighted the need to cultivate and support a cadre of career public servants who have broad multidisciplinary experience in risk analysis. The need for analytical resources is pressing in all fields but especially in the subfield of ecological risk assessment—the most immature aspect of this growing discipline (Barnthouse 1994).

Looking much more broadly, it is increasingly apparent that the concept of risk needs to be integrated into the way scientists and professionals are trained. Otherwise, the needs of the public and private sectors for experts and keen decision makers will not be met. In the long run, the nation's commitment to risk analysis needs to be expressed not only in the education of scientists and professionals but in the curricula used to educate young children in math, science, and economics. Perhaps this more analytical citizenry is the ultimate cure for the prevailing syndrome of paranoia and neglect about risk.

NOTES

Helpful suggestions were made by John Evans, Robert Hahn, James Hammitt, Jennifer Hartwell, March Sadowitz, Paul Slovic, and Jonathan Wiener. The views are exclusively those of the author.

1. Interestingly, several years ago the federal government embraced a form of "variability analysis" of economic costs when it required that regulatory impacts on small businesses be highlighted in rulemaking notices.
2. Other categories of possible health benefits related to the reduction of hazardous air pollutants were noted but not quantified.
3. Interview with Mr. Barry Felrice, Office of Rulemaking, National Highway Traffic Safety Administration, Washington, D.C., 1994.
4. Note that those calculations exclude the epidemic control benefits resulting from fewer infected citizens.

REFERENCES

Abelson, Philip H. "Pesticides and Food." *Science* 259 (1993): 1235.

Ames, Bruce N. "Pollution, Pesticides, and Cancer." *Journal of AOAC International* 75 (1992): 1–5.

———, M. Profet, and Lois S. Gold. "Dietary Pesticides (99.9% All Natural)." *Proceedings of the National Academy of Sciences, USA* 87 (1990): 7777–81.

Archibald, S. O., and C. K. Winter. "Pesticides in Our Food: Assessing the Risks," in C. K. Winter, J. N. Seiber, and C. F. Nuckton, eds., *Chemicals in the Human Food Chain*. New York: Van Nostrand Reinhold, 1990.

Barnthouse, L. W. "Issues in Ecological Risk Assessment: The CRAM Perspective." *Risk Analysis* 14 (1994): 251–56.

Brain, J. D., B. D. Beck, A. J. Warren, and R. A. Shaikh, eds. *Variations in Susceptibility to Inhaled Pollutants: Identification, Mechanisms, and Policy Implications*. Baltimore: Johns Hopkins University Press, 1988.

Breyer, Stephen G. *Breaking the Vicious Circle*. Cambridge: Harvard University Press, 1993.

———. *Regulation and Its Reform*. Cambridge: Harvard University Press, 1982.

Burack, T. S. "Of Reliable Science: Scientific Peer Review, Federal Regulatory Agencies, and the Courts." *Virginia Journal of Natural Resources Law* 7 (1987): 27–110.

Business Roundtable. *Toward Smarter Regulation*. Washington, D.C.: Business Roundtable, 1994.

Carnegie Commission on Science, Technology, and Government. *Risk and the Environment: Improving Regulatory Decision Making*. New York: Carnegie Commission, June 1993.

Considine, T. J., G. A. Davis, and D. Marakovits. "Costs and Benefits of Coke Oven Emission Controls." Final Report to U.S. EPA, December 17, 1992.

Cooke, R. M. *Experts in Uncertainty: Opinion and Subjective Probability in Science*. New York: Oxford University Press, 1991.

Cross, F. "The Public Role in Risk Control." *Environmental Law* 24 (1994): 888–969.

Department of Health and Human Services. *Health USA*. Washington, D.C.: Government Printing Office, annual.

———. *Healthy People: National Health Promotion and Disease Prevention Objectives*. Washington, D.C.: Government Printing Office, September 1990.

Drummond, M. F., G. L. Stoddart, and G. W. Torrance. *Methods for the Economic Evaluation of Health Care Programmes*. New York: Oxford University Press (Oxford Medical Publications), 1987.

Dunlap, R. E. "Trends in Public Opinion toward Environmental Issues: 1965–1990." *Society and Natural Resources* 4 (1991): 285–312.

Eddy, D. M. "Screening for Cervical Cancer." *Annals of Internal Medicine* 113 (1990): 214–226.

Environmental Law Review Committee. *Environmental Legislation: The Increasing Cost of Regulatory Compliance to the City of Columbus*, Report to the Mayor and City Council of Columbus, Ohio. May 13, 1991.

Environmental Protection Agency. *The Dioxin Reassessment*. External Review Draft. Washington, D.C., June 1994a.

———. *A Guidebook to Comparing Risks and Setting Environmental Priorities*. Washington, D.C.: Government Printing Office, September 1993b.

———. "National Emission Standard for Hazardous Air Pollutants for Source Categories: Organic Hazardous Air Pollutants from the Synthetic Organic Chemical Manufacturing Industry and Other Processes Subject to the Negotiated Regulation for Equipment Leaks." 40 CFR Part 63, 1994c.

———. "National Emission Standards for Hazardous Air Pollutants; Benzene; Rule and Proposed Rule." *Federal Register* 54 (September 14, 1989): 38044–72.

———. "National Emission Standards for Hazardous Air Pollutants for Source Categories and for Coke Oven Batteries." *Federal Register* 58 (1993a): 57898–935.

———. "National Emission Standards for Hazardous Air Pollutants for Source Categories: Aerospace Manufacturing and Rework." *Federal Register* 59 (1994b): 29216–51.

———. "Regulation of Fuels and Fuel Additives: Standards for Reformulated and Conventional Gasoline." *Federal Register* 59 (February 16, 1994d).

———. *Report of the Director of the Science Advisory Board*. Washington, D.C.: Government Printing Office, annual.

Environmental Protection Agency, Science Advisory Board. *Reducing Risk*. Washington, D.C.: Government Printing Office, 1990.

Federal Focus Inc. *Toward Common Measures: Recommendations for a Presidential Executive Order on Environmental Risk Assessment and Risk Management Policy*. Washington, D.C.: Federal Focus Inc., 1991.

Fischhoff, Baruch. "Acceptable Risk: A Conceptual Proposal." *Risk: Health, Safety and Environment* 5 (1994): 1–28.

———, et al. "How Safe is Safe Enough? A Psychometric Study of Attitudes toward Technological Risks and Benefits." *Policy Sciences* 8 (1978): 127.

Fischhoff, B., S. Lichtenstein, P. Slovic, S. L. Derby, and Ralph L. Keeney. *Acceptable Risk*. New York: Cambridge University Press, 1981.

Florini, K. L., and E. K. Silbergeld. "Getting the Lead Out." *Issues in Science and Technology* 9 (Summer 1993): 33–39.

Foster, K. R., D. E. Bernstein, and Peter W. Huber, eds. *Phantom Risk: Scientific Inference and the Law*. Cambridge: MIT Press, 1994.

Freeman, A. M. *The Measurement of Environmental and Resource Values: Theory and Methods*. Washington, D.C.: Resources for the Future, 1993.

Gelles, G. M. "Costs and Benefits of HIV-1 Antibody Testing of Donated Blood." *Journal of Policy Analysis and Management* 12 (1993): 512–31.

Goldstein, Bernard D., M. Demak, M. Northridge, and D. Wartenberg. "Risk to

Groundlings of Death Due to Airplane Accidents: A Risk Communication Tool." *Risk Analysis* 12 (1992): 339–41.

Graham, John D. "The Economics of Controlling Outdoor and Indoor Air Pollution," in L. Tomatis, ed., *Indoor and Outdoor Air Pollution and Human Cancer.* New York: Springer-Verlag, 1993.

———. "New Directions for Chemical Risk Assessment." *Regulation* (Fall 1991b): 14–18.

———. "The Safety Risks of Fuel Economy Legislation." *Risk: Issues in Health and Safety* 3 (1992): 95–126.

———, ed. *Harnessing Science for Environmental Regulation.* Westport, Conn.: Greenwood Publishing Co., 1991a.

Graham, John D., and J. K. Hammitt. "Refining Comparative Risk Assessment for Priority Setting in the Federal Government," in Terry Davies, ed., *Comparative Risk.* Washington, D.C.: Resources for the Future, in press.

Graham, John D., and Jonathan Wiener. *Risk versus Risk: Tradeoffs in Human Health and Environmental Protection.* Cambridge: Harvard University Press, 1995.

Graham, John D., L. Green, and Marc J. Roberts. *In Search of Safety: Chemicals and Cancer Risk.* Cambridge: Harvard University Press, 1988.

Hegner, R. E. "Does Protecting for Human Health Protect Ecological Health?" *Risk Analysis* 14 (1994): 3–4.

Jasanoff, Sheila. *The Fifth Branch: Science Advisors as Policymakers.* Cambridge: Harvard University Press, 1990.

Laden, F., and G. M. Gray. "Toxics Use Reduction: Pro and Con." *Risk: Issues in Health and Safety* 4 (1993): 213–34.

Landy, M. K., Mark J. Roberts, and S. R. Thomas. *EPA: Asking the Wrong Questions.* New York: Oxford University Press, 1990.

Larson, J. L., D. C. Wolf, and B. E. Butterworth. "Induced Cytotoxicity and Cell Proliferation in the Hepatocarcinogenicity of Chloroform in Female B6C3F1 Mice: Comparison of Administration by Gavage in Corn Oil vs. ad Libitum in Drinking Water." *Fundamental and Applied Toxicology* 22 (1994): 90–102.

Lippman, M. "Role of Science Advisory Groups in Establishing Standards for Ambient Air Pollutants." *Aerosol Science and Technology* 6 (1987): 93–114.

McGinnis, J. M., and W. H. Foege. "Actual Causes of Death in the United States." *Journal of the American Medical Association* 270 (1993): 2207–12.

Melnick, R. Shep. *Regulation and the Courts: The Case of the Clean Air Act.* Washington, D.C.: Brookings Institution, 1983.

Mendeloff, J. M., and R. M. Kaplan. "Are Large Differences in 'Lifesaving' Costs Justified? A Psychometric Study of the Relative Value Placed on Preventing Deaths." *Risk Analysis* 9 (1989): 349–63.

Merkhofer, M. W. *Decision Science and Social Risk Management.* Boston: D. Reidel Publishing Company, 1987.

Morgan, M. G., and M. Henrion. *Uncertainty: A Guide to Dealing with Uncertainty in Quantitative Risk and Policy Analysis.* New York: Cambridge University Press, 1991.

Municipality of Anchorage. *Paying for Federal Environmental Mandates: A Looming Crisis for Cities and Counties.* Anchorage: September 1992.

National Committee for Injury Prevention and Control. *Injury Prevention: Meeting the Challenge.* New York: Oxford University Press, 1989.

National Highway Traffic Safety Administration. *Development of the Functional Capacity Index.* Washington, D.C.: Department of Transportation, July 1994.

National Research Council. *Environmental Epidemiology: Public Health and Hazardous Wastes.* Washington, D.C.: National Academy Press, 1991.

———. *Human Exposure Assessment to Airborne Pollutants.* Washington, D.C.: National Academy Press, 1991.

———. *Issues in Risk Assessment.* Washington, D.C.: National Academy Press, 1992.

———. *Science and Judgment in Risk Assessment.* Washington, D.C.: National Academy Press, January 1994.

———. *The Structure and Performance of the Health Effects Institute.* Washington, D.C.: National Academy Press, 1993.

Office of Technology Assessment. *Health Risk Assessment.* Washington, D.C.: Government Printing Office, 1994.

Portney, Paul R. "Economics and the Clean Air Act." *Journal of Economic Perspectives* 4 (Fall 1990): 173–81.

———, ed. *Public Policies for Environmental Protection.* Washington, D.C.: Resources for the Future, 1990.

Roth, E., M. G. Morgan, B. Fischhoff, Lester Lave, and A. Bostrom. "What Do We Know about Making Risk Comparisons?" *Risk Analysis* 10 (1990): 375–87.

Samet, J. M., and J. D. Spengler, eds. *Indoor Air Pollution: A Health Perspective.* Baltimore: Johns Hopkins University Press, 1991.

Singer, Eleanor, and Phyllis M. Endreny. *Reporting on Risk.* New York: Russell Sage Foundation, 1993.

Stone, Richard. "Can Carol Browner Reform EPA?: One Year after Becoming EPA Administrator, Browner Has a Lot to Do to Fulfill Her Promise to Make Science the Centerpiece of Environmental Regulation." *Science* 263 (1994): 312–14.

Tengs, Tammy O., Miriam E. Adams, Joseph S. Pliskin, Dana Gelb-Safran, Joanna E. Siegel, Michael C. Weinstein, and John D. Graham. "Five-Hundred Life-Saving Interventions and Their Cost-Effectiveness." *Risk Analysis* 15 (1995): 369–90.

Viscusi, W. Kip. *Fatal Tradeoffs: Public and Private Responsibilities for Risk.* New York: Oxford University Press, 1992.

Warren, M. "Reforming the Federal Regulatory Process: Rhetoric or Reality?" Working Paper, Center for the Study of American Business, Washington University, June 1994.

Wilson, R. "Analyzing the Risks of Everyday Life." *Technology Review* 81 (1979): 40–46.

Zeckhauser, Richard J., and W. Kip Viscusi. "Risk within Reason." *Science* 238 (1990): 559–64.

Zimmerman, Rae. "Social Equity and Environmental Risk." *Risk Analysis* 13 (1993): 649–66.

Chapter 10

REGULATORY REFORM
What Do the Government's Numbers Tell Us?

Robert W. Hahn

OVERVIEW

The political earthquake that shook Washington in November of 1994 brought with it a call for regulatory reform. The call came not just from conservative Republicans, although they vigorously supported reform. The call also came from many Democrats, who recognized that Washington bureaucracies were not working very well and in many instances were standing in the way of progress. The bipartisan support for some kind of regulatory reform stemmed from the public's growing awareness of the potential excesses of government regulation. Philip Howard highlighted some of those potential excesses in his best-selling book on regulation, *The Death of Common Sense* (1995). In that book Howard showed how laws and regulations deterred Mother Teresa and the Missionaries of Charity from building a homeless shelter in the South Bronx and prevented Amoco from reducing five times as much benzene at its Yorktown refinery at one-fifth the current cost. The message is clear—our regulatory system is broken and needs to be fixed.

But how to fix it? In this chapter I focus on the central issue in both the regulatory and political debates—the role of cost-benefit analysis in regulatory reform. Republicans have generally argued that increasing the use of "improved" cost-benefit analysis is essential to regulatory reform, particularly the regulation of health, safety, and the environment. Moreover, some Republicans have urged using a test that requires that the benefits of a regulation justify or exceed the incremental costs. Democrats, particularly those in the administration, have been more reserved. While endorsing cost-benefit analysis in principle, they argue that President Clinton's Executive Order 12886 already requires cost-benefit analysis to the extent it is consistent with existing law.

Several scholars have argued for making better use of cost-benefit analysis in developing regulations (DeMuth 1995; Hahn 1995b). But how much of a difference in policy would that really make if it were required? The answer depends, in part, on the way in which policy makers use cost-benefit analysis and on the number of regulations introduced that would fail cost-benefit tests.

The principal objective of this chapter is to provide a comprehensive review of major federal regulations that address the environment, health, and safety. To my knowledge, this is the most comprehensive analysis to date. In particular, it includes an analysis of most major rules from 1990 to the present.[1] This analysis covers proposed and final rules[2] from the Environmental Protection Agency, the Occupational Safety and Health Administration, the Consumer Product Safety Commission, the National Highway Traffic Safety Administration, and the Mine Safety and Health Administration.[3]

This database will provide useful information on a host of issues: the current role of cost-benefit analysis in analyzing major rules, the costs of regulation, the net benefits of regulation, the cost-effectiveness of regulation, factors affecting the cost-effectiveness of regulation, and the opportunity for reallocating regulatory expenditures to save more lives or to achieve other social objectives. The results I report are part of a broader research project aimed at assessing the costs and benefits of regulation. As such, those results represent a summary of my findings to date in the area of health, safety, and environmental regulation. We should view the findings presented in this study as preliminary; at the same time, I have tried to focus on those findings that will be robust in the sense that they are unlikely to change significantly as I uncover new information on the period under study.

First, I review the literature and describe the research methodology. Then I present the major analytical results on cost-benefit analysis, the cost-effectiveness of regulations, and the potential for reallocating environmental, health, and safety expenditures more efficiently. Finally, I offer some conclusions, policy recommendations, and suggestions for future research.

Review of Literature and Methodology

A large literature evaluates the impact of federal regulation on the economy (Weidenbaum and DeFina 1978; Litan and Nordhaus 1983; Hahn and Hird 1991; Hopkins 1991). The specific focus of this study builds on pathbreaking work done at the Office of Management and Budget beginning in the early 1980s (Morrall 1986). That work ranked health, safety, and environmental regulations in terms of cost-effectiveness.

In addition, this study draws on several other areas of regulatory research that evaluate the impact of government regulation and offer suggestions for improving the regulatory process. One area focuses on improving estimates of the costs and benefits of specific regulations and programs (Crandall et al. 1986; Viscusi 1992). A second area identifies appropriate institutions and tools for improving the regulatory process (Noll 1971; Lave 1981). A subset of that literature examines the effectiveness of the regulatory oversight mechanism (DeMuth and Ginsburg 1986; Smith 1984; Fraas 1991; Hahn 1994; Breyer 1993). A third area attempts to identify factors that help explain the cost-effectiveness of regulations (Van Houtven and Cropper 1994; Morrall 1986). A fourth area assesses the role of economic analysis in decision making (Derthick and Quirk 1985; Farrow 1991; Hird 1991). A final area evaluates the total costs and benefits of regulation and deregulation (Hahn and Hird 1991; Hopkins 1991; Winston 1993).[4]

This study develops a unique database that provides a systematic account of the impact of major federal rulemakings on social regulation.[5] A primary data source for this chapter is the regulatory impact analysis or RIA, which various executive orders dating back to 1981 have required. While small numbers of RIAs have been examined for selected periods (General Accounting Office 1984; EPA 1986a), this is the first research project aimed at synthesizing the data on costs and benefits for a large number of RIAs. Agencies generally do such a regulatory analysis for each "major" rule whose annual impact on the economy is estimated to exceed $100 million.[6]

Typically, the agency proposing the regulation performs the regulatory impact analysis, often with the help of outside consultants. The analysis is supposed to include a statement of the potential need for the proposal, an examination of alternative approaches, an assessment of benefits and costs, the rationale for choosing the proposed regulatory action, and a statement of statutory authority. Thus, the regulatory impact analysis provides a rich source of data for examining the costs and benefits of regulation. Moreover, the analysis can provide some insight into how existing regulations might have fared if congressional reform proposals requiring that a regulation's incremental benefits justify or exceed its incremental costs had been in force.

In this chapter I focus primarily on the period from 1990 to the present because researchers have not systematically analyzed that time frame. I analyze all regulatory impact analyses that I could locate for that period. In the twenty-two cases where RIAs were not available, I examine the preamble of the *Federal Register* notice in lieu of the RIA. The preamble typically summarizes the information that the regulatory impact analysis presents.

The methodology I use to estimate cost and effectiveness is similar to that of Morrall (1986). Unlike Morrall, however, this study attempts to avoid introducing adjustments to individual studies based on a detailed analysis of the RIAs. My analysis has an advantage over Morrall's in that an interested third party can more easily reproduce it. The disadvantage of my analysis is that the numbers are more likely to be "biased" in support of a regulation. In particular, I am concerned that agencies could overstate the benefits of a program and understate the costs.[7] To address that issue, I perform some general sensitivity analyses. In addition, where possible, I complement that formal analysis by evaluating OMB comments on specific proposed regulations that highlight sources of disagreement between the OMB and a particular agency.

This chapter also examines regulations before 1990, including most of the major regulations considered by Morrall since 1980. The part of the analysis that includes data before 1990 focuses primarily on issues of cost-effectiveness.

The methodology I use to examine cost-effectiveness is also similar to that described in Tengs and Graham (1996) and Tengs et al. (1995). The analysis differs from that of Tengs and Graham in several important respects, however. First, I discount benefit streams to better account for the timing of benefits; second, I use a different measure of cost-effectiveness; third, my focus is on original source material wherever possible. Thus, while Tengs et al. (1995) sometimes rely on information summarized in other studies (for example, Van Houtven and Cropper 1994), I have examined the regulatory impact analyses. Finally, Tengs and Graham focus on the potential to reallocate resources more effectively within the United States, while I quantify the potential for saving more lives or money by reallocating resources to developing nations.

Results

This section provides an overview of the data, a detailed analysis of costs and benefits, an examination of the cost-effectiveness of selected regulations and factors affecting the cost-effectiveness of regulation, and some estimates of the potential to allocate expenditures on environmental, health, and safety regulation more efficiently.

Overview of the Data

In table 10-1 I present an overview of the major rules reviewed for this part of the study. The table shows the number and percentage of regulations for which some part of costs and benefits were quantified.[8] It also shows the fraction of regulations that the agency found would pass a cost-benefit test, in other words where quantified monetary benefits would exceed quantified costs.[9] The last row of the table shows the percentage of regulations that would pass a cost-benefit test, using the total number of regulations examined here as the denominator.[10]

I reviewed a total of ninety-two rules: seventy from the EPA, fourteen from OSHA, six from NHTSA, and one each from the CPSC and MSHA.[11] In 99 percent of the cases agencies reported information on costs or costs and cost savings. All agencies other than the EPA quantified some measure of health benefits for all rules examined here. In many cases that quantification was incomplete, however. Moreover, none of the agencies, except the EPA and the CPSC, attempted to monetize the benefits of particular rules. The CPSC did monetize benefits for the single rule I examine, and the EPA monetized benefits for 30 percent of the rules examined. For some agencies such as OSHA and NHTSA, the cost-benefit framework was precluded. While those agencies did not monetize benefits during the period under study, they

Table 10-1 Regulatory Scorecard, 1990 to Mid-1995

	All	Final	Proposed	CPSC	MSHA	NHTSA	OSHA-Health	OSHA-Safety	EPA
Number of regulations reviewed	92	58	34	1	1	6	9	5	70
Costs/savings assessed	91 (99%)	57 (98%)	34 (100%)	1 (100%)	1 (100%)	6 (100%)	9 (100%)	5 (100%)	69 (99%)
Benefits quantified[a]	80 (87%)	48 (83%)	32 (94%)	1 (100%)	1 (100%)	6 (100%)	9 (100%)	5 (100%)	58 (83%)
Health	51 (55%)	33 (57%)	18 (53%)	1 (100%)	1 (100%)	6 (100%)	9 (100%)	5 (100%)	29 (41%)
Pollution reduction	41 (45%)	24 (41%)	17 (50%)	0 (0%)	0 (0%)	0 (0%)	0 (0%)	0 (0%)	41 (59%)
Benefits monetized	23 (25%)	11 (19%)	12 (35%)	1 (100%)	0 (0%)	0 (0%)	0 (0%)	0 (0%)	22 (31%)
Agency finding that monetized benefits exceed costs	17 (18%)	9 (16%)	8 (24%)	1 (100%)	0 (0%)	1 (17%)	1 (11%)	1 (20%)	13 (19%)

Note: CPSC=Consumer Product Safety Commission; MSHA=Mine Safety and Health Administration; NHTSA=National Highway Traffic Safety Administration; OSHA=Occupational Safety and Health Administration; EPA=Environmental Protection Agency.
a. This category includes health benefits, benefits from pollution reduction, and any other benefits that were quantified or monetized.

often highlighted significant cost savings.

Using the agency numbers on benefits and costs, I found that 18 percent—seventeen of ninety-two—of all rules examined would pass a cost-benefit test. Seven rules pass a cost-benefit test without monetizing benefits because of net cost savings.[12] Of the rules that monetize benefits, ten of twenty-three pass a cost-benefit test.[13]

Table 10-2 shows a more detailed breakdown for the EPA. All but one rule involving a water pollution regulation assess costs. Twelve of the rules did not quantify benefits. Of those, many were process-oriented.[14] Two-fifths of the regulations quantify health benefits, and just under three-fifths quantify pollution reductions. Interestingly, while 88 percent of the Clean Air Act regulations quantify emissions reductions, only 29 percent actually monetize the benefits. Below, I shall consider the impact of monetizing more of those agency benefits. Of the twenty-two rules that monetize benefits, nine pass the cost-benefit test when I use agency numbers. An additional four rules pass the test without monetizing benefits because of significant cost savings.

This overview of agency analyses suggests that there is considerable variation in the type of analysis agencies perform for individual rules. In addition, there is considerable variation in the assumptions underlying the analysis and in the quality

Of the rules that monetize benefits, ten of twenty-three pass a cost-benefit test.

of analysis itself. The discount rate used varies across regulations, and agencies do not always indicate the timing of the costs and benefits. Agencies may only show that information in particular years instead of presenting full streams of costs and benefits.[15] We should keep those characteristics of the data set in mind when we interpret the results.

The Cost-Benefit Analysis

The preceding analysis of costs and benefits suffers from a lack of consistency across and within agencies. To make the analysis consistent across different programs and regulations, I convert dollar estimates to 1994 dollars, and I introduce a common discount rate as well as a consistent set of values for reducing health risks. In table 10-3 I summarize values for key parameters.

Table 10-2 Regulatory Scorecard: Breakdown for Environmental Statutes, 1990 to Mid-1995

	EPA	CAA	CWA	SDWA	FIFRA	TSCA	RCRA	CERCLA
Number of regulations reviewed	70	42	10	6	1	1	8	2
Costs/savings assessed	69 (99%)	42 (100%)	9 (90%)	6 (100%)	1 (100%)	0 (0%)	8 (100%)	2 (100%)
Benefits quantified[a]	58 (83%)	38 (90%)	7 (70%)	6 (100%)	1 (100%)	0 (0%)	6 (75%)	0 (0%)
Health	29 (41%)	11 (26%)	5 (50%)	6 (100%)	1 (100%)	0 (0%)	6 (75%)	0 (0%)
Pollution reduction	41 (59%)	37 (88%)	4 (40%)	0 (0%)	0 (0%)	0 (0%)	0 (0%)	0 (0%)
Benefits monetized	22 (31%)	12 (29%)	4 (40%)	2 (33%)	0 (0%)	0 (0%)	4 (50%)	0 (0%)
Agency finding that monetized benefits exceed costs	13 (19%)	8 (19%)	1 (10%)	2 (33%)	0 (0%)	0 (0%)	2 (25%)	0 (0%)

Note: CAA=Clean Air Act; CWA=Clean Water Act; SDWA=Safe Drinking Water Act; FIFRA=Federal Insecticide, Fungicide, and Rodenticide Act; TSCA=Toxic Substances Control Act; RCRA=Resource Conservation and Recovery Act; CERCLA=Comprehensive Environmental Response, Compensation, and Liability Act.

a. This category includes health benefits, benefits from pollution reduction, and any other benefits that were quantified or monetized.

Table 10-3   Key Parameters of the Model

	Low Value	Base Value	High Value
Discount rate	3%	5%	7%
Implicit value of life	$3,000,000	$5,000,000	$7,000,000
Value of pollution benefits ($/ton)			
Carbon monoxide	0	0	100
Hydrocarbons	100	1,000	2,500
Nitrogen dioxide	100	1,000	2,500
Particulate matter (PM 10)	2,500	10,000	30,000
Sulfur dioxide	100	700	1,000

Notes: All dollar figures have been adjusted to 1994 dollars using implicit price deflators (*Economic Report of the President*, 1995). See the discussion of the implicit value of life in the text.

The real discount rate for the base case is 5 percent. That rate lies between the OMB's suggested 7 percent rate and the real Treasury rate, which I approximate at 3 percent (Lyon 1990; GAO 1991; Hartman 1988; OMB 1992). I examine the 3 percent and 7 percent scenarios in the sensitivity analyses.

Valuations of reductions in mortality risks and nonfatal health risks, such as work injuries, are based on research summarized by Viscusi (1992). His work estimates what individuals are willing to pay for an increase in the probability that they will avoid certain kinds of risks. That payment is summarized in a measure that is referred to as the "value of life."[16] The value of life is a shorthand way of describing the amount one would be willing to pay to save an additional life, say, by investing in some activity that reduces risks.[17] In my calculations the value of life for the base case is $5 million. The sensitivity analyses examine a range of $3 million to $7 million.[18]

To monetize nonfatal injuries or diseases, I introduce a fatality index based on work summarized in Viscusi (1992). I value a chronic disease or disabling injury at one-third of a life, workday-lost injuries at one-hundredth of a life, and non-workday-lost injuries at one-two-hundredth of a life. I adjust nonfatal injuries from car accidents by using NHTSA's equivalent life calculation.

Willingness to pay for reductions in pollution is likely to vary dramatically by region, depending on population, severity of the problem, and the nature of the impacts. Here I develop some very general estimates based on my best judgment, but I fully appreciate the difficulties in making such estimates. My estimates are based on work by Harrison et al. (1992) and Rowe et al. (1995) as well as on selected numbers from the EPA's regulatory impact analyses.

Unless otherwise specified, I presume that regulations have been in force for at least twenty years. Where the RIA specified a longer time frame, I use that information. If benefits accrued over a longer time frame because a disease or illness has a latency period, I discount the benefits back to the present. If the stream of benefits is not given, I discount the average annual benefits by using average latency periods.[19]

If the agency specified a preferred alternative or scenario in the RIA or *Federal Register* notice, I evaluate that alternative or scenario. If the agency did not specify a preferred alternative, I examine an average of the most likely set of alternatives or scenarios.

My analysis of the RIAs takes agency cost numbers as given. It also takes agency estimates of the impact of rules as given.[20] I then use those numbers to estimate the present value of the costs and benefits of a particular regulation or regulatory alternative.[21] All dollar estimates are in 1994 dollars. The estimates I develop below are thus based on agency numbers, but with additional assumptions designed to help increase the level of consistency as well as to monetize a greater fraction of the benefits.

In table 10-4 I summarize the net benefits of regulation on the basis of the information in the RIAs and the *Federal Register*.[22] The table provides aggregate estimates for each agency as well as a combined estimate for all agencies. I divide OSHA into two parts to study regulations dealing with health and regulations dealing with safety. The first part of the table summarizes the results for final rules, the second part summarizes the results for proposed rules, and the third part combines the two categories. For each part, I list the number of regulations considered, the number of regulations for which cost or cost and benefit information was available, and aggregate information on benefits and costs.

To obtain net benefits, one typically takes the difference between benefits and costs. The table distinguishes between gross costs and net

**Table 10-4   Net Benefits of Regulations, 1990 to Mid-1995
(present value in billions of 1994 dollars)**

	All	CPSC	MSHA	NHTSA	OSHA-health	OSHA-safety	EPA
Final							
Number of regulations[a]	54	1	1	4	5	3	40
Monetized benefits exceed costs[b]	23	1	1	4	2	3	12
Net costs	220.4	0.7	0.3	16.9	24.5	−4.9	182.9
Gross costs	267.1	1.2	0.3	22.7	24.5	11.7	206.7
Benefits	499.2	5.5	0.4	164.2	46.5	28.8	253.8
Net benefits[c]	278.8	4.9	0.1	147.3	22.0	33.7	70.9
Proposed							
Number of regulations	29	0	0	2	4	2	21
Monetized benefits exceed costs	15	0	0	1	3	2	9
Net costs	−23.1	0.0	0.0	9.5	−89.8	4.4	52.8
Gross costs[d]	181.9	0.0	0.0	9.5	96.9	4.4	71.2
Benefits	492.7	0.0	0.0	63.0	277.2	81.2	71.3
Net benefits	515.8	0.0	0.0	53.6	367.0	76.7	18.5
All							
Number of regulations	83	1	1	6	9	5	61
Monetized benefits exceed costs	38	1	1	5	5	5	21
Net costs	197.2	0.7	0.3	26.3	−65.3	−0.4	235.7
Gross costs	449.1	1.2	0.3	32.2	121.4	16.1	277.9
Benefits	991.9	5.5	0.4	227.2	323.7	110.0	325.1
Net benefits	794.7	4.9	0.1	200.9	389.1	110.4	89.4

Note: Aggregate totals may not add owing to rounding.
a. Includes regulations that have either quantified costs or benefits.
b. Benefits are monetized by using base-case values. See table 10-3.
c. Net benefits are calculated by subtracting net costs from benefits.
d. The huge difference in net and gross costs for proposed rules is a result of one rule—the indoor air quality rule proposed by OSHA in 1994. The net cost of the rule is −$92 billion, while the gross cost of the rule is $94 billion. The cost savings are attributed to productivity gains.

costs because agencies frequently distinguish between compliance costs and cost savings resulting from a rule. Gross costs are direct compliance costs.[23] Net costs represent the difference between gross costs and any cost savings or additional costs associated with the rule. For example, cost savings generally take the form of avoided costs of cleanup or damage, savings from waste minimization, productivity gains, or fuel economy benefits. I compute net benefits as benefits minus net costs.[24]

Benefits fall into two main categories. About 60 percent of the total benefits results from reductions in the risk of death, disease, and injury.[25] The remaining 40 percent results from reductions in pollution, with about 14 percent coming from reductions in sulfur dioxides and 13 percent coming from reductions in volatile organic compounds, a primary contributor to urban ozone.[26]

The analysis provides several interesting insights into government agencies' use of cost-benefit analysis. First, on the basis of agency numbers, there are about $280 billion in net benefits for final rules[27] and $515 billion for proposed rules.[28] The positive aggregate for totals also carries over to the agencies. Where agencies have promulgated proposed or final regulations, their numbers suggest that those regulations would result in net benefits.

At the same time, however, not all agencies' rules would pass a cost-benefit test, even if we used their numbers.[29] Focusing on final rules, I find that twenty-three out of fifty-four, or 43 percent, would pass such a test. For proposed rules, fifteen of twenty-nine, or 52 percent, would pass such a test. Note that the agency numbers themselves have only eight proposed rules and nine final rules passing a cost-benefit test (see table 10-1). The higher number of rules that pass when I use such an analysis is largely due to the fact that I monetize benefits in several cases where the agencies have not done so.

Figure 10-1 provides an overview of the distribution of net benefits. The left side of the figure shows the number of rules with net costs that fall in various categories. The right side of the figure shows the number of rules with net benefits that fall in various categories. Most rules with net benefits tend to be in the $10 billion to less than $100 billion category or $1 billion to less than $10 billion category. In contrast, most rules with net costs fall in the category of $0 to less than $1 billion or the $1 billion to less than $10 billion category.[30] While less than half of all final rules pass a cost-benefit test, aggregate

Figure 10-1   Distribution of Net Benefits of Fifty-four Final Regulations, 1990 to Mid-1995

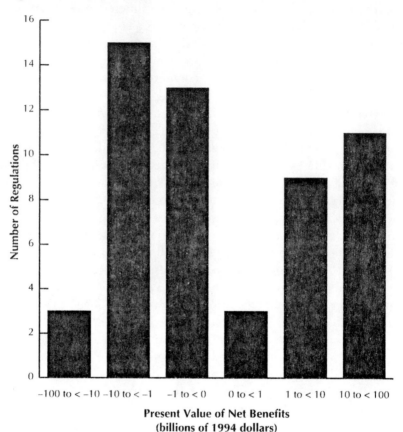

net benefits are positive because many of the rules that do pass have substantial benefits. Ten final rules account for just over $320 billion in net benefits. While those ten rules make up about 30 percent of the total net costs, they represent nearly 80 percent of total benefits for all final rules.

The agencies' numbers suggest that a substantial number of their own regulations should not be promulgated if cost-benefit analysis were the sole criterion for judgment.[31] Using agency estimates of costs and benefits, I calculate the extent to which net benefits would increase if I excluded rules failing a cost-benefit test. I find that net benefits would increase by $115 billion if agencies did not implement final rules failing a cost-benefit test. While all safety regulations pass a cost-benefit test, health regulations pass less frequently. In the case of OSHA health regulations, only two of five final regulations would pass a cost-benefit test; in the case of EPA regulations, only twelve of forty would pass such a test. This analysis suggests that there could be significant gains from applying a cost-benefit test to individual regulations.

Because the EPA accounts for about three-quarters of the final rules, table 10-5 analyzes EPA rules in more detail on the basis of specific statutes. Focusing on final rules reveals some interesting patterns. First, four of six statutes have regulations that result in net costs. Only regulations based on the Clean Air Act and the Safe Drinking Water Act yield positive net benefits.[32] Second, the Clean Air Act has significantly greater benefits than any of the other programs. The data I used to construct table 10-5 show that two of fifteen final regulations would pass a cost-benefit test for statutes other than the Clean Air Act, whereas ten of twenty-five final regulations would pass for the Clean Air Act. Proposed regulations show a similar pattern with a wide range of net benefits for regulations. While six final regulations have net benefits between $10 billion and $50 billion, only three have net costs between $10 billion and $20 billion.

There is a great deal of uncertainty in the actual numbers. Table 10-6 examines the impact of varying the discount rate and the value of benefits for final rules. A reduction in the value of benefits from the base scenario to the "low" scenario reduces net benefits from $279 billion to –$17 billion. An increase in net benefits to the "high" scenario increases net benefits to $653 billion. Variations in the discount rate also have an important impact. A decrease in the discount rate would tend to increase net benefits because many of the benefits occur far out in the future. Decreasing the discount rate from 5 percent to 3 percent increases net benefits by $53 billion, while increasing the discount rate from 5 percent to 7 percent decreases net benefits by $53 billion.[33]

Table 10-6 also shows how the number of rules passing a cost-benefit test varies with assumptions about the discount rate and the valuation of benefits. The number of rules that pass a cost-benefit test is most dependent on the value of the benefits. When I use low values at a 5 percent discount rate, ten fewer final rules pass a cost-benefit

Table 10-5 Net Benefits of Regulations: Breakdown for Environmental Statutes, 1990 to Mid-1995 (present value in billions of 1994 dollars)

	EPA	CAA	CWA	SDWA	FIFRA	TSCA	RCRA	CERCLA
Final								
Number of regulations[a]	40	25	3	3	1	0	6	2
Monetized benefits exceed costs[b]	12	10	0	1	0	0	1	0
Net costs	182.9	121.7	6.5	25.2	0.8	0.0	7.6	21.1
Gross costs	206.7	135.8	6.5	25.2	0.8	0.0	17.2	21.1
Benefits	253.8	209.5	0.5	43.7	0.0	0.0	0.1	0.0
Net benefits[c]	70.9	87.8	-6.1	18.5	-0.8	0.0	-7.4	-21.1
Proposed								
Number of regulations	21	13	4	3	0	1	0	0
Monetized benefits exceed costs	9	8	1	0	0	0	0	0
Net costs	52.8	25.6	1.9	24.6	0.0	0.8	0.0	0.0
Gross costs	71.2	40.9	4.9	24.6	0.0	0.8	0.0	0.0
Benefits	71.3	71.0	0.0	0.2	0.0	0.0	0.0	0.0
Net benefits	18.5	45.4	-1.8	-24.3	0.0	-0.8	0.0	0.0
All								
Number of regulations	61	38	7	6	1	1	6	2
Monetized benefits exceed costs	21	18	1	1	0	0	1	0
Net costs	235.7	147.3	8.4	49.8	0.8	0.8	7.6	21.1
Gross costs	277.9	176.8	11.5	49.8	0.8	0.8	17.2	21.1
Benefits	325.1	280.6	0.5	43.9	0.0	0.0	0.1	0.0
Net benefits	89.4	133.2	-7.9	-5.9	-0.8	-0.8	-7.4	-21.1

Note: Aggregate totals may not add owing to rounding.

a. Includes regulations that have either quantified costs or benefits.

b. Benefits are monetized by using base-case values. See table 10-3.

c. Net benefits are calculated by subtracting net costs from benefits.

Table 10-6   Impact of Varying Key Parameters on Net Benefits of Final Rules

Values of Benefits	Discount Rate					
	3%		5%		7%	
Low values	−15	(14)	−17	(13)	−27	(13)
Base values	332	(22)	279	(23)	226	(23)
High values	774	(26)	653	(26)	543	(26)

Notes: Present value of net benefits in billions of 1994 dollars. The number of final rules that pass a cost-benefit test is given in parentheses.

test than in the base case. That result is predominantly driven by the values of pollution reduction, as eight fewer Clean Air Act rules pass the test.[34] When I use high values at a 5 percent discount rate, three additional rules, all from the Clean Air Act, pass a cost-benefit test. In other words, changes in the value of pollution reductions considered here have a marked effect on the net benefits of Clean Air Act rules. The analysis also reveals that the number of rules passing a cost-benefit test does not change dramatically when I vary the discount rate for a given value of benefits.[35]

This analysis treats a single regulation as the unit of analysis. Yet such a treatment glosses over a potentially very important issue. Not all parts of a regulation may result in net benefits, even if the impact of the entire rule is positive. Thus, it may be appropriate to target those parts of a rule that result in net benefits.

Two examples will be used to illustrate the potential importance of targeting. First, the EPA had a 1991 rule aimed at reducing exposure to lead and copper in drinking water. The first part of the rule aimed at controlling corrosion had net benefits of about $60 billion or a benefit-to-cost ratio of over fifteen.[36] Depending on the effectiveness of corrosion control, the second part of the rule required the replacement of lead pipe. For that part of the rule, the EPA found that benefits only exceeded costs at the extreme high range of benefits and low range of costs. The point is simply that the first part of the rule seems to be an economic winner, while the second part is an economic loser.

The analysis for limiting asbestos in a 1989 rule also illustrates the potential gains from targeting. Using the assumptions contained in the regulatory impact analysis for a likely scenario, the cost-effectiveness of banning selected products ranges from −$.03 million per cancer case avoided for banning asbestos in specialty paper to more than $800 million per cancer case avoided for banning asbestos in automatic transmission components. Again, targeting the regulation to yield the most cost-effective risk reductions could help.[37]

Interpretation of the Data

Without a detailed evaluation of each individual regulatory impact analysis or *Federal Register* preamble, it is difficult to say how individual analyses are likely to be biased. Such an analysis is beyond the scope of this study. Nonetheless, I shall argue below on the basis of theoretical and empirical considerations that the aggregate net benefit estimates presented here are likely to substantially overstate actual net benefits relative to what a "neutral" economist would have estimated. I divide my argument into two parts: theoretical reasons for believing that agency estimates are biased in a particular manner and evaluations of particular laws and regulations that suggest that net benefits are overestimated.

The two principal reasons for believing that agency estimates tend to overstate net benefits are related. One is based on public choice analysis, and the second is based on the enabling statutes, which frequently do not permit a balancing of benefits and costs.

Simply stated, the public choice argument would suggest that agency bureaucrats have an incentive to expand the size of their program (Niskanen 1971). They can achieve that objective by expanding their regulatory reach. To the extent that higher net benefits increase the likelihood that a regulation is passed, those bureaucrats have an incentive to overstate benefits and understate costs.

A related argument is that regulations typically have concentrated benefits and diffuse costs. The groups that receive the lion's share of the benefits have an incentive to overstate those benefits relative to the costs. Those groups will organize and mobilize more effectively because members stand to gain more than the average citizen (Olson 1971).

The legal argument is really a reflection of the political argument. Many of the enabling statutes for environmental, health, and safety regulation do not permit a balancing of costs and benefits. Therefore, to the extent that an executive order requires cost-benefit analysis, Congress and the regulators may try to circumvent that order. One way to circumvent it is to bias the cost-benefit analysis in favor of showing higher net benefits.

While the political arguments tend to point toward an upward bias, the economic arguments are less clear (Hahn and Hird 1991). Direct compliance costs may overstate actual compliance costs because the available engineering cost estimates do not reflect how an industry behaves when it has to comply with a regulation. The argument is that industry will find ways to reduce the cost of compliance relative to an engineering cost estimate developed when the regulation is not yet in force. Also, industry has an incentive to overstate the costs. On the other hand, the regulator need not—and frequently does not—use the industry cost estimates. Moreover, the cost estimates often do not consider transaction costs, such as litigation and paperwork, as well as potential impacts on investment, productivity, and growth (Hazilla and Kopp 1990; Hahn 1995a; Robinson 1995).

On the benefit side, a neutral economist might find that net benefits are understated because some benefits, such as the chronic health effects of air pollution and most benefits to ecosystems, are hard to quantify in monetary terms. At the same time, however, agencies may overstate the beneficial impacts of those parts of a rule that can be quantified to make the rule appear more attractive.

On balance, the theoretical arguments point in the direction that agencies are likely to overstate net benefits, particularly for rules where most of the net benefits are relatively easily quantified. Nonetheless, the theoretical arguments are not unambiguous. It is thus helpful to assess the data. I use two approaches—one that considers groups of regulations and a second that considers specific regulations.

We can apply some consistency checks to the data at the aggregate level. First, consider the total benefits and costs of social regulation. Hahn and Hird (1991) conclude that the benefits and costs of social regulation through 1988 are comparable. If that assessment is correct, and most regulations with the highest net benefits were generally implemented at the outset, we have reason to believe that most regulations implemented since 1990 would not pass a cost-benefit test.

More to the point, consider the case of the 1990 Clean Air Act Amendments. Involved in the formulation of that act, I did a cost-benefit analysis for the Council of Economic Advisers (Hahn 1990). That analysis suggested that the act, when fully implemented, would result in substantial net costs to the economy—on the order of $10 billion to $20 billion annually (Hahn 1994; Portney 1990). Those estimated net costs are hard to square with the estimate obtained here of a present value of $50 billion in net benefits that are associated with regulations based on the 1990 Clean Air Act Amendments. I find a large discrepancy between what economists have estimated for net costs of the 1990 legislation and what agencies have estimated as net benefits for individual regulations, when I use the base-case values for pollution reduction.

As noted above, the net benefits of regulations are quite sensitive to assumptions about the value of pollution reductions. For example, using the low values, we find that the Clean Air Act regulations would result in net costs of $90 billion, which is more in line with economists' estimates. Using the high values, we find that benefits would be about $220 billion, which seems highly implausible.[38]

A final example relates to cost savings. The agencies frequently point out cost savings resulting from avoided costs of cleanup, avoided costs of property damage, and savings from productivity gains or fuel economy benefits. In seven cases they find that those cost savings are sufficiently large that the rule actually results in net savings. This means that it would be in the interest of firms to adopt those rules for purely economic reasons. Thus, the agencies effectively claim that firms are not maximizing profits without government intervention.

One must be skeptical about government officials' identifying new profit opportunities that businesses are not already pursuing. After all, those companies are in the business of making money, while the government is not. The large cost savings associated with those regulations suggest that the government may have substantially over-estimated net benefits. At the same time, I do not wish to suggest that there are not potential cost savings from rules; I am merely skeptical of taking at face value the government estimates of the magnitude of those savings.

A review of selected individual regulations paints a similar picture. Below I consider three examples that illustrate different problems with the agencies' calculations.

One common problem relates to the discounting of costs and benefits. In 1990 the EPA proposed a rule regulating hazardous waste from facilities that make wood preservatives. The EPA's initial risk assessment found 300 cancer cases over 300 years and described that risk as an average of one cancer case per year. The OMB (1990a) pointed out that there was no risk until after 2090 and that the risk did not exceed one per year until 2215. The EPA calculated the discounted compliance costs to be as low as $800,000 per undiscounted cancer case prevented. When the OMB accounted for the timing of benefits, the agency calculated the cost as $7.2 trillion per statistical cancer case avoided.

A second common problem is the use of worst-case scenarios to derive estimates of expected risks (Nichols and Zeckhauser 1986; Hendee 1996). In a 1987 formaldehyde regulation OSHA argued that the cancer risk was five per 100,000 persons exposed for forty-five years. The OMB (1986) argued that OSHA greatly overestimated the risk and that the actual cancer risk was closer to one in a billion. The OMB noted that OSHA used a pattern of worst-case scenarios in determining exposure assumptions, model selection, and the use of administered dose rather than delivered dose.

Combining those errors with the fact that OSHA did not discount the benefits to account for the long latency period before the onset of a cancer, the OMB obtained significantly different results for cost-effectiveness. While OSHA found that the cost per cancer case avoided ranged from $5 million to $41 million, the OMB estimated that the number should be in the neighborhood of $70 billion per cancer case avoided.

A third problem is the failure to specify a clear baseline from which to measure proposed changes in policy. Failure to specify a clear baseline makes it difficult to determine whether benefit and cost estimates are sensible. In addition, absence of a clear baseline can lead to problems with double counting of benefits. Such double counting can occur when the benefits of a rule are misspecified or when a rule takes credit for benefits that result from another rule. One example of double counting occurred in the 1990 EPA rule to identify and list hazardous waste for petroleum refineries. In response to the rule, the OMB (1990b) argued that the EPA failed to consider the risk-reducing effects of other EPA regulations, so that the EPA significantly overstated the benefits of that rule. The EPA attributed three-fourths of the estimated cancer prevention benefits and more than three-fourths of the estimated noncancer health benefits to avoided contamination of public drinking water wells; however, mandatory treatment requirements promulgated under the Safe Drinking Water Act had already yielded those benefits. Thus, the majority of human health risks that the EPA claimed for that rule had already been substantially reduced or eliminated.

My analysis of the costs and benefits of regulation since 1990 yields several important conclusions. First, net benefits exhibit a wide range. Second, even using agency numbers, net benefits would increase substantially if agencies rejected rules that did not pass a cost-benefit test. Third, aggregate estimates of agency net benefits are positive when agency data are used. Fourth, the total level of net benefits is quite sensitive to the presumed value of benefits as well as to the discount rate. Fifth, the number of regulations passing a cost-benefit test is sensitive to the values of the benefits, especially the values of pollution reductions. Sixth, we have strong theoretical and empirical reasons to believe that the government substantially overstates its estimates of net benefits. Moreover, it is plausible that the aggregate expected net benefits for the final regulations studied here are actually negative. Finally, it is quite likely that several final and proposed rules would pass a net benefit test, even if a neutral economist performed it. At the same time, fewer regulations would pass an economist's cost-benefit test than the agency analysis suggests.

Cost-Effectiveness

The cost-effectiveness of a regulation is one measure of the efficiency with which resources are being spent. In environmental, health, and safety regulation, one common measure of cost-effectiveness is the resources used for each statistical life that is saved.[39] The subsequent analysis will examine how that measure varies within and across agencies. The analysis also identifies patterns in the data on cost-effectiveness. Unlike previous analyses, which tend to focus on the association of a single variable such as cancer with cost-effectiveness, this analysis uses multiple regression to sort out the impact of different factors on cost-effectiveness.

Before examining the data, I need to define the measure of cost-effectiveness. I define costs as direct costs. I exclude cost savings from the base case because I believe that those savings are generally questionable. Indeed, in seven cases, including cost savings in the analysis leads to regulations that would save a company money, which means that the company is not maximizing profits. While those savings are possible, I consider them unlikely to be achieved. Nonetheless, I shall also consider the case in which the analysis includes those cost savings.

I measure effectiveness in terms of "adjusted" lives and life-years, where adjustments account for significant nonfatal diseases and injuries by using the fatality index I previously discussed. I calculate life-years by multiplying the number of lives saved by the expected remaining life-years at the time of the premature death.[40] I use that conversion because it better accounts for the time of the premature death or health effect. For example, a life-year calculation would account for the fact that a child has a greater expected remaining life than an elderly person. I compute cost-effectiveness by dividing the annualized cost by the annualized effectiveness.[41] The discount rate for the base case is 5 percent.

Cost-effectiveness is quite sensitive to the measure that is used. An example will illustrate this point. Consider a NHTSA regulation requiring an antilock braking system for selected vehicles. The costs per adjusted life and life-year—the measures used here—are $1,000,000 and $60,000, respectively. If we net out nearly $500 million in annual property damage savings so that we use a measure of net costs, the annual cost-effectiveness per adjusted life is $330,000. If we exclude nonfatal health effects from the denominator, the cost-effectiveness measure changes dramatically: we obtain a value of $1,860,000 when property cost savings are not included and $610,000 when cost savings are included. Finally, if we include the impact of nonfatal health benefits in the numerator instead of in the denominator, yet another measure emerges. Monetizing nonfatal health benefits and including them in the numerator yields –$3,800,000, while adding nonhealth savings to that calculation yields –$5,050,000, which implies that the regulation actually results in net savings.

The preceding example suggests that we need to interpret cost-effectiveness measures with great care. More important, calculations that rely on cost-effectiveness to reallocate resources may be misleading because the ordering of cost-effectiveness measures may not be highly correlated with the ordering of net benefits associated with those measures. We can solve that problem by working directly with benefit and cost numbers rather than with cost-effectiveness numbers if the benefit information is available.

Figure 10-2 summarizes information on the cost-effectiveness of final regulations. The figure graphs the cost-effectiveness of each reg-

Figure 10-2   Cost-Effectiveness ($/life) of Selected Final Regulations, 1984 to Mid-1985

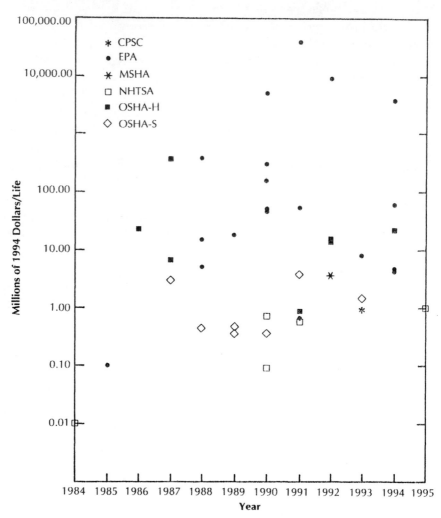

ulation against time on a logarithmic scale. I identify the date of each regulation by the year of promulgation. The data include virtually all major environmental, health, and safety regulations with adequate cost and effectiveness information since 1990, but only selected major regulations before that time.[42] From the figure we can see that cost-effectiveness exhibits a wide variation over time, within agencies and across agencies. Cost-effectiveness ranges from $10,000 to $36 billion per life saved, with a median value of about $6 million per life saved. The level of those expenditures and the differences in cost-effectiveness across regulations suggest that there is significant potential for achieving much greater risk reduction at a lower cost to society, a point made by Tengs and Graham (1996) and many other economists that I shall consider below.

To put those cost-effectiveness numbers in perspective, if we spent the entire GNP on reducing accidental deaths and environmentally induced cancers, the maximum we could spend per life saved is $65 million.[43] If we applied that "GNP test" to all final regulations, only 20 percent—eight of forty—would fail. For the EPA, 43 percent—six of fourteen—would fail the test since 1990.[44]

> **The differences in cost-effectiveness across regulations suggest that there is significant potential for achieving much greater risk reduction at a lower cost to society.**

In other words, for a significant number of regulations, we would spend money at a rate that would exhaust the GNP simply on investments aimed at reducing fatal accidents and a small portion of cancers. To make such imprudent investments would leave no money for the basic necessities of life.

The preceding figures suggest that EPA regulations tend to be relatively poor in terms of cost-effectiveness compared with other agencies' regulations. The median final EPA regulation is about $50 million per life saved. That is more than three times higher than the median for OSHA health regulations and more than fifty times higher than the median for all safety agencies besides MSHA.

Figure 10-2 also reveals that regulations involving safety are more cost-effective on average than regulations involving health. For example, OSHA health regulations are more expensive per life saved than OSHA safety regulations in all but one instance. A similar pattern, not shown in the figure, emerges for life-saving regulations involving cancer compared with those that do not involve reductions in cancer cases. The median cancer regulation is almost seventy times as large as the median noncancer regulation.[45]

The plot of the data as a function of time does not reveal any obvious trend. The absence of a trend came as somewhat of a surprise. One might expect cost-effectiveness to worsen over time as agencies implement the most cost-effective regulations first. Part of the reason for the absence of a time trend may be that I do not consider regulations before 1984 because of a lack of data. In addition, there are several other factors. Agencies may identify new areas that had not been analyzed where regulations could be relatively cost-effective. Moreover, technological improvements can lower the cost of regulation. Another possibility is that this type of social regulation may have already reached the point of diminishing returns in the early 1980s. A more complete time series going back to the early 1970s might show a time trend.

An alternative explanation for the absence of a time trend is simply that concerns with cost-effectiveness rarely drive agencies' agendas. Instead, they are driven by laws that Congress passes as well as crises that spring up from time to time. I have found some evidence that agencies do not set priorities based on relative risks or cost-effectiveness. For example, the EPA only began seriously examining the relative rankings of risks a few years ago (EPA 1987b). Even to this day, the agency has done very little work on prioritizing regulations in terms of cost-effectiveness. The same can be said of the other agencies, although NHTSA with the Federal Highway Administration has done retrospective analyses of its programs (NHTSA-FHWA 1991). Moreover, regulatory agencies that have primary responsibility for protecting the environment, safety, and health of the public have paid scant attention to developing strategic plans that would implement the most cost-effective regulations first.

I use the information shown in figure 10-2 along with information based on work by Morrall (1986), updated in Lutter and Morrall (1994) and Viscusi (1996), to examine some of those hypotheses more formally with an ordinary least squares regression. The dependent variable in the regression is the natural log of the cost-effectiveness of regulation[46] as measured by the cost per life-year saved or cost per life saved.[47] Regulations include both proposed and final rules. Table 10-7 summarizes three regressions, one based on the data assembled for this study, a second based on Morrall's earlier calculations, and a third that pools the two data sources.

The first regression uses three explanatory variables: a dummy variable for whether the rule is primarily aimed at reducing cancer risks (1 if yes, 0 otherwise); a dummy variable for whether the EPA promulgated the rule (1 if yes, 0 otherwise); and a time variable asso-

Table 10–7 Comparison of Regressions Using Three Datasets

Data Set		n	R Square	Constant	Cancer	Year	EPA	Morrall
Hahn	Natural log of cost-effectiveness ($/life-year)	56	0.654	−155.14	4.22[a] 6.02	0.08 0.67	2.08[a] 3.03	
Morrall	Natural log of cost-effectiveness ($/life)	59	0.600	−326.44	5.86[a] 6.34	0.16[a] 2.42	−0.70 −0.75	
Pooled	Natural log of cost-effectiveness ($/life)	94	0.647	−158.45	4.42[a] 8.46	0.08 1.42	1.02 1.97	0.76 1.28

Note: The t-statistics are given in parentheses.
a. The t-value is significant at the 5 percent level using a two-tail test.

ciated with the year the rule is listed in the *Federal Register* (for example, if the year is 1987, the value of that variable is 1987).

The hypothesis is that the sign of the cancer dummy will be positive because agencies appear to be willing to regulate cancer risks more stringently than noncancer risks. On the basis of a review of the data, I expect the sign of the dummy for the EPA to be positive. Finally, I hypothesize that the time variable is positive because I presume that cost-effectiveness declines over time as agencies use the low-cost options for saving lives first.

The first regression provides support for two of the three hypotheses. Each of the variables has the expected sign, which is positive. All explanatory variables are significant, with the exception of the time trend variable.[48]

The second regression is based on Morrall's (1986) extended data set. The data include some minor rules not included in my data set, as well as some regulations before the development of formal regulatory impact analyses. Although the regression uses the same basic measure of cost-effectiveness, Morrall has adjusted the agency numbers on the basis of a detailed analysis of specific rules. The regression reported here takes the same basic form as the first regression. Unlike the first regression, the coefficient on the EPA variable is negative, but insignificant, and the time variable has the expected sign and is significant.[49]

The EPA dummy is negative and insignificant because of the introduction of a few OSHA rules and one Food and Drug Administration rule that are all in the high range of cost-effectiveness and not in my database. Four of those rules are from the 1970s. Yet the time variable is significant because agencies promulgated numerous safety rules between 1967 and the early 1980s that were relatively cost-effective.

The third regression pools the Morrall data with my data set. Where I have computed cost-effectiveness numbers, I use those numbers with the cost-per-life measure in the regression; otherwise, I use Morrall's numbers. I add a dummy variable to the regression that takes on a value of 1 when I use Morrall's cost-effectiveness data. We expect the sign of the Morrall dummy to be positive if we believe that agencies overstate benefits and understate costs, since Morrall would have adjusted the numbers accordingly. Of course, his data include several rules from the 1970s and early 1980s when it was likely that less costly risks were still available to regulate.

The pooled regression is significant for cancer but insignificant for the EPA, year, and Morrall dummies.[50] All explanatory variables have the expected sign. In the case of cancer, pooling the data further accentuates the results of the initial regressions, while in the case of the year and EPA dummies, the results of the pooled data fall somewhere in between.

In addition to examining the impact of the determinants of cost-effectiveness, I did a preliminary analysis of proposed rules for which "no action" was taken.[51] As one might expect, there is a relationship between the decision not to take action on a rule and its expected cost-effectiveness. As the cost-effectiveness of a rule increases, it is less likely that action will be taken on that rule. In my database, for example, there is a .5 correlation between taking no action and the cost-effectiveness of a rule.[52] That suggests that the decision not to take action is driven, at least in part, by the cost-effectiveness of the proposal. I plan to explore that relationship in more detail in later work.

I can now summarize the implications of that analysis for the determinants of cost-effectiveness. The cancer dummy variable generally appears to be significant. Agency rules dealing with reducing cancer generally have a poorer cost-effectiveness than those that do not, and that finding is fairly robust to the particular specification of the log-linear regression.[53] The time trend does not generally appear to be significant. The variable on the EPA is also significant in some cases, but not in others, depending on the time frame and data.

Saving More Money and Lives

Given the relatively poor cost-effectiveness of some regulations, it is worth exploring how to reallocate resources to save more lives or money (Goklany 1992). Here, I develop a calculation similar to that described in Tengs and Graham (1996), but I focus on the developing world. If one is really concerned about using public investments to save lives, then the developing world is a logical place to look. The question I examine is the extent to which one can save lives, money, or both by reallocating U.S. expenditures to other life-saving activities in the developing world.

In table 10-8 I summarize a crude calculation for the United States and the rest of the world. The table compares the cost and effectiveness numbers for the United States and the developing world

Table 10-8   The Efficiency of Life-Saving Investments in the United
States and the Developing World (1994$)

Region	Costs (billions)	Life-Years Gained (millions)	Average Cost per Life-Year	Life-Saving Efficiency Ratio[a]
United States[b]	$8.3	0.1	$96,865	1
Mexico	$8.7	2.5	$3,456	28
Middle-income[c]	$7.2	21.8	$330	293
Low-income[d]	$5.8	93.4	$62	1,569

Note: The reader should be aware that there are large uncertainties associated with
the numbers, but they are the best available.
a. Defined as U.S. cost-effectiveness divided by developing-region cost-effectiveness.
b. Based on final regulations from 1990 to mid-1995. Gross costs are used here.
c. The middle-income region is based on data from Latin America and the
Caribbean countries. Note that this region includes Mexico but is based on an analysis different from the calculation done specifically for Mexico.
d. The low-income region is based on data from sub-Saharan Africa.

for selected regions. Given data availability, I consider three areas—
low-income countries with data from sub-Saharan Africa, middle-
income countries with data from Latin America and the Caribbean
nations, and Mexico.[54]

I base the cost and effectiveness measures for the United States
on all twenty-seven final regulations in my database on federal regulations. Costs, which are about $8 billion, represent the sum of annual-
ized gross costs. That expenditure yields about 90,000 life-years gained
at a cost per life-year of just under $100,000.

For the rest of the world, I use a comparable measure of effectiveness called "disability adjusted life-years" saved. That represents the
number of years saved as a result of the intervention.[55]

The calculations for the low-income countries and the middle-
income countries are based on very crude estimates. The calculations
for Mexico are based on more refined estimates.[56] In addition, the
assumptions differ across the calculations.[57] Nonetheless, the calculations are useful for providing estimates of the order of magnitude of
potential efficiency gains, and they are the best numbers available now.

The column labeled "life-saving efficiency ratio" provides some
insight into the potential for saving more lives, money, or both by

reallocating resources. The ratio represents the number of life-years that can be saved with a $1 investment in developing countries versus spending that same dollar on an average recent federal regulation in the United States. In Mexico, a dollar expenditure on a life-saving activity is about thirty times as effective as spending that amount on a recent average federal regulation; in the low-income countries it is over 1,500 times as effective; and in the middle-income countries, it is almost 300 times as effective.

Those life-saving efficiency numbers strongly suggest that other regions could achieve substantially more savings in life-years for less money than is spent in the United States.[58] While the average numbers highlight those savings, I have constructed a total cost curve that more completely characterizes the data. For the regions examined here, we could save 114 million life-years at a cost of about $27 billion.[59] The first 100 million life-years could be saved in low-income and middle-income regions at a cost of less than $100 per life-year. An additional ten million life-years could be saved at less than $1,000 per life-year. That includes a few interventions in Mexico.[60] While most of the life-years could be saved rather

> **In Mexico, a dollar expenditure on a life-saving activity is about thirty times as effective as spending that amount on a recent average federal regulation.**

cheaply, saving the last 4,000 life-years would cost more than $100,000 per life-year and would include thirteen U.S. regulations with a cost per life-year saved of more than $1,000,000. As expected, U.S. regulations are at the high end of the cost-effectiveness curve.[61]

When resources spent in the United States are reallocated to the rest of the world, the potential for saving more lives is substantial. We could save more than 110 million additional life-years by reallocating recent U.S. expenditures of about $8 billion to life-saving activities in other countries.[62] Furthermore, since we could save 90,000 life-years for about $2 million by using one intervention that treats sexually transmitted diseases in low-income countries, nearly all of the $8 billion represents potential cost savings.

If we focus solely on the United States, we reach a similar qualitative conclusion. Tengs and Graham (1996) consider substituting nonregulatory interventions for some costly regulatory interventions in the United States. While their data are not directly comparable to mine, they find that $500 million spent on medical interventions in the United States could be reallocated to save an additional 350,000 life-years annually for an average cost-effectiveness of about $1,000 per life-year saved, a figure comparable to some developing nations.

There is also some potential to save lives by diverting expenditures from existing regulations to some proposed regulations. For example, the requirement that employees wear seat belts appears to be a relatively cost-effective investment. Agency estimates suggest that the measure could save more than 14,000 life-years at a cost per life-year of less than $20,000. When compared with a median cost per life-year saved of $600,000 for recent major federal regulations, that investment looks quite attractive.

This analysis shows that there is great potential for increasing lives saved by reallocating expenditures to more cost-effective interventions within the United States or to developing nations. It also shows that the same number of lives could be saved at substantially lower cost by reallocating resources. We shall need to refine such analysis to develop a better understanding of precisely which interventions and regulations offer the highest returns.

Although the potential for saving lives cost-effectively in developing countries is substantially greater than in the United States, it may not be economically efficient to do so. Willingness to pay for risk reductions is likely to vary substantially across countries (Lutter and Morrall 1994). Whether those differences in willingness to pay exceed differences in cost-effectiveness is an empirical issue.[63]

Even if we can realize efficiency gains by reallocating expenditures across nations or even programs, U.S. citizens and special interests may be reluctant to make such trade-offs. For example, labor unions supporting particular safety regulations are unlikely to endorse spending money on life-saving interventions in Mexico if doing so stymies their preferred regulations. The case is probably easier to make for reallocating expenditures within U.S. regulatory programs, but even there we can expect fierce resistance from parties that perceive themselves as losers.

Conclusions, Recommendations, and Areas for Future Research

This chapter provides the most comprehensive analysis of the benefits and costs of recent environmental, health, and safety regulation based on studies by government agencies. Several conclusions emerge from the analysis. First, using government agency data, it would appear that there is a present value of about $280 billion in net benefits to government regulation in those areas since 1990. Second, it is likely that those estimates of net benefits are substantially overstated. Third, about half the final rules would not pass a cost-benefit test, even when we use government agencies' numbers. Fourth, eliminating final rules that would not pass a cost-benefit test could increase the present value of net benefits by more than $115 billion when we use government agencies' numbers. Fifth, the quality of the cost-benefit analyses exhibits a wide variation from very poor to very good. Agencies could dramatically improve average quality by following a few simple guidelines. Sixth, we could save a substantial number of lives and money by reallocating resources from ineffective domestic regulations to other life-saving interventions in the United States or in the developing world. In addition, we could realize significant gains by more carefully targeting regulations. Seventh, agencies could improve regulations by implementing a strategic planning process that uses net economic benefits as a criterion in deciding how to allocate agency resources. Finally, the cost-effectiveness of regulations exhibits some distinct patterns. On average, environmental regulations and cancer-reducing regulations are not so cost-effective as other social regulations, and the decision to take action on a proposed rule is related to the expected cost-effectiveness of the rule.

The analysis presented here is the first part of a broader research project aimed at assessing the benefits and costs of regulation, the regulatory impacts of specific regulations and agencies, and the design and evaluation of regulatory reform proposals. We can fruitfully expand the current analysis in several ways. First, we can obtain more information on the quality of the underlying analyses, both within and across agencies. Second, we can construct a larger database of regulations, both for rules from other agencies such as the FDA and for rules before 1990. Third, we can develop a better understanding of how regulatory oversight has affected policy outcomes. Finally, we can refine and extend some of the benefit estimates.

This analysis uses as its main source of data regulatory analyses that were done before the enactment of regulations. It would be useful to compare those analyses with what actually occurred to determine likely biases in the estimates. That is a laborious exercise, but one that could identify systematic biases associated with doing prospective analyses of proposed policies.

If one takes the agency numbers of net benefits developed here at face value, there is reason to be gleeful. They basically say that the federal government has done more good than harm in promulgating regulations since 1990; however, the government could do an even better job if it took its own agency estimates of benefits and costs more seriously.

There are reasons *not* to take the agency numbers at face value. Both theory and empirical evidence suggest that agencies are likely to overstate substantially the aggregate numbers for net benefits. That leads to an important insight for reformers interested in promoting economically efficient regulation. Simply requiring that agencies do more cost-benefit analysis is not likely to have much impact.

If cost-benefit analysis is to play a greater role in agency rule making, the quality of the analysis should be improved dramatically. Changes that would improve the quality of analysis include: making key assumptions explicit—something that current regulatory impact analyses do not frequently do; summarizing key assumptions; using best estimates and appropriate ranges to reflect uncertainty; providing estimates of the net present value of costs and benefits with common assumptions; introducing peer review of the analyses and putting more weight on peer-reviewed scholarship; and summarizing sensitivity analyses and base-case results. Some of those changes are embodied in regulatory reform bills that the 104th Congress is considering.

Agencies could improve the quality of their analysis if they used a common set of economic assumptions, as I have done here. Using common baseline assumptions would make it easier to compare results for different regulations. Variables for which common assumptions should be used include the social discount rate, the value of reducing risks of dying and accidents, and the value associated with improvements in health. An agency, such as the OMB, should be given the responsibility for developing key values for different variables based on the best economics and science. The use of a common set of assumptions should not preclude the introduction of other values for variables where such values may be appropriate.

An agency such as the OMB should also develop a standard format for presenting results in a clear and succinct manner. A good summary and clear analysis will make it easier for policy makers and interested parties to evaluate results. In addition, transparency is necessary if such analysis is to enjoy broad public support.

Improving the quality of cost-benefit analysis is an important step for improving public policy. For such analysis to be taken seriously, however, policy makers must change the rules of the game. They should require agency heads to put more weight on the economic results of regulatory analyses. There are several mechanisms for achieving that end, including a legislative requirement that benefits justify or exceed costs.[64] In addition, policy makers should expand the scope of regulatory oversight to include regulations in place and of regulatory review to include all regulatory agencies. Moreover, policy makers should allow interested parties to sue if they can argue that an agency did not select an alternative that could achieve the same goal at a much lower cost or if they believe that the benefits from a proposed regulation fall far short of costs. Finally, policy makers could create a technocratic elite to regulate the regulators (Breyer 1993) and could consider securing legislation requiring Congress to approve each major regulation before it becomes law.

None of those proposals is a panacea, but all of them deserve serious consideration. Increased judicial review would be helpful, but the statute needs to be crafted carefully to allow for limited challenges. Increasing the scope of executive regulatory oversight should promote more economically efficient regulation. Requiring benefits to justify costs is likely to be helpful. If an agency head has to justify costs in a written statement, that would force him to think more carefully through the economic issues at stake. It is easy to imagine, however, that some of those proposals may lead to less efficient policies. The performance of a technocratic elite depends to some extent on the directions from its political master—who may not be an advocate for economic efficiency.[65] Congress may not be willing to vote against regulations where benefits are concentrated and costs are diffuse.

One simple proposal that has merit is to require regulatory agency heads to plan their agenda for developing regulations based on economic considerations, including cost-effectiveness and net benefits. Agency heads should do that planning annually or biannually, and policy makers should encourage the OMB to review the economic portion of the planning process. Such a planning exercise, if required by Congress, could be helpful in ensuring that agencies pick the low-hanging fruit before climbing to pick the fruit at the top of the tree.

Current planning in most regulatory agencies places insufficient emphasis on the likely benefits and costs of regulations and excessive emphasis on politics and deadlines. Congress should consider changing that emphasis by explicitly asking agencies to consider broad economic impacts in formulating their policy agendas.

Another sensible proposal is to allow for the explicit consideration of costs and benefits in the development of all regulatory policies. Sections of some statutes explicitly prohibit the balancing of costs and benefits in the development of environmental, health, and safety regulations. For example, the Clean Air Act requires that national emission standards for hazardous air pollutants be set to protect human health without considering costs, and the Delaney Clause imposes a zero-risk tolerance for pesticides in food additives. Congress should remove those prohibitions to allocate resources more efficiently.

Unfortunately, process changes, such as those requiring greater use of cost-benefit analysis, will always have significant limitations. In the end, there is no substitute for rewriting the substantive laws in a way that promotes efficiency and reduces the current reach of the federal government (Hahn 1995c). That means devolving certain functions where the problems are local, such as the disposal of waste and the treatment of drinking water; it also means changing the nature of the role of the regulators. It may, for example, be more appropriate for the EPA and OSHA to provide information in areas such as energy efficiency and worker safety than for those agencies to impose arbitrary requirements that are frequently costly and ineffective.

The debate on cost-benefit analysis has become excessively polarized. Many Democrats claim to support cost-benefit analysis, but only so long as it does not change policy outcomes. Many Republicans support cost-benefit analysis because they believe it can improve bureaucratic decision making and help roll back the seemingly inexorable growth of the regulatory state. The Democrats can "talk the talk" on cost-benefit analysis, but cannot "walk the walk" because they fear that using cost-benefit analysis would reduce the role of government and thus hurt their core constituencies. The Republicans, however, are guilty of putting excessive faith in the tool. Cost-benefit analysis is not the equivalent of stepping on a scale to find out one's weight to the nearest pound, as many Republicans and economists sometimes might suggest.[66] For the regulatory issues examined here, cost-benefit analysis is more like guessing the balance in one's checking account when he knows the number of checks he has written but is missing several entries in his checkbook. In short, there is typically a great deal of uncertainty in cost-benefit analysis, and reasonable people will often disagree about best estimates and appropriate ranges (Lave 1996).

So what is an appropriate role for cost-benefit analysis in the regulation of health, safety, and the environment? Because the amounts we are spending are in the hundreds of billions of dollars annually, cost-benefit analysis should play a more prominent role in public policy formation than it has to date. That does not mean that all regulatory proposals should require a detailed cost-benefit analysis. Rather, the level of the analysis should be tailored to the problem. Big issues, in terms of their economic impact, should receive more scrutiny and analysis than relatively small economic issues.[67]

> **Performed well and taken seriously, cost-benefit analysis can and should aid in the selection and design of more economically efficient policies.**

Today we make a useful distinction between major and minor rules, but we should refine that distinction, perhaps by adding some other categories where a "back-of-the-envelope" analysis or less than full-blown analysis is required.

Despite my enthusiasm for cost-benefit analysis, I am leery about proposals that require the agency head to implement regulations solely on the basis of whether benefits exceed costs. Given the uncertainties in the analysis, we should not ask too much of the tool. A standard that benefits justify costs gives the agency head more leeway but is more sensible.

Agency heads should not be bound by a strict cost-benefit test because there may be other factors that an agency head will want to consider in a decision. It is important, however, that the agency head and elected officials be held accountable for decisions that are expected to impose significant costs on consumers without commensurate benefits. Ideally, the burden of proof should be shifted so that elected officials and agency heads have to use a great deal of scarce political capital if they wish to advance laws or regulations that impose a net economic burden on society.

We should view cost-benefit analysis as an accounting tool that can help point out the implications of a policy. It can identify winners and losers from a policy, and it can help rank policies in terms of their likely impact on economic efficiency. Performed well and taken seriously, cost-benefit analysis can and should aid in the selection and design of more economically efficient policies.

NOTES

This research was supported in part by a grant from the National Science Foundation, Decision, Risk and Management Science Program. I would like to thank Jonathan Siskin for his excellent research assistance and analytical insights. I also would like to thank Mia Chough, Ed Dale, Elizabeth Drembus, Jonathan Feldman, Leigh Tripoli, and Andrew Wong for providing analytical support and editorial assistance. In addition, I would like to thank Jose-Luis Bobadilla, Peter Cowley, Art Fraas, Harold Furchtgott-Roth, John Graham, David Harrison, Randy Lutter, Randy Lyon, Al McGartland, John Morrall, Bob Shelton, Brett Snyder, Cass Sunstein, Jens Svenson, Tammy Tengs, Leigh Tripoli, W. Kip Viscusi, and Clifford Winston for their help in framing various parts of the analysis. This chapter represents my views and does not necessarily reflect the views of any individuals or institutions with which I am affiliated.

1. I use the words *rule* and *regulation* interchangeably in this chapter.
2. A proposed rule is simply a proposal for adopting a rule or regulation. A final rule is the actual regulation.
3. I am extending this analysis to other agencies and will report on the results in future work.
4. Another important strand of research examines the long-term impacts of regulation on growth and productivity. See, for example, Hazilla and Kopp (1990), Jorgenson and Wilcoxen (1990), and Robinson (1995).
5. My database includes a few rules that were not considered major in their final form; however, regulatory impact analyses were prepared for those rules on the presumption that they could be major.
6. While the definition of a "major" or "significant" rule has changed somewhat over time, it is generally a regulation that is expected to have one or more of the following characteristics: an annual impact on the economy of $100 million or more; a major increase in costs or prices for consumers or business; or significant effects on competition, employment, investment, productivity, or innovation. Recently, that definition has been expanded under President Clinton's Executive Order 12886.
7. Agency costs almost never take into account long-term impacts on productivity and investment. Moreover, agency estimates rarely take into account other costs of regulation such as expenses incurred in litigating regulations and managerial time spent on compliance (Hahn 1995b). Agencies could overstate the costs of technology-based control options if there is flexibility in the standards; such flexibility is often quite limited, however.
8. I wish to alert the reader to the fact that the cost and benefit numbers developed throughout this chapter are based on those estimates, many of which are fre-

quently incomplete. Nonetheless, the numbers summarize the official information that was available to the government at the time of the decision.

9. In most cases an agency presents a range of benefits. Unless the agency has given a best-guess estimate, I have used the average over the range.

10. In future research I shall examine the number of rules that consider alternatives.

11. While the CPSC is not subject to OMB review, I included one rule from that agency that would have likely been placed in the major category if it had been reviewed.

12. One EPA rule, which would have passed a cost-benefit test on the basis of net cost savings or monetized benefits, is counted as one of the ten rules that monetized benefits. In addition, two of the rules with net cost savings were EPA rules that were aimed at easing compliance with existing regulations.

13. An additional four rules would pass a cost-benefit test if the high end of the agency range were used to estimate benefits.

14. Examples include a rule assessing the extent to which general federal actions conform to state or federal implementation plans under the Clean Air Act, a rule outlining the operating permits program of the Clean Air Act, and a rule setting requirements for lead-based paint activities. Those rules only qualitatively describe benefits.

15. I plan to more carefully document some sources of variation in future research.

16. This terminology is somewhat misleading and has led to unnecessary controversy. Economists are really trying to measure what people are willing to pay for small changes in the probability of reducing different kinds of health and safety risks.

17. See Viscusi (1996) for a more extended discussion.

18. The implicit value-of-life number should probably vary depending on a variety of contextual factors, such as the nature of the risk, the population at risk, whether the risk is new, and whether it is voluntary. I ignore such issues in the interest of simplicity.

19. Average latency periods represent rough approximations of broad categories of diseases. I have assumed the following average latency periods: lung cancer, twenty-five years; benzene and other toxic-related cancer, ten years; and lead-related effects, two years.

20. That introduces some obvious biases into the analysis. On one hand, agencies have an incentive to overstate benefits and understate costs if they believe that their preferred regulation or regulatory alternative is more likely to be approved if it has higher net benefits. On the other hand, some benefits are difficult to quantify or monetize, such as noncancer health effects. Benefit categories that do not provide estimates are not included in the analysis.

21. All net present values are adjusted to the year 1995. For example, if an agency has a net present value calculation starting in 2000, I discount that calculation back to 1995. I obtained information on implementation dates from the *Federal Register*. Unless they are specified, I assume that all final regulations are implemented one year after their promulgation; I assume that proposed regulations are implemented in 1996. Note that the time period between the proposed and final stages can vary greatly. Some rules proposed in the early 1990s have not become

final and may never be finalized. In addition, some rules will be changed sub-stantially before they become final.

22. Table 10-1 covers six more regulations than does table 10-4. I count regulations in table 10-4 only if I understand the basis for agency estimates. For a regulation to be counted in table 10-1, it merely has to be listed in the *Federal Register*.

23. Compliance costs as normally used in RIAs represent some combination of equipment costs, training costs, paperwork costs, and costs to government agen-cies. Sometimes RIAs present another measure referred to as "social costs," but the definition of those costs is not always made clear. To maintain consistency, I have used the compliance cost estimates. If a measure of social costs were avail-able for all RIAs, and that measure actually represented changes in producer and consumer surplus, then I would have preferred to use that measure.

24. I show gross costs here because there is some skepticism about the estimates of net costs that government agencies use for selected regulations. I examine that issue in more detail below.

25. I did not include disease and injury benefits that did not clearly fit into fatality index categories. Thus, benefits may be understated. Those excluded benefits may include reductions in diseases unique to only one or a few regulations, such as reductions in the incidence of reduced IQ levels as a result of lead exposure or reductions in exposures to other noncarcinogens. In future analyses I shall try to incorporate those values into my calculations.

26. I derive the pollution benefits from a wide variety of categories including both health and welfare benefits. Health benefits may include both mortality and morbidity effects, while welfare effects may include visibility aesthetics, materi-als damage, and agricultural benefits.

27. Although included in table 10-1, this part of the analysis does not explore two rules on stratospheric ozone that, according to the EPA, have very large net ben-efits. The regulatory impact analysis on the accelerated phaseout of chlorofluo-rocarbons estimates that the present values of costs through 2075 could be near-ly $45 billion. The EPA estimates that the present value of benefits is between $10 trillion and $40 trillion, which is a huge number. The agency's analysis is based on a large number of deaths caused by skin cancer far into the future. It is quite possible that a cure for such cancers will be developed. I plan to explore the sensitivity of the net benefits of that rule to key changes in assumptions in subsequent work.

28. Most of my analysis in this section will focus on final rules for two reasons. First, many proposed rules may change substantially before they are made final. There-fore, costs and benefits from proposals may not reflect the final decision. Fur-thermore, some of the proposed rules will never become final. Second, the year of implementation for proposed rules is unknown, which makes the timing of the costs and benefits unclear.

29. In this and subsequent sections, when I discuss cost-benefit results based on agency numbers, the cost-benefit numbers are really based on agency numbers along with my assumptions concerning a discount rate and valuation of benefits. As noted in the preceding section, the agency does not always specify such assumptions.

30. Eleven rules with net costs did not clearly quantify any substantial benefits.
31. I do not wish to overstate this conclusion. Recall that I examine in detail only one agency alternative for each proposed or final regulation. Other alternatives not considered in the regulatory impact analysis or not analyzed here might pass such a test, at least using the agency numbers.
32. In the case of the Safe Drinking Water Act, one regulation addressing lead and copper accounts for 98 percent of the benefits of all Safe Drinking Water Act regulations.
33. Similar patterns appear for other proposed regulations and all regulations taken together.
34. In assessing individual regulations, we should view the values for pollution reductions used here as very rough approximations. For example, if many of the proposed emission reductions occur in areas that are already in compliance with the air quality standards, the values used in the base case probably overstate the benefits. One example where the benefits are likely to be overstated is for reductions in nitrogen oxide emissions in the Northeast.
35. In general, as the discount rate increases, future costs and benefits are valued less. If benefits occur farther in the future than costs, which is generally the case, net benefits should decrease. The opposite should hold when the discount rate is decreased. In this calculation, however, some cost and benefit streams that are annualized are also affected directly by the discount rate. A machine whose costs are annualized at the discount rate or lives that are converted to life-years are affected by the discount rate. That leads to the theoretical possibility that the net benefits of a rule can increase or decrease with changes in the discount rate, which is what I observe here.
36. The regulatory impact analysis does not give the year dollar, so I have not updated those figures to 1994 dollars.
37. It might also make sense to set up a market aimed at reducing exposure to products containing asbestos. The right to use asbestos could be bought and sold. Appropriate weights would need to be developed for the different uses of asbestos, on the basis of their expected impact on human health.
38. Another key parameter I have not examined is the predicted reductions in emissions.
39. Another measure, frequently used in environmental regulation, is the cost per ton of pollutant removed. That measure is typically used for Clean Air Act regulations. Here I use the cost-per-life-saved measure because it applies to a broader class of regulations in the database.
40. I took values for the average age of death from Tengs (1994). I took remaining life-years at a given age from the U.S. National Center for Health Statistics (1992). The average age of death, with remaining life-years in parentheses, is as follows: birth, 0 (75); accident, 35 (43); fire, 37 (41); worker injury, 40 (38); heart attack, 60 (21); and cancer, 66 (17). Those assumptions do not take into account that the average age of death may vary greatly within the categories. For example, different types of cancer may exhibit a wide range on average age of death. In addition, I use the average age of death as a proxy for the occurrence of nonfatal health effects. Varying assumptions on the average age of death did not significantly affect the results.

41. As with lives, I discounted life-years at the specified discount rate.

42. I believe that I have included most regulations with cost-effectiveness data, but I continue to work on completing that part of the data search.

43. I base that number on data from 1992. GNP is from the *Economic Report of the President* (1995) and has been updated to 1994 dollars. Numbers of deaths from both cancer and accidents are taken from U.S. National Center for Health Statistics (1995). I assume that 1 percent of cancer deaths are environmentally induced (Ames and Gold 1996).

44. Four of the rules that would not pass a cost-benefit test since 1990 are regulations from the Resource Conservation and Recovery Act of 1976.

45. The relationship between health and safety across all regulations is similar but less pronounced. Health regulations consist of all cancer regulations and four other regulations that address noncancer risks, mainly lead-related. The cost-effectiveness of the health regulations exhibits a wider range because some of the lead regulations are relatively cost-effective.

46. Initially, I used the value for cost-effectiveness, but none of the results was significant. Thus, I tried using a logarithmic function.

47. Cost per life-year is a more precise measure. I use it in the first regression reported here. The latter two regressions use cost per life because the cost per life-year data are not available for some of the earlier regulations.

48. I define significance at the 5 percent level using a two-tail t-test. I ran several other regressions with this data set, both with different independent variables and different subsets of the cost-effectiveness data. In nearly all cases the basic qualitative results were the same. For example, I added a dummy for health regulations, and the signs and significance results were similar, but the health dummy was insignificant—probably reflecting the fact that the cancer dummy and health dummy are correlated. As expected, the t-statistic on the cancer variable went down when I introduced the health dummy. In all three regressions the health dummy is both positive and significant when the cancer dummy is dropped from the regression, yet the R square is not so high. That reflects the fact that some health rules that address risks such as lead can be quite cost-effective. When I considered net costs rather than gross costs, I ran a truncated regression, which dropped rules with net cost savings. The signs and significance results again were similar. When I ran an adjusted net costs scenario, the EPA dummy was no longer significant. Finally, when I used the cost per life measure instead of the cost per life-year, the results were basically unaffected.

49. As with the first regression, I examined some variations—including adding a dummy for health. Those changes did not substantially alter the basic results.

50. As with the other regressions, I examined some variations—including adding a dummy for health and using both net costs and cost per life-year. Those changes did not substantially alter the basic results, except that when I used the cost per life-year measure for my results, the Morrall dummy was significant.

51. "No action" means that the status quo is selected explicitly. In some cases agencies propose rules for which no action is likely. I have not included those rules in this category because I have not been able to obtain sufficient information on that group of rules.

52. The correlation using Morrall's database is .4 and the correlation using the pooled database is .6.
53. This finding concerning a relatively poor cost-effectiveness for cancer regulations may not hold for nonregulatory interventions. I shall address that issue in subsequent research.
54. Information for low- and middle-income countries is based on Bobadilla et al. (1994). Information for Mexico is based on Bobadilla et al. (1995). Regions of the world are defined in the World Bank's *World Development Report* (1993).
55. Unhealthy life-years are given lower weights than healthy ones, depending on the degree of disability. This concept is similar to the fatality index discussed above, but the actual applications are likely to differ because a standard set of numbers is not used for both cases.
56. I applied middle- and low-income numbers to 80 percent of the population in that region. I used the 80 percent base because I assumed that it would be significantly more expensive to target the last 20 percent of the population. The numbers on Mexico are more refined in the sense that local conditions have been more thoroughly taken into consideration. Developing-world cost-effectiveness numbers are extremely sensitive to location and can vary greatly even within a single country. Population figures are obtained from the World Bank's *World Development Report* (1993).
57. For example, the other studies discount future life-years back to the present at 3 percent as opposed to the 5 percent discount rate used in my base case.
58. Other authors have made this point, but I am unaware of serious efforts aimed at quantifying the magnitude of those potential gains. See, for example, Easterbrook (1994).
59. Since the middle-income region includes Mexico, there is a problem with overlap. In this calculation I have netted out Mexico from the middle-income region and used country-specific numbers on Mexico.
60. Low-cost interventions in Mexico include programs to control alcohol abuse and tobacco use and to promote breast feeding. Most interventions in Mexico range between $1,000 and $5,000 per life-year saved.
61. Three U.S. safety regulations are less expensive than a few life-saving interventions in Mexico.
62. As noted above, one would expect those regions to have some similarities to other regions in the world. Thus, the potential for saving life-years, costs, or both is probably much higher than estimated here.
63. I plan to explore that issue in more detail in subsequent research.
64. Some statutes, such as antidiscrimination statutes, may not be designed to pass cost-benefit tests. For such statutes, it is still appropriate to achieve the specified objectives at the lowest possible cost.
65. Goldstein (1996) makes a similar argument concerning risk assessment.
66. The scope of the cost-benefit analysis should also depend on the likelihood that the resulting information will affect the ultimate decision. If the analysis is unlikely to affect the policy outcome, then the resources devoted to the analysis should be "small." Conversely, if the analysis is likely to affect the policy outcome, there is a justification for devoting more resources to assessing the impacts of different regulatory proposals.

REFERENCES

Ames, Bruce N., and Lois S. Gold. "The Causes and Prevention of Cancer: Gaining Perspectives on the Management of Risk," in Robert W. Hahn, ed., *Risks, Costs, and Lives Saved: Getting Better Results from Regulation*. New York and Washington, D.C.: Oxford University Press and AEI Press, 1996.

Bobadilla, José-Luis, Peter Cowley, Philip Musgrove, and Helen Saxenian. *The Essential Package of Health Services in Developing Countries*. Washington, D.C.: World Bank, 1994.

Bobadilla, José-Luis, Juilo Frenk, Peter Cowley, Beatriz Zurita, Julio Querol, Enrique Villarreal, and Rafael Lozano. "The Universal Package of Essential Health Services." *Economia y Salud*. Tlalpan: Mexican Foundation for Health, 1995.

Breyer, Stephen G. *Breaking the Vicious Circle: Toward Effective Risk Regulation*. Cambridge: Harvard University Press, 1993.

Council of Economic Advisers. *Economic Report of the President, 1995*. Washington, D.C.: Government Printing Office, 1995.

Crandall, Robert, Howard Gruenspecht, Theodore Keeler, and Lester Lave. *Regulating the Automobile*. Washington, D.C.: Brookings Institution, 1986.

DeMuth, Christopher C. "Testimony on the Comprehensive Regulatory Reform Act of 1995," March 17, 1995.

———, and Douglas Ginsburg. "White House Review of Agency Rulemaking." *Harvard Law Review* 99 (1986): 1075.

Derthick, Martha, and Paul J. Quirk. *The Politics of Deregulation*. Washington, D.C.: Brookings Institution, 1985.

Easterbrook, Gregg. "Forget PCB's. Radon. Alar. The World's Greatest Environmental Dangers Are Dung, Smoke, and Dirty Water." *New York Times Magazine*, September 11, 1994.

Environmental Protection Agency. *EPA's Use of Benefit-Cost Analysis 1981–1986*. Washington, D.C.: Government Printing Office, 1987a.

———. *Unfinished Business: A Comparative Assessment of Environmental Problems*. February 1987b.

Farrow, Scott. "Does Analysis Matter? Economics and Planning in the Department of the Interior." *Review of Economics and Statistics* 73 (1991): 172–76.

Fraas, Arthur. "The Role of Economic Analysis in Shaping Environmental Policy." *Law and Contemporary Problems* 54 (1991): 113.

General Accounting Office, Office of the Chief Economist. "Discount Rate Policy." 17.1.1. May 1991.

General Accounting Office, Resources Community and Economic Development Division. "Cost-Benefit Analysis Can Be Useful in Assessing Environmental Regulations, Despite Limitations." RCED-84-62, April 6, 1984.

Goklany, Indur. "Rationing Health Care While Writing Blank Checks for Environmental Hazards." *Regulation* (Summer 1992): 14–15.

Goldstein, Bernard D. "Risk Assessment as an Indicator for Decision Making," in Robert W. Hahn, ed., *Risks, Costs, and Lives Saved: Getting Better Results from Regulation*. New York and Washington, D.C.: Oxford University Press and AEI Press, 1996.

Graham, John D. "Making Sense of Risk: An Agenda for Congress," in Robert W. Hahn, ed., *Risks, Costs, and Lives Saved: Getting Better Results from Regulation.* New York and Washington, D.C.: Oxford University Press and AEI Press, 1996.

Hahn, Robert W. "The Politics and Religion of Clean Air." *Regulation* (Winter 1990): 21–30.

———. "A Preliminary Estimate of Some Indirect Costs of Environmental Regulation." Unpublished paper, American Enterprise Institute, Washington, D.C., February 1995a.

———. "Regulation: Past, Present and Future." *Harvard Journal of Law and Public Policy* 13 (1994): 167–229.

———. "Regulatory Reform: A Legislative Agenda." Testimony for the Committee on Governmental Affairs, U.S. Senate, February 8, 1995b.

———. "Regulatory Reform—The Whole Story." *Wall Street Journal,* February 27, 1995c, A12.

———, and John A. Hird. "The Costs and Benefits of Regulation: Review and Synthesis." *Yale Journal on Regulation* 8 (1991): 233–78.

Harrison, David, Jr., Albert L. Nichols, John S. Evans, and Douglas J. Zona. *Valuation of Air Pollution Damages.* National Economic Research Associates, Inc., March 1992.

Hartman, Ray W. "One Thousand Points of Light Seeking a Number: A Case Study of CBO's Search for a Discount Rate Policy." Washington, D.C.: Congressional Budget Office, 1988.

Hazilla, Michael, and Raymond J. Kopp. "The Social Cost of Environmental Quality Regulations: A General Equilibrium Analysis." *Journal of Political Economy* 98 (1990): 853–73.

Hendee, William R. "Modeling Risk at Low Levels of Exposure," in Robert W. Hahn, ed., *Risks, Costs, and Lives Saved: Getting Better Results from Regulation.* New York and Washington, D.C.: Oxford University Press and AEI Press, 1996.

Hird, John A. "The Political Economy of Pork." *American Political Science Review* 85 (1991): 529–56.

Hopkins, Thomas D. "Cost of Regulation." RIT Public Policy Working Paper, Rochester Institute of Technology, 1991.

Howard, Philip K. *The Death of Common Sense: How Law Is Suffocating America.* New York: Random House, 1995.

Jorgenson, Dale W., and Peter J. Wilcoxen. "Environmental Regulation and U.S. Economic Growth." *RAND Journal of Economics* 21 (1990): 314–40.

Lave, Lester. "Benefit-Cost Analysis: Do The Benefits Exceed the Costs?" in Robert W. Hahn, ed., *Risks, Costs, and Lives Saved: Getting Better Results from Regulation.* New York and Washington, D.C.: Oxford University Press and AEI Press, 1996.

———. *Strategy of Social Regulation Decision.* Washington, D.C.: Brookings Institution, 1981.

Litan, Robert, and William Nordhaus. *Reforming Federal Regulation.* New Haven: Yale University Press, 1983.

Lutter, Randall, and John F. Morrall. "Health and Health Analysis: A New Way to Evaluate Health and Safety Regulation." *Journal of Risk and Uncertainty* 8 (1994): 43–66.

Lyon, Randolph F. "Federal Discount Rate Policy, the Shadow Price of Capital, and Challenges for Reforms." *Journal of Environmental Economics and Management* 18 (1990): S29–S50.

Morrall, John F., III. "A Review of the Record." *Regulation* 10 (November/December 1986): 25–34.

National Highway Traffic Safety Administration and the Federal Highway Administration. "Moving America More Safely: An Analysis of the Risks of Highway Travel and the Benefits of Federal Highway, Traffic, and Motor Vehicle Safety Programs." September 1991.

Nichols, Albert L., and Richard J. Zeckhauser. "The Perils of Prudence: How Conservative Risk Assessments Distort Regulation." *Regulation* 10 (November/December 1986): 13–24.

Niskanen, William A. *Bureaucracy and Representative Government.* Chicago: Aldine, 1971.

Noll, Roger G. *Reforming Regulation: An Evaluation of the Ash Council Proposals.* Washington, D.C.: Brookings Institution, 1971.

Office of Management and Budget. "Circular A94: Guidelines and Discount Rates for Benefit-Cost Analysis of Federal Programs." October 29, 1992.

———. "Comments on OSHA's Proposed Rule Making: Occupational Exposure to Formaldehyde." March 1986.

———. "Letter of Return to EPA Concerning Hazardous Waste Management System: Wood Preservatives." November 15, 1990a.

———. "Letter of Return to EPA Concerning Hazardous Waste Management Systems: Identification and Listing of Hazardous Waste; CERCLA Hazardous Substance Designation—Petroleum Refinery Primary and Secondary Oil/Water/Solids Separation Sludge Listings (F037 and F038)." September 6, 1990b.

Olson, Mancur, Jr. *The Logic of Collective Action.* New York: Schocken Books, 1971.

Portney, Paul R. "Economics and the Clean Air Act." *Journal of Economic Perspectives* 4 (1990): 173–81.

Robinson, James C. "The Impact of Environmental and Occupational Health Regulation on Productivity Growth in U.S. Manufacturing." *Yale Journal on Regulation* 12 (1995): 387–434.

Rowe, Robert D., Lauraine G. Chestnut, Carolyn M. Lang, Stephen S. Bernow, and David E. White. *The New York Environmental Externalities Cost Study: Summary of Approach and Results.* RCG Hagler Bailly, January 1995.

Smith, V. Kerry. *Environmental Policy under Reagan's Executive Order: The Role of Benefit-Cost Analysis.* Chapel Hill: University of North Carolina Press, 1984.

Tengs, Tammy O. Personal communication, November 15, 1994.

———, and John D. Graham. "The Opportunity Costs of Haphazard Social Investments in Life-Saving," in Robert W. Hahn, ed., *Risks, Costs, and Lives Saved: Getting Better Results from Regulation.* New York and Washington, D.C.: Oxford University Press and AEI Press, 1996.

Tengs, Tammy O., Miriam E. Adams, Joseph S. Pliskin, Dana Gelb-Safran, Joanna E. Siegel, Michael C. Weinstein, and John D. Graham. "Five-Hundred Life-Saving Interventions and Their Cost-Effectiveness." *Risk Analysis* 15 (1995): 369–90.

U.S. National Center for Health Statistics. "Advance Report of Final Mortality Statistics, 1992." Vol. 43, No. 6, Supplement, March 22, 1995.

———. *Vital Statistics of the United States*, annual and unpublished data. Washington, D.C.: Government Printing Office, 1992.

Van Houtven, George L., and Maureen L. Cropper. "When Is a Life Too Costly to Save?" Policy Research Working Paper 1260, World Bank, Environment, Infrastructure, and Agriculture Department, 1994.

Viscusi, W. Kip. "The Dangers of Unbounded Commitments to Regulate Risk." In Robert W. Hahn, ed., *Risks, Costs, and Lives Saved: Getting Better Results from Regulation*. New York and Washington, D.C.: Oxford University Press and AEI Press, 1996.

———. *Fatal Tradeoffs: Public and Private Responsibilities for Risks*. New York: Oxford University Press, 1992.

Weidenbaum, Murray, and R. DeFina. *The Cost of Federal Regulation of Economic Activity*. American Enterprise Institute Reprint No. 88. Washington, D.C.: American Enterprise Institute, 1978.

Winston, Clifford. "Economic Deregulation: Days of Reckoning for Microeconomists." *Journal of Economic Literature* 31 (1993): 1263–89.

World Bank. *World Development Report 1993: Investing in Health*. New York: Oxford University Press, 1993.

SUBJECT INDEX

AUTHOR INDEX

William M. Landes
Clifton R. Musser Professor of
Economics
University of Chicago Law School

Sam Peltzman
Sears Roebuck Professor of Economics
and Financial Services
University of Chicago
Graduate School of Business

Nelson W. Polsby
Professor of Political Science
University of California at Berkeley

George L. Priest
John M. Olin Professor of Law and
Economics
Yale Law School

Murray L. Weidenbaum
Mallinckrodt Distinguished
University Professor
Washington University

Research Staff

Leon Aron
Resident Scholar

Claude E. Barfield
Resident Scholar; Director, Science
and Technology Policy Studies

Cynthia A. Beltz
Research Fellow

Walter Berns
Resident Scholar

Douglas J. Besharov
Resident Scholar

Robert H. Bork
John M. Olin Scholar in Legal Studies

Karlyn Bowman
Resident Fellow

John E. Calfee
Resident Scholar

Lynne V. Cheney
W. H. Brady, Jr., Distinguished Fellow

Dinesh D'Souza
John M. Olin Research Fellow

Nicholas N. Eberstadt
Visiting Scholar

Mark Falcoff
Resident Scholar

John D. Fonte
Visiting Scholar

Gerald R. Ford
Distinguished Fellow

Murray F. Foss
Visiting Scholar

Diana Furchtgott-Roth
Assistant to the President and Resident
Fellow

Suzanne Garment
Resident Scholar

Jeffrey Gedmin
Research Fellow

Patrick Glynn
Resident Scholar

Robert A. Goldwin
Resident Scholar

Robert W. Hahn
Resident Scholar

Thomas Hazlett
Visiting Scholar

Robert B. Helms
Resident Scholar; Director, Health
Policy Studies

Douglas Irwin
Henry Wendt Scholar in Political
Economy

Glenn Hubbard
Visiting Scholar

James D. Johnston
Resident Fellow

Jeane J. Kirkpatrick
Senior Fellow; Director, Foreign and
Defense Policy Studies

Marvin H. Kosters
Resident Scholar; Director,
Economic Policy Studies

Irving Kristol
John M. Olin Distinguished Fellow

Dana Lane
Director of Publications

Michael A. Ledeen
Resident Scholar

James Lilley
Resident Fellow; Director, Asian
Studies Program

John H. Makin
Resident Scholar; Director, Fiscal
Policy Studies

Allan H. Meltzer
Visiting Scholar

Joshua Muravchik
Resident Scholar

Charles Murray
Bradley Fellow

Michael Novak
George F. Jewett Scholar in Religion,
Philosophy, and Public Policy;
Director, Social and
Political Studies

Norman J. Ornstein
Resident Scholar

Richard N. Perle
Resident Fellow

William Schneider
Resident Scholar

William Shew
Visiting Scholar

J. Gregory Sidak
F. K. Weyerhaeuser Fellow

Herbert Stein
Senior Fellow

Irwin M. Stelzer
Resident Scholar; Director, Regulatory
Policy Studies

W. Allen Wallis
Resident Scholar

Ben J. Wattenberg
Senior Fellow

Carolyn L. Weaver
Resident Scholar; Director, Social
Security and Pension Studies

Printed in the United States
6863

9 780195 211740